ANIMAL LIBERATORS

ANIMAL LIBERATORS

RESEARCH AND MORALITY

Susan Sperling

UNIVERSITY OF CALIFORNIA PRESS

Berkeley   Los Angeles   London

#17767285

12-89

University of California Press
Berkeley and Los Angeles, California

University of California Press, Ltd.
London, England

Copyright © 1988
by The Regents of the University of California

Library of Congress Cataloging in Publication Data
Sperling, Susan
    Animal liberators
    Bibliography: p.
    Includes index.
    1. Animals, Treatment of—United States.   2. Animal
experimentation—United States. I. Title.
HV4764.S68   1989   179'.3'0973   88–10639
ISBN 0–520–06198–5 (alk. paper)
Printed in the United States of America

1 2 3 4 5 6 7 8 9

For Marc

Contents

Preface

In writing this book, I have tried to avoid the polemical approach that characterizes much of the literature on animal rights, but many readers will want to know my position on the issues raised by the movement. There are elements of the movement's argument with which I agree, and I sometimes felt I had found a resonant voice in my informants. Animal rights groups have focused public attention on the treatment of laboratory animals; they have been—and continue to be—successful in bringing about much-needed regulation of research practices. Research on animals *must* be carefully regulated, with the goal of minimizing pain and discomfort and replacing inappropriate animal models with other research strategies wherever possible.

But I also have strong reservations about key aspects of animal rights ideology. First, I find disturbing comparison of animal rights to abolitionism. Western society's scientific and folk taxonomy has analogized the categories *race* and *species* with dire results in the past. In a subtle way, the comparison of black liberation from slavery and animal liberation reflects and plays on this conflation of human race with animal species. As an evolutionary anthropologist, I know that part of the work of a good introductory class in human evolution is to disabuse students of the notion that race and species are similar categories. To foster continuing ambiguity on this point, even in the name of an enlightened ethical precept like fair treatment of animals, is a mistake.

Second, the central assertion of animal liberation—that animals and humans share equal moral status—glosses over the complexity of human relationships to animals worldwide. Peter Singer, the Australian philosopher and animal rights advocate, posits a dichotomy only comprehensible to urban inhabitants of the industrialized West and few other societies when he writes, "We treat [animals] as if they were things to be used as we please, rather than as beings with lives of their own to live" (1985). The recognition of animals as sentient beings in the world of nature and yet different from humans in moral status is implicit in the attitudes and behavior of people in many other cultures. For instance, among the !Kung San, gatherer-hunters of southern Africa, the hunter is pragmatic about his desire for meat but asks forgiveness of the animal's spirit after the kill. In this example, the animal is neither a thing nor the equal of a human being. This duality is still present in the West in rural and agrarian communities, and it is surprising only to those who live in an environment devoid of wild animals or work animals but crowded with anthropomorphic projections onto them. Pets are the animals with whom many of us have habitual contact, and they are in many respects our fantasy projections of human kin (Shell 1986). Animal liberation posits too ethnocentric and narrow a view of the human-animal relationship, a view that has little application outside the privileged enclaves of the industrial West.

Animals have specific historical meanings to those of us living in the industrialized West of the late twentieth century. Since Darwin and the other nineteenth-century evolutionists described human origins as reaching into the animal world, we have read animals for signs about our past, present, and future. Animals inhabit our imagination in a variety of contexts, from Disney's anthropomorphized mice to little Hans's castrating projections of his father onto the horses of fin de siècle Vienna, as described in Freud's seminal analysis. Darwin and Freud inscribed the animality of humans onto twentieth-century thought—not only our physical similarity to animals but our emotional primitiveness as well. How these images relate to the older meanings that animals have for human beings has been largely unexamined. Animal liberation is one aspect of the complex reconstruction of our modern natural cosmology which incorporates both old and new concepts of what an animal is. The animal rights movement is as embedded in Western cultural constructs of human and animal as is the scientific tradition of using animal models in research. Neither scientific vivisection nor animal liberation can be understood without examining the culture in which they have arisen.

But "anthropologizing" the problem does not remove the moral imperative to make personal and collective decisions about the use of animals by science in our society. The question of when it is justifiable to experiment on animals is extremely problematic; compassionate people argue vehemently on both sides of this issue. I have come to see it as a subject on which reasonable people may disagree, and I am far from resolving my own internal debate. Some animal experiments are, in fact, unnecessary and should be eliminated, but it is also clear that the use of animal models has greatly enhanced the quality of human existence. Many people are alive because of medical techniques or vaccines developed using animal subjects. Would these technologies have been developed without the use of animals? We can only know what happened; speculations about what *might* have been, given a completely different emphasis in Western science, are impossible to argue in the absence of historical data. Many animal liberationists find these medical advances insufficient justification for experimenting on animals. An education in evolution has left me with a strong conviction of human uniqueness, and I cannot view animals and humans as moral equals.

But in taking the view that humans and animals are not equal, I do not imply that animals should be fair game for human abuse. Animal liberation ideology rests on certain Christian cosmological assumptions: all those who are within the Covenant are "brothers"; animals, in order to be treated well, must therefore be viewed essentially as equals. (Not all proponents of the animal rights movement agree that humans and animals are moral equals, but this position is currently central to the movement's ideology). Within this cosmology, there are no rules governing the treatment of nonkin (Shell 1986). This has led to many well-documented atrocities perpetrated by Western societies on "others," that is, human beings defined as nonbrothers and thus outside of God's Covenant. According to Christian cosmology, there are two alternatives only: a being may be within the Covenant and therefore a brother or outside the Covenant and therefore prey to any form of exploitation. The ideology of animal rights, which posits the absolute equality of human and animal as the basis for kindness, is embedded in the Christian cosmological taxonomy of kin and nonkin.

This is not the only approach within Western culture to the question of how humans ought to deal with other species. The Old Testament allows that there are extraspecies members of the Covenant: animals and humans are both within the Covenant, although inhabiting different places in it (Shell 1986). Human stewardship and kindness that have reference to real individual and social needs need not rest on the concept that animals and humans are alike in moral status. Bettyann Kevles, my editor at the University of California Press, told me about a conversation she had with a rabbi on the subject of kindness to animals. According to Jewish law, a deaf person cannot be a ritual slaughterer because he would be unable to hear the pain of an animal being killed. In listening to the cries of suffering beings and making decisions that balance intricate human needs and responsibilities, we shoulder the unique and terrible burden of being consciously moral beings.

An anthropologist studying such highly charged issues within her own society must confront head-on the question of ethnographic objectivity, a problem central to the discipline. As a participant in the same culture as my informants in the animal rights movement, I share with them strong responses to current practices in science and medicine. We are all suspended in the same web of culture. The futility of ethnographic objectivity—for researchers of exotic as well as familiar cultures—has been the subject of a refined discourse in recent anthropology. I have tried to offer some mutual interpretations of the central themes of this book through the words of my informants in the animal rights movement, in conversations with whom I frequently experienced a radical unsettling of my attitudes and perspectives. By interpreting these discourses and their historical and cultural roots, I hope to contribute to a sense of the exoticism of Western culture. Our science, our politics, and our social ideologies are as peculiar as those of Highland New Guinea, or any other place constructed by culture, history, and the ethnographic imagination. It is in this spirit that I invite the reader to consider with me the recent passionate debate about animals and our relationship to them.

Acknowledgments

I am grateful to many people for their contributions to the completion of this book. Phyllis Dolhinow, my graduate advisor at Berkeley, supported my intellectual enthusiasm for a topic which others might have found eccentric. Her perspectives on the complex issues involved in studying behavior continue to inform my work. Burton Benedict gave me critical assistance throughout my initial research on the animal rights movement, and Irving Zucker lent his judgment and wit to reading a long and unwieldy dissertation manuscript. I wrote much of this book while a postdoctoral fellow in the Medical Anthropology Program at the University of California, San Francisco. I particularly wish to thank Margaret Clark and Joan Ablon, as well as Priscilla Ednalgan, for their help and support.

Micaela di Leonardo of Yale University critiqued an early version of the manuscript from a feminist and cultural anthropological perspective. I am deeply indebted to her for intellectually rigorous and enlightening suggestions. Donna Haraway of the University of California, Santa Cruz, generously read and critiqued parts of the manuscript. Her advice has added an important historical contextualization to the book.

I could not have understood animal rights ideology in any depth without the help of activists in the animal rights movement, many of whom interrupted busy schedules to welcome me into their homes and offices. Nikki Simpson, the administrative analyst at the Berkeley Committee for the Protection of Animal Subjects, and Sandra Bressler, Executive Director of the California Biomedical Research Association, made much useful data available to me. Steven Landes encouraged my early interest in anthropology and lent his language expertise to commenting on the manuscript. Ronald Goldstein brought Cohn's *Pursuit of the Millennium* to my attention, and I am grateful to him for our many discussions of millenarianism.

My friends Mallory Jones and Pascale Judet lent support during the period of my research and writing. In this context I also thank my friends and colleagues Yewoubdar Beyene, Regina Garrick, and Karen Pliskin, postdoctoral fellows at the University of California, San Francisco. My son Gregory Landes has given me support and inspiration; his ideas about animals and people have influenced me during the years of my research on antivivisection. That we share an abiding interest in animals is a source of deep joy for me. I wish to thank my mother, Roselle Sperling, my first anthropology teacher, who taught me to observe people by saying time and again, "look at that," rather than "it's none of your business." Marc Janowitz, my companion, was the oak upon which I leaned during the most trying phases of manuscript preparation, only he can know the extent of my gratitude to him.

My final thanks goes to Bettyann Kevles, my editor at University of California Press. It is a rare priviledge to know someone like Bettyann in any context. It has been my good fortune to have met her as an editor. Her wisdom and advice have been invaluable to the completion of this work.

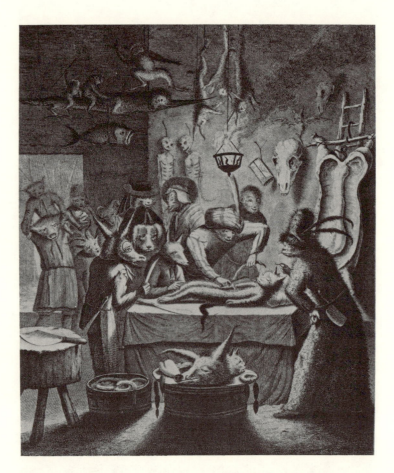

"Karikatur auf eine Sektion," n.d., plate 328, Wolf-Heidegger and Cetto, 1967 *Die Anatomische Sektion in Billicher Darstellung*. S. Karger, Basel, p. 572.

1

Introduction

Wee, sleekit, cow'rin', tim'rous beastie,
O, what a panic's in thy breastie!
—Robert Burns

On a spring day in 1983, a large crowd gathered at the locked gate surrounding the Primate Research Center of the University of California at Davis to condemn the activities of the scientists within. Similar demonstrations were staged simultaneously at several of the other regional centers for biomedical and behavioral research on nonhuman primates. These impassioned and bitter demonstrations were the fruits of the efforts of a new kind of social activist, the animal rights advocate. The nationwide protests were organized by Mobilization for Animals, an efficient and politically sophisticated coalition whose leaders had succeeded in attracting groups representing a broad spectrum of political and social ideologies. Outside the Primate Research Center, holistic health groups, radical feminists, nuclear freeze and ecology advocates, Buddhists, and antifluoridation adherents joined in common cause to decry the use of animals in research. Fliers passed from hand to hand condemning the brutality and triviality of repetitive experiments, the suffering of animal subjects, and the greed and savagery of the animal experimentation history.

Feminists for Animal Rights circulated a flier that juxtaposed a photograph of a naked woman bound to a chair and a picture of a kitten strapped into a restraining device awaiting experimental surgery. It bore the caption, "Why have women abandoned animals to the crimes of the patriarchy?" The fund-raising circular of a group calling itself Buddhists Concerned for Animals asserted, "The very state of mind which will permit the testing of radioactive weapons on live monkeys permits the vivisection of our planet for the same purpose." What had inspired radical feminists and Buddhists to join forces outside the research center? A new ideology of protest was evolving, and people with diverse concerns were finding a common ground in the condemnation of animal experimentation.

While small antivivisection groups have always existed in the United States, the strength of the new animal rights movement, which began to develop during the late 1970s, has no parallel in modern history. In the last several years significant changes have occurred in the relationship between the research community and a segment of the public increasingly active in its opposition to research with animal subjects. The animal rights movement, which has arisen in a number of Western technological societies, bears a superficial resemblance to the traditional humane groups that have functioned in these same societies for a century. On close examination, however, important differences in both ideology and method of operation emerge which distinguish the new animal rights groups from the traditional animal welfare movement. The reform-oriented humane societies have attempted to improve the treatment of animals in a variety of settings and to educate the public about humane concerns. In contrast, adherents of the recent grass roots animal rights groups question assumptions about the human relationship to animals that have been fundamental to Western culture in the modern period. Animal rights activists do not merely ask for reform in the treatment of animals but attack the very premise that it is moral or necessary to experiment on other species. Another point of departure between the older, reform-oriented humane movement and the new groups is that animal rights advocates have focused protest specifically on the issue of research using animal subjects. This emergence of groups devoted to radical changes in research practices, if not to total abolition of the use of animals by science, is a social phenomenon of potentially great impact.

Manifestations of the movement's growth are omnipresent. Many state legislatures adopted pound seizure laws in the decades after World War II which allowed university and other research facilities access to abandoned animals. Over the last few years, a growing number of states have repealed these laws following successful campaigns waged by recently formed animal rights groups. In university communities, rallies and demonstrations organized by local animal rights groups are now a frequent occurrence. All this has wrought a fundamental change in the traditional relationship between academic science and the lay community. In the San Francisco Bay area, the extremely active animal rights movement has had a significant impact on the University of California at Berkeley. Recently, for example, state funding of a new, multimillion-dollar animal care facility there was almost denied by the California legislature as a result of a successful campaign by the animal rights community. This campaign included some tactics that surprised the university administration, for example, purloining of private correspondence between the administration and research faculty on the matter of deficiencies in current housing for laboratory animals. One of the new groups was able to obtain, and subsequently publish, these exchanges.

The scientific research community has paid increasing attention to—and shown growing alarm at—this burgeoning movement. Before the growth of animal rights sentiment in the late 1970s, biomedical scientists could expect approval from the public for experimental work that was perceived as seeking to alleviate human suffering or as furthering the understanding of human biology and behavior. There are many signs of the erosion of this approval on the part of the general public as well as animal rights activists. With increasing frequency in recent years, scientists have faced outright threats of loss of funding and institutional support for research with animal subjects as a result of pressure from animal rights groups. Such encounters have left many researchers angry and shocked. The scientific research community has responded to these events in a variety of ways. Scientific journals have published an increasing number of articles on issues related to the use of animal subjects. There have been numerous symposia on the subject (e.g., New York Academy of Sciences, 1982), with resulting publications. Universities have initiated lobbying efforts in many state legislatures to protect their research interests and have formed university committees charged with enforcing the various agency guidelines for the treatment of research animals.

At the same time, the animal rights movement has grown increasingly sophisticated in its tactics and has successfully kept the issue of laboratory research before the public through appeals to the media. Newspapers, popular magazines, and the electronic media have dramatically increased their coverage of animal rights protests over the last several years. In addition, many of the new groups produce their own publications, and with the aid of professional direct mail consultants, they have developed substantial mailing lists. The movement has also sought, and found, adherents within the academic community who have sometimes joined in protesting university practices. In fact, the movement may be said to have an academic wing, composed chiefly of philosophers, who have developed an ethical theory of animal rights, and a number of academic veterinarians.

Finally, a radical component of the movement espouses direct action such as the "liberation" of animals from laboratories. Such incidents are now fairly common in Great Britain, which has a very active animal rights movement, and are on the increase in the United States. In 1984, one of the new groups, the Animal Liberation Front (ALF), raided a research project at the University of Pennsylvania funded by the National Institutes of Health (NIH). On the basis of information gathered in the raid, and subsequent protest to NIH, the secretary of the Department of Health and Human Services suspended funding to the laboratory. For the first time, an administration official had intervened in the allocation of a grant from NIH, the largest source of funding for biomedical research in the United States. The Pennsylvania case has inspired controversy, anger, and fear in the research community. A number of activists openly espouse terrorism as the necessary mode of action for what they view as the moral equivalent of the destruction of European Jewry during the Holocaust or the oppression of blacks under slavery. Activists frequently make an analogy between the work of abolitionists before emancipation and the efforts of animal rights activists. This analogy between racism and "speciesism" (a neologism coined by philosopher Richard Ryder to describe the human prejudice toward the rights of animals) is invoked in a recent essay by Singer (1985), an architect of the movement, in the *New York Review of Books*. One activist in the San Francisco Bay area movement made such a comparison:

> "We talk about remembering the Holocaust so it won't happen again, and I'd like to know, when it does happen again, how are we going to know it? Does it have to happen to European Jews? Or does it have to happen to people? I say it's happening now and we don't recognize it."

Clearly, the issue of research with animal subjects is an emotionally volatile one for many people.

During my graduate training in anthropology, my research was with nonhuman primates. My work involved observing monkey behavior in an effort to illuminate the evolutionary basis of important human behaviors. The emergence of a movement questioning the morality and utility of my future work had a strong impact on me, and as I became familiar with the animal rights movement, I began to realize that it provided potentially fertile ground for anthropological analysis. As a graduate student at Berkeley, I had many different kinds of experiences with animals. During my first year, traditionally a time of having one's strengths tested by faculty, a famous scientist whose ideas I had studied and greatly admired asked me to work on a project with him. I was enormously flattered and full of both hope and fear about the work I would do under his supervision. I had written a seminar paper about sex differences in the human pelvis; specifically, the ways in which the structure of the pelvis had changed over the course of human evolution, creating differences between female and male. Was this sexual dimorphism of the bony pelvis a uniquely human evolutionary phenomenon or did these differences exist in other species? If so, some of the models for the evolution of these changes in humans might be wrong and might need rethinking.

The scientist suggested that we start with some dissections of a small and available species of animal that gives birth to well-developed, "precocial" young; that is, offspring that might impose some stresses on the female's pelvis during birth. This was a way of starting to gain baseline data on a number of different kinds of animals and their pelvic structures. The morning of our first dissection, as I crossed to the Life Science Building, where a pool of commonly used research animals was maintained for researchers on the campus, I was full of anxiety and ambition. Four live guinea pigs stared at me through holes in a box handed over the counter by a young laboratory technician. I filled out the appropriate forms, and seeing that the guinea pigs were needed for dissection, the technician asked me if we wanted them "put down," the common laboratory term for killing an animal. Were they two males and two females, the sex ratio we wished to dissect first? The technician admitted that it was difficult to sex guinea pigs as both male and female had a ubiquitous genital pouch, but he had done his best. Hesitating, because my supervisor and I had not discussed how we would kill the animals, I told him to put them down. The box came back minutes later, filled with four carcasses; I carried them back to the little basement laboratory in which we worked.

I remember that the bodies of the fat, white guinea pigs were still quite warm and limp and that they reminded me very much of the many guinea pigs I had kept as pets throughout childhood: short-haired, white ones very similar to these, exotic Peruvian long-hairs in beautiful colors; all constantly munching and scrambling about. I even thought briefly of the tiny guinea pig that my friend and I had secretly shared at age ten by pooling our allowance money. She lived in an apartment, so we kept our pet in a box in the attic of my house and crept upstairs to play with it all afternoon. Later that evening, I found my father, always tender with animals, hunched over the guinea pig's box gently stroking it.

But in the lab, we were seeking knowledge, not the warm experience of stroking a furry body. It was harder than I anticipated to dismember and dissect those animals. I remember feeling tested, feeling that I would show the great man I was capable of being a scientist. This was the early seventies, and women had much to prove in the sciences in general. We labored over the four bodies of the dead animals, and as we exposed the genitalia and pelvis, we found that all four animals were males. We had no basis for comparison without looking at both sexes. I ran back for four more guinea pigs, but this time I did not move with such an uplifted spirit. The technician assured me he would do his best to give us some females this time. Sweating from my exertions, hunched over the table under the gaze of the scientist, I found again that all of the animals were males. By the time we finished late that afternoon, our empty labor had given birth to eight dead male guinea pigs whose dissected bodies now littered the table.

I remembered a grotesque, frequently told story about an early piece of research by a famous physical anthropologist. While working in a hospital lab, the scientist had experimented with rats or mice by amputating their forelimbs to see if they would run bipedally in order to test hypotheses about the evolution of bipedalism in our own species. The story had it that a number of these bipedal rodents had escaped and scurried on their hind legs through the dark building one night and into the psychiatric ward, where horrified patients, barely able to distinguish reality from their own hallucinations, stared at the monstrosities. I felt that I had entered a dark world inhabited by corpses and grotesque chimera. Would this be my life as a scientist? A number of successful students in my department had been sent to do neurobehavioral research on a Caribbean island that housed a large social colony of vervet monkeys. In the mid-1970s, there was a flurry of interest in the evolution of the brain, and monkey models were being widely used in an attempt to understand which areas of the primate brain controlled various social behaviors. A typical research strategy of the time, commonly used on the island, was to ablate, or surgically remove, a part of the brain, release the animal back into its social group, and then observe changes in its behavior. If the animal became more aggressive, for instance, this observation would be used as data about the neural control of aggression in primates.

I wanted to succeed and make important discoveries about primate social behavior and human evolution. I left the basement laboratory that afternoon in a state of emotional turmoil; my head ached and my stomach felt queasy. I thought that it might help me to work off some tension by running around the track at the women's gym nearby. I did not have my sneakers with me, so I ran barefoot. As I went around the track, the sky seemed to darken, and clouds raced across the late afternoon sun. It was a warm day in early fall, yet I felt chilled. Suddenly, I felt a stab of pain in one foot. I stopped to examine it and realized that I had been stung by a yellow jacket. As I held my throbbing foot, a tiny brown field mouse appeared in my path; its beaded eyes seemed to stare intensely into my own, and I was transfixed by a sense of sorrow and loss. This small, beautiful creature had a life here in the field, its heart beat incredibly rapidly, it lived out the small passions of a rodent's existence, as Robert Burns had said long ago in his poem. The weight of the guinea pig corpses lay heavily on me, and I felt a kind of primitive fear that I had committed a transgression. Was knowledge worth the death of a beautiful creature whose heart beat its own unique rhythm and lived out its own struggle here in the field? I was frightened by what I had done, by its irrevocability, and afraid to go to sleep that night and dream about the dead animals. I knew that I would never go to the Caribbean island and that, in a certain sense, I would disappoint the famous man.

Later, another important scientist from an eastern university implanted electrodes in the brains of gibbons and released them for telemetric stimulation and monitoring on another Caribbean island. One of his research assistants, a graduate student, reported that a number of the rare, endangered apes had wandered into the ocean and drowned. As I matured as a young anthropologist and as a human being, I came to see the bankruptcy of these research strategies; they were not only cruel but also bad science. A primate is a complex social animal, and to implant electrodes or ablate the brain and release the animal constitutes a disruption of such major proportions that little sensible data can be gained about social repercussions. The animals were so disrupted that other variables could not be isolated, and this would affect the outcome of all their social interactions.

I have come to believe that in many cases, cruelty is not isolated from the validity of the research. I now believe that this is often, but not always, the case in behavioral research and that some of the worst examples of pain inflicted on research animals come from bad research design. For example, in certain kinds of behavioral research, the theoretical model is really all that is important, and species differences are not taken into consideration. In such research traditions, the animal may be used as a model for learning processes that are assumed to be universal. These kinds of studies have rarely considered the nature of the animal species but have been aimed at uncovering basic principles of behavior. Animal suffering has resulted from experimental design that is flawed science and that uses animal subjects inappropriately, without reference to their biological and behavioral status as individuals or species. While there are some universal aspects of animal behavior, good behavioral research design must always take into account the particular adaptations of the species in question. As I saw a connection between abuse and poor research design in biobehavioral science, I began to come to an uneasy peace with myself about my revulsion to certain kinds of experiments and to honor it as more than a girlish weakness. I had little doubt that the moral issues involved in clinical research with animals had to be weighted in the direction of human health and life over the inevitability of animal suffering. But what about good, well-conceived basic research that explored important questions about animal biology and behavior without necessarily leading to clinical benefits for humans? The ethical dimensions of this question seemed enormous.

I later learned that my experience with the guinea pigs was not unique, that many graduate students and seasoned researchers had similar stories. During my graduate training, I studied with a talented and successful comparative psychologist whose research on endogenous "time-clocks" in rodents had illuminated important neural mechanisms by which sexual behavior is regulated. During my first visit to his lab, he introduced me to a young woman at work at a table who he referred to as the project's vivisector. She was pregnant at the time and leaned over her large, protruding abdomen while she worked calmly on the anesthetized body of a sleeping rodent, her hands moving as deftly and gracefully as those of an expert seamstress. A scrupulously honest examiner of himself and others, the psychologist told me he did not think the issue of the human use of animal subjects was a simple one, yet he believed that on balance his work was right and that our need to understand nature was fundamental and could not be denied. He made no pretense that his work had clinical applications to human suffering or disease, but he felt he was exploring the frontiers of vital knowledge about life. At the same time, he said that in conversations with other animal researchers, many had admitted being upset and even had nightmares relating to their work. I felt the psychologist was someone willing to confront the ambiguous moral dilemmas of using animals for human knowledge, to accept responsibility, and to struggle with these issues. I had come to believe that confronting this kind of ambiguity was one of the most distinctively human enterprises, imposed on us by our knowledge that we are part of nature and separate from it at the same time. And it seemed to me, increasingly, that much of anthropology centered around resolution of this conflict about the ambiguous place of human beings in the world of nature.

I was, after all, an anthropology student reading the theories of Lévi-Strauss and others about the human relationship to nature. According to some classic works in anthropology, the distinction between humanity and the world of nature is at the heart of human culture; culture defines that distinction and ritualizes anxieties when boundaries between humans and nature are crossed. Thus, some rites of passage have been interpreted as relieving human anxieties at crucial boundaries between culture and nature encountered during the human life cycle. (This construction of nature and culture as opposite poles is a particular feature of Western tradition, and anthropologists, as products of this tradition, have used these paired constructs in their exegesis of other societies. The extent to which structuralist interpretations of the nature/culture dichotomy represent cross-cultural universals is currently much debated. However, this opposition clearly has enormous implications for anyone studying Western culture.) As I read the intellectual inheritance of my discipline, I too was caught up in the uncertainty of my own ambiguous relationships—as a woman, and as a human being, to the work of modern science in its radical manipulations of nature and animals.

My interest in primate social behavior led me to research with monkeys that was of a very different kind from the dissections and ablations that had so revolted me both emotionally and intellectually. I began to study under the guidance of Phyllis Dolhinow, a primatologist who had done pioneering work observing the behavior of langur monkeys during the early years of modern primate field studies. One of the first women to do primatological fieldwork, she had traveled to India and observed and recorded the behavior of monkeys under the rigorous, and sometimes dangerous, conditions of the field. She had carefully avoided interfering in any way with her subjects. When, after a time, the animals became so accustomed to her presence that the younger ones attempted to initiate play by pulling on her skirt, she did nothing to encourage their enticements. Her work was a model of thorough and painstaking observation that provided data on what was, at that time, a little-known species. The burgeoning field of modern primatology had explored the subfamily of Old World monkeys called cercopithecines. Baboons and macaques remain the most widely studied and best known monkeys. The social behaviors of the other major branch of Old World monkeys to which the Indian langur belonged, the colobines, were largely unknown.

Now Dolhinow worked with a colony of langur monkeys housed in large enclosures in the Berkeley hills. The langurs had come from a group at the San Diego Zoo and lived at the research facility in the kinds of social units that they form in natural settings. I began to go daily to the primate behavior station, sitting quietly on a bench watching a group of langur monkeys amid the fragrant eucalyptus of the hills. At first, certain animals stared at me and threatened by slapping the ground and grimacing, but eventually I learned the passive gaze and manner of the observer, and like the other researchers, I attracted very little attention. I came to know each monkey and its personal quirks. Despite my attempts at dispassionate objectivity, I found it impossible not to form certain attractions and dislikes. Three monkeys stand out in my memories of that period. Big Female was a fat old langur with many offspring in the colony, and she reminded me of a bedraggled but comfortable woman who might be watching soap operas in her bathrobe and hair curlers. Wave was an elegant young female who seemed distracted and distant. Short-tail was quite ugly in comparison to Wave, but I came to secretly attribute to her a kind of valiant honor. She would rush to the defense of certain animals, throwing herself between two animals in aggressive encounters. Of course, I was careful to keep these impressions within the bounds of humorous fantasy, and my observations of behavior were objective and recorded in the operationally defined mode that had come to characterize modern primatological methodology.

Many different studies were undertaken during my years at the Primate Behavior Station. Through it all, I learned by experience and observation much about the humane treatment of animals in captivity. My mentor loved animals. There was no other way to describe her relationship to the monkeys and a host of stray birds, squirrels, and other living things that came her way. The langurs were minimally interfered with, except when an injury occurred, at which time great energy went into the medical care of the hurt animal. Many nights were spent watching anxiously over a sick monkey. Once, when a young female was having a difficult time giving birth, and another student and I sat past midnight on the chill runway, watching and waiting, our teacher came with a small bottle of brandy. We three huddled together, cheered by the wonderful gift of the liquor with its slightly burning warmth. I was not present the following day when the mother gave birth successfully, but I felt that I had shared a great privilege during that long birth watch.

Our research group began to examine the specific reactions of infant langurs to brief separations from their mothers. Infant and maternal attachment had long been an area of interest, and a wide body of literature existed on cercopithecine separation studies; however, no research had ever examined whether or not the reactions to separation were different for the colobines. In many colobine species, females other than the mother would handle and care for infants, often from immediately after birth. So, unlike most cercopithecine monkeys, infants would have much experience with females other than their biological mother. Would the infant langurs become despondent when separated from the mother? Would they exhibit the behavioral and physiological "depression" that Harlow had observed in his famous studies of separated rhesus macaque infants? Since the reactions of macaques were being used as models for examining human infant mother-loss, it seemed important to know whether or not they characterized all nonhuman primates or just certain species. We were testing hypotheses about an important issue: the well-being of a young primate who temporarily or permanently loses contact with its mother.

In the langur separation studies, a mother would be removed temporarily from the social group and housed elsewhere. Later, the mother would be returned. The infant's and mother's activities were recorded during separation and following reunion. Much interesting data emerged from this research about differences in attachment among langurs. For instance, the infant langurs did not suffer like rhesus babies because they easily "adopted" other females. Might this call into question some of the generalizations that people had made from the rhesus separation

studies to human infant rearing? Our research had obvious implications for situations in which young primates are normally exposed to multiple caretakers and then separated from the mother.
One must always be very careful about analogies between monkeys and humans, and clearly the species differences among nonhuman primates in response to separation had to be taken into
consideration when human evolution was discussed.

There were inevitable losses during the research. Two infants
out of the many studied died during the separation studies. In a
setting in which the life of each animal was highly valued, death
was never taken lightly. However, there is one fact that helps miti-
gate the sense of loss when a monkey dies. For a field primatologist, the reality of the hardship and mortality of nonhuman primate life in nature is always close at hand. The mortality rate at
the behavior station was always much lower than rates for langurs
anywhere in the wild.

Several years later, as the animal rights movement became important in the university community, researchers began to be
scrutinized by activists and publicly condemned. To my surprise,
Dolhinow, whose work had always seemed a model of humane
concern, was roundly condemned by the local movement. In fall
1984, during a public talk on primates and evolution, one activist
loudly heckled her from the audience and tried to keep her from
continuing her paper. Pandemonium broke out when another
man tried to make the animal rights activist sit down and the activist swung at him with a camera. In a short time, the campus police
entered the auditorium and arrested the protester, a middle-aged
veterinarian active in the local movement. Dolhinow continued
her talk, apparently unperturbed, but those of us who knew her
saw that she was shaken.

Outside the building, a group of animal rights adherents
marched with placards condemning her as a murderess. One
woman, with a small, rhinestone-collared dog on a leash, thrust a
leaflet into my hands which asked how a mother (Dolhinow had a
child) could kill baby monkeys. A crowd milled around restlessly,
listening and talking. I heard a heated argument between another
well-known Berkeley researcher and one of the activists. The researcher kept asking the protestor to agree that people could
calmly disagree about animal research and still communicate with

each other. But there seemed to be little communication that afternoon. Indeed, there seemed to be no real communication between the research community and the new movement in general. I left feeling deeply disturbed by the attack on a woman who I knew to be a humane and responsible researcher. I came to feel strongly that, among other things, it was her gender that had singled her out for protest. Only later, when I began to examine the symbolic links between animals and women in the protest of animal experimentation, did it occur to me that the activists felt particularly angered by a woman whom they perceived to be an instrument of harm to animals.

The atmosphere surrounding discussions about animal experiments had become so charged that rationality seemed lost in the loud static of accusations and counter-accusations. Many researchers recognized that some inappropriate laboratory facilities and abuses existed, but they had become defensive in the face of the indiscriminate attacks launched by the animal rights movement. Issues of reform could not be addressed in this atmosphere. Humane basic research, and applied research with animals that had brought about profound improvements in the treatment of human disease, were condemned. The new animal rights groups questioned the fundamental right of human beings to use other species to forward human goals.

Western culture has been particularly concerned with defining the human relationship to animals and to the world of nature of which animals are a part. The formal study of boundaries and relationships between these cosmological categories has been a dominant theme in Western science since the scientific revolution of the seventeenth century. Anthropologists have long studied the natural cosmologies of "traditional" societies but have less frequently examined the natural cosmology of their own society. Examining the animal rights movement provided an opportunity to study formation and change in the natural cosmology of modern technological culture since the movement disputes some of the fundamental assumptions informing Western attitudes toward animals since the Enlightenment. In a number of traditional cultures, animals have been described as symbolic mediators on the border between that which is human and that which is not in the world of nature (Douglas 1973). In our society, the symbolic role of animals has varied historically, often reflecting ambiguous and fluctuating attitudes toward nature. Recently, animals have assumed a crucial symbolic role for many as representatives of a natural world increasingly besieged by technology. The modern urban dweller may have his most intimate contact with nature in the form of a pet. Pets thus have an important meaning for many, which is reflected in the alarm they feel when confronted with the concept of experimentation with dogs and cats.

I became fascinated by the animal rights movement, for it seemed to involve profoundly anthropological and culture-specific issues about the border between human and animal and the human relationship to nature. I came to see it as related to much that concerned me as an anthropologist. As a discipline, primatology focuses on the borderline between our species and the world of nature. When anthropologists study apes and monkeys, they do so within the scientific discourse about human nature that has been a feature of our society since the Enlightenment. The nonhuman primates are our closest relatives in the animal world, and ideas and theories about their relationship to us are intimately linked to larger cultural constructs of human and animal. In the last decades, primate studies have had an important role in defining our relationship to animals and hence to important distinctions within our natural cosmology.

Christian cosmology sharply defined the border between animal and human (although as the historian Keith Thomas [1983] points out, attitudes have fluctuated during different periods in Western history, incorporating folk traditions that constructed the relationship between human and animal more ambiguously). Cartesian dualism in the seventeenth century added a scientific dimension to the traditionally sharp theological boundary; animals were conceived formally as automata without mind or soul. The dominant view of animals within our tradition has thus been of their "otherness." We have studied them as exemplars of nature from which we stand apart by virtue of the unique human attributes of soul and reason. At the same time, the study of animals has, with increased urgency at specific historic moments during the last century, provoked questions about the strict dividing line between our species and others. Modern animal behavior studies, particularly those of the nonhuman primates, have recently had a role in blurring the traditional Western boundary between human and nonhuman. For many people today, the dividing line between ape and human has changed to an uncertain border, as information about chimpanzee language and cognitive abilities and complex social behavior has received wide popular dissemination.

Fifty years ago, most people in the developed world had a limited exposure to wild animals. This usually consisted of a trip to the zoo to view socially isolated lions, bears, and monkeys in cages. An exponential growth in popular accounts of animal life in the wild has brought the subject into public prominence. In the decades since the 1960s, our interest as a society in studies of animals has been manifested in a wide scholarly and popular literature. The complex social behavior of apes, dolphins, and some of the social carnivores is now part of the popular imagination of our culture. As I pursued my research, I began to see a relationship between the increased focus on animals and their behavior and the development of the animal rights movement. The ideology of the new animal rights movement reveals aspects of the recent scientific and popular discourse about animal behavior that has become a familiar feature of our society.

As I examined the symbolic role of animals in our culture and its relationship to animal rights, the analytical imperative of a comparative case led me to the late Victorian period in Great Britain. During this period, an extremely active movement arose to protest the use of animals in research. While it is hard for us to think of the Victorian world in terms of being a technological society, in fact, it was perceived as such by many of its contemporaries. Important features of modern technological culture had their birth during this era. Great Britain was the first modern industrial society. The Victorian antivivisection movement arose at a time when many people felt alarm at new technologies that they perceived as antithetical to nature. The 1880s saw the consolidation of a new science-intensive medicine in Great Britain which many viewed as dangerous. The vivisectional method had recently become the most important technique of the new physiology, and concurrently the image of the traditional clinician as advisor and family friend was replaced by that of the specialist, basing his diagnosis on physiological research data rather than on a long and personal relationship with the patient (French 1975).

Through vivisection, the new physiology made an implicit analogy between the human body and those of other mammals. These changes in the theory and practice of medicine were profoundly upsetting to the antivivisectionists, who accused medical science practitioners of setting the concerns of the body above those of the spirit and of placing technical expertise above compassion. Analysis of the Victorian antivivisection movement reveals its profound similarity to the modern animal rights movement as well as the historical specificity of each protest. Essentially, people were upset about the same thing—the perceived manipulation and corruption of nature by human technology, for which the scientific use of animals is a key symbol. In both periods, research with animals has been viewed as the symbol of more pervasive social evils and the revitalization of society believed to hinge on the abolition of the abuse of animals. Similar attributes have been ascribed to researchers during both periods. They are seen as powerful, corrupt, and lacking in empathy. Their cruelty represents a dangerous social trend. In the modern literature, the researcher is often viewed as part of a conspiracy of powerful individuals and institutions who resist the abolition of animal research because it would mean the end of profits and prestigious careers. It is impossible to look at the protests against animal research in both periods without being struck by their millennarian tone: the abolition of research using animals is a pivotal act that will help reverse the dangerous corruption in the human relationship to nature and achieve a millennium in which the human species lives once again in harmony with nature.

In both periods, interventive medical science has been viewed as dangerous and a return urged to clinical observation rather than experimentation with animals. Vaccines and pharmaceuticals have been believed to be dangerous and polluting by many adherents who urge a noninterventive medicine of homeopathy, nutrition, and hygiene. Activists have claimed that if the body is in harmony with nature, interventive techniques developed through animal research are unnecessary. These themes are expressed through symbolic discourses specific to each period. The Victorian literature linked women to the cause of animals through the nineteenth-century concept of greater female naturalness and emotionality. This association was employed by proponents of antivivisection and also by their critics, who accused the anti-vivisectionists of irrationality and hysteria. No other anti-vivisectionist better expressed the millennarian vision of the Victorian movement than its leading architect, Frances Power Cobbe. Her writings exemplify the yearning of many in the movement for a spiritual regeneration of society through a return to the values of the heart as opposed to the cold intellect of science. She spoke and wrote of the vivisectionists' animalistic obsession with bodily processes, the divine ordination of suffering as a means of achieving grace, and medicine's interference with the order of nature. She wrote:

> To contend against vivisection is, then, not against any exceptional or transitory evil, but against those besetting sins of the age of which it is the outcome . . . overestimate of the body as compared to the soul; overestimate of knowledge as compared to love.

Nineteenth-century Evangelicalism, which stressed the value of feeling over rationality, was an important influence on the anti-vivisection movement and a number of other Victorian protest movements. Cobbe wrote of a "millennium of mercy" in which these values would prevail against the cold logic of the new research science. The modern animal rights movement has also linked women to animals but has employed the analytical framework of ecological feminism, one trend in modern feminism. This perspective connects the abuse of animals to the patriarchal oppression of women and nature. The millennial themes in the modern movement are expressed deploying meanings specific to the last decades of American life. Thus, Michael Fox (1980) writes of a "return to Eden" in the lexicon of the human potential movement:

> Human salvation is wholly dependent upon the liberation of nature from our selfish treatment. Human liberation will begin when we understand that our evolution and fulfillment are contingent on the recognition of animal rights. The dawning of a New Eden is to come. (P. xiv)

While certain themes (i.e., women and animals as exemplars of nature) are important to both movements, these are expressed in historically and culturally specific ways.

Both antivivisection and animal rights activists have been concerned with the revitalization of societies that they have perceived as morally diseased and dangerous. Animal experimentation is the key metaphor for the abuses by technological society of living organisms and the ecology. In both periods, adherents have referred to an earlier time when humans lived in a state of nature, without disease or strife, a common theme in millennarian sects throughout European history. This state of nature will be restored with the abolition of animal abuse and the achievement of animal rights.

As part of my research on the modern movement, I conducted interviews with many of the key activists in the San Francisco Bay area animal rights movement. These discussions with activist informants provided a unique opportunity to learn about the ideology of a social protest movement in its nascent stages. The modern animal rights movement has explicit links to several other modern movements that criticize various aspects of technological society. Thus, informants in the new groups have developed both ideological and political or organizational ties to holistic health groups, the antinuclear movement, ecology, and radical feminism. As one activist said:

> "Agitation for animal rights is part of a revolutionary process aimed at restructuring the major institutions of society . . . the same forces in our society which allowed slavery to exist in America and elsewhere, which caused the Vietnam War, are the forces responsible for the pathetic place of animals in our culture."

In both periods, protest has had charismatic properties. Charisma involves a phenomenon of involvement, often oppositional involvement, with the active centers of social order (Shils 1982). In modern Western societies, science and its practitioners are such a center and repository of symbols, beliefs, and values. In both the Victorian and modern periods, the protest against animal research has situated the adherent in a profoundly oppositional position to the central zone of science and its hyperrational values. It is partly the charismatic animus of this opposition that has made dialogue between researcher and adherent so frustrating for each. Interactions take place across an abyss. The university under siege from animal rights protest attempts reforms through the establishment of committees for the protection of animal subjects. Like her Victorian predecessor, the activist sees the struggle in very different terms. The perceived corruption, greed, and cruelty of the researcher are part of an impending ecological apocalypse. The university administrator talks about cleaner cages, while the activist challenges the fundamental assumption of border between human and animal as false and emblematic of a hubris that is destroying the world.

Adherents in both periods have frequently focused on the pollution of nature by modern technology. For the Victorian activist, it was the human body whose natural functions were disordered by the invasive technologies developed by progress in physiological and immunological science of that period. Thus, vaccination and other interventive medical techniques were viewed by most antivivisectionists as polluting and dangerous. In the modern period, this theme has continued to be an important one in the protest of animal research. But the modern period has expanded the concern with the disorder and pollution of the human body to the pollution of the environment. This modern ecological critique explicitly ties the harmful potential of pharmaceuticals, chemical additives, and other agents tested on animals to the ecological crisis in industrialized society, in which the earth itself is the victim. The common focus in Victorian and modern ideology on "inner" and "outer" nature and their potential pollution, on the moral aspects of this pollution, and, finally, on the central symbolic role of animals in both movements are themes that lend themselves to symbolic analysis. Such an analysis makes the movement adherents' world view coherent by illuminating aspects of it that have been either ignored or written off as hyperbole. It also helps to explain why protest against research with animals emerges forcefully at certain times, and why it is directed to concerns beyond the pain and suffering of animals.

How have animals become symbolically linked to apocalyptic visions of a future dominated by destructive technologies? The symbolic environment of Christian cosmologies gives heavy emphasis to the paired structural terms *human/animal* and *culture/ nature*; these oppositions have preoccupied Western popular and scientific discourse since the seventeenth century. In both the Victorian and modern periods, the boundary between human and animal has been contested by important developments in scientific ideology and research practice. The technological products of human culture have been perceived as transgressing the natural bodies of humans—and the animals with which humans identify. Thus, machines and medical technologies have been viewed by both protests as disordering and manipulating nature in the form of human and animal bodies; the world views of activists in both periods reflect anxiety about these perceived invasions. Antivivisection and animal rights are social responses to these events by individuals particularly sensitive to these changes for specific reasons. It is important to realize, however, that the claims of both movements cannot simply be dismissed as irrational anxieties. These beliefs reflect both rational criticisms of the costs of technology and deep anxieties about changing relationships among humans, animals, and machines.

Animals were an important topic in Victorian society. The middle-class membership of the Royal Society for the Prevention of Cruelty to Animals (RSPCA) had waged battle since the early years of the century against working-class abuses of animals (a great irony of the period was the humane movement's lack of success in addressing the brutal habits of the upper classes in their treatment of animals, most notably in the hunt). Over the course of the nineteenth century, the humane treatment of animals had been elevated to the status of a great moral imperative for British children. Sunday school lectures and essay contests encouraged children to think about the topic. The prize for a winning essay might well have been a copy of Sewell's classic, *Black Beauty,* with its metaphoric association between the loyal and obedient horse and the loyal worker (Lansbury 1985). A popular literature on animals and their behavior, in which dogs and horses figured prominently, had a wide readership. The keeping of pets by city dwellers became common in this same period, and pet-keeping, with its anthropomorphic transformations, was an important influence on antivivisectionist thought.

The Victorian period in Great Britain was also one of great debates about the human/animal border (Himmelfarb 1962; Thomas 1983; Turner 1980). Evolutionary theory questioned the strict dividing line between human and animal; Darwin and others proposed a continuum not only for morphological evolution but for the evolution of human consciousness as well. The antivivisectionists responded to the theory of evolution in complex and ambivalent ways. They invoked Darwinian concepts to bolster their arguments, at the same time attacking the theory of evolution as a degradation of human uniqueness. The urban Victorians who made up the antivivisection movement lived in a social milieu in which animals had recently come to represent many different qualities from those that had been projected on them in earlier periods.

As in the Victorian period, animals are an important focus of current American society. Modern animal ethology, particularly primate studies, provides a contextual background for analysis of the influence of scientific trends on popular attitudes in the animal rights movement. A literature has developed over the last two decades that anthropomorphizes primates, animalizes humans, and fits monkeys and apes into the role formerly occupied by "primitive humans" in the writings of social evolutionists. The influence of sociobiology in accounts of primate behavior since the 1970s has added impetus to these transformations. Sociobiology explicitly links human behavior to sets of genetic regulators for all animal and human behavior. These and other modern primate studies have remodeled the category "primitive" as signified by monkeys and apes rather than by traditional tribal societies. In scholarly and popular accounts, as well as various hybrid texts, nonhuman primates have been used in evolutionary model building to replace the technologically simple human groups of the early years of cultural evolutionism.

According to the cultural evolutionists of the late nineteenth and early twentieth centuries, tribal groups represented living examples of earlier stages of culture through which humans had passed on the road to Western culture. Modern cultural relativism made it untenable to stack living cultures into evolutionary totem poles with Europeans on top. But an analogous process has occurred in modern primate studies and their popularizations. Nonhuman primates are in many respects our "primitives," occupying a role that is structurally similar to the one formerly occupied by Trobriand Islanders or Crow Indians in older evolutionary schemata. This remodeling of the category "primitive exemplar," or link between nature and culture, has occurred with increasing frequency since the 1960s in both popular and scholarly treatments of human evolution. The availability of detailed data from field studies, the entrenchment of cultural relativism within modern anthropology, and the rise of new analytical tools in animal ethology have all fueled this trend. The animal rights movement must be examined with reference to the meaning in our society of this recent discourse about the animal nature of humans and the human nature of animals.

This volume examines the animal rights movement in the context of the social determinants of beliefs about animals and their symbolic meaning at two important moments in modern Western history. It addresses both the question of why the animal rights movement has arisen at the present time in our society and the broader issue of how our ideas about animals and nature alter over time. Changes in ideas and social institutions occur slowly in fragmented ways. I have not attempted to search for consistent or neat ideological structures, for they do not exist to order the complex and ambiguous ways in which we have viewed our relationship with animals and nature. It is through an examination of these "contradictions, tensions and paradoxes" (Jordanova 1980) that patterns emerge. Both Victorian antivivisection and modern animal rights protests have arisen at moments of broad cultural debate about boundaries between human and animal and between organism and machine, paired dichotomies of great significance in modern Western culture.

The animal rights movement is part of the landscape of late twentieth-century life; I have tried to examine both the tree and the forest in which it grows with a wide-angle lens. If the picture is revealing, I hope that future work fills in the detail that is inevitably lost when such an encompassing perspective is attempted.

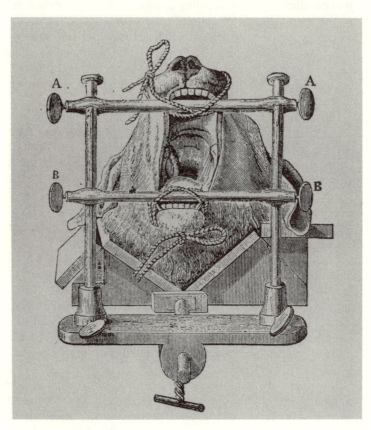

"Illustrations of Vivisection," a pamphlet by F. P. Cobbe. *American Antivivisection Society,* Philadelphia, 1888.

2

The Victorian Antivivisection Movement

. . . when we think of what earth might become were the tiger passions within our race to be bred out at last.
—Frances Power Cobbe, 1884

In nineteenth-century Great Britain, Anna Kingsford, one of the first women of her era to attain a medical degree, a feminist, and a vegetarian, shocked the intelligentsia by offering herself as a vivisectional subject to spare the suffering of animals. Frances Power Cobbe, an intellectual who corresponded with Darwin on the subject of instinct versus learning in the behavior of dogs, drew vivid comparisons in her essays between the role of women and that of animals in society. Stephen Coleridge, grandson of Lord Coleridge, the great parliamentary reformer, decried in numerous pamphlets the dangers of polluting the human body with vaccines derived from animal research. All three of these activists were Victorian antivivisectionists and architects of the movement that posed a serious threat to the experimental science of their time.

During my research on the Victorian movement, I spent afternoons in the dusty stacks of Doe Library on the Berkeley campus reading the lives and letters of these three luminaries and of their cohorts in the great British protest that took place a century ago. At such times, bent over a cracking leather binding, I developed a persistent fantasy. In my daydream, Kingsford, Cobbe, and Coleridge are lifted out of their historical context and cast into the spring sunshine outside the Primate Research Center on an April day of protest organized by the modern animal rights movement. The Victorians are surprised by the dress and demeanor of the modern protesters, but after the initial shock, the three link arms with the others in recognition of their common cause.

The modern animal rights movement is the ideological heir to the passionate and powerful nineteenth-century movement to abolish the scientific use of animals. Strikingly similar fears and convictions inspired the actions of a great many people who protested animal research during the crucial, formative years of British physiological research using animal subjects. For both movements, the act of vivisecting an animal is symbolic of what is viewed by adherents as the central moral dilemma of society: the technological manipulation of living things by institutions antithetical to the natural order. As such, both protests express some of the most characteristic anxieties of human beings living in modern industrial cultures, confronted daily with the incursions of machines and new technologies into the natural world. The Victorian antivivisectionists have frequently been dismissed as a group of eccentric spinster ladies devoted to dogs, cats, and "budgies," all functioning as surrogate children. Nothing could be further from the truth. The Victorian movement was intellectually sophisticated, highly organized, and powerful. The antivivisectionists articulated the same critique of science and medicine, and of the values they are perceived by many to promulgate, as has the modern animal rights movement.

An examination of the rise of British antivivisectionism reveals the intense feelings about animals, science, and technology that sparked the protest of animal experimentation in the late nineteenth century. This diachronic approach illuminates the social determinants of the beliefs about animals in both periods of passionate protest, or, as the anthropologist Mary Douglas (1973) puts it, "the way in which social pressures reach an individual and structure his consciousness" (p. 112). Because animals are rich symbols of nature, attitudes toward animals in a given culture often expose beliefs and fears about the relationship of humans to the natural world. In our culture, when people have perceived technology as threatening to overwhelm natural systems, feelings about animals have surfaced forcibly to make their way into the social and political arenas.

Although there was sporadic antivivisection activity in some sections of the United States during the nineteenth century, the issue of vivisection did not have the importance in this country that it had in Great Britain. Because the United States lagged behind Britain in both industrial and scientific development, antivivisection was a much later and less significant phenomenon in America. One reason for the predominance of the British movement is that vivisection was rare in nineteenth-century America (Turner 1980), whereas, by the 1870s, it had become the most important research methodology in British physiology (French 1975). Although a parallel movement did exist in a number of Western societies in the nineteenth century, it is the British movement that was the intellectual antecedent of all others. By mid-nineteenth century, Great Britain was the world's first mature industrialized society. It is within its urban commercial economy that antivivisection developed as a powerful movement.

It is necessary to define antivivisection and to distinguish it from the general category "humane movement," because the antivivisection movement was fundamentally different in ideology and organization and was a response to very different anxieties. Antivivisection protests specifically the surgical cutting of living animals for purposes of experimental research. In a more general sense, it includes all potentially painful experiments with animals. Humane movements derive from the historical goal of the general protection of animals against all forms of cruelty. A review of the history of the humane movement for animal welfare clarifies the distinction between traditional humane groups and groups devoted to the abolition of animal experimentation. In the nineteenth century, as now, the former represent a traditional reform-oriented movement, like the great humanitarian reform movements of the nineteenth century that abolished slavery and child labor. Both antivivisection and animal rights, in contrast, are radical attempts to realign aspects of the human relationship to nature.

Nineteenth-century antivivisectionists felt themselves to be completely separate from, and often at odds with, the mainstream humane movement. Similarly, the modern animal rights advocates consider themselves to be distinctly different from the local humane society. Adherents of antivivisection and animal rights have viewed their mission as having vastly broader implications that go to the very heart of what is perceived as wrong with their societies. Both have focused protest specifically on the use of animals by science, rather than on the general issue of human treatment of animals in all contexts. Humane societies for the prevention of cruelty to animals developed in both the United States and Britain in the nineteenth century, in each case following the abolition of slavery. The temporal connection between the antislavery issue and the growth of animal protection is not coincidental. The antislavery movement was the prototype for other reform movements, which learned to use the methods developed by the abolitionists for focusing and mobilizing public opinion. These tactics included dissemination of tracts, sponsorship of lectures, and the use of parliamentary pledges in Great Britain (French 1975). In addition, nineteenth-century animal protection explicitly referred to abolition for its ethical framework in much of its literature in the Anglo-American world (Coleman 1924; Coleridge 1918; Turner 1980). Before midcentury, the issue of kindness to animals was part of the larger social question of reform in response to industrialization and urbanization. After midcentury in Great Britain, a deepening anxiety about the human relationship to nature occurred in response to events in science and medicine (French 1975; Turner 1980). It is at this time, and in response to a new set of circumstances, that antivivisection sentiment developed.

The growth of humane attitudes toward animals in Europe provides a backdrop for the development of the late Victorian protest of vivisection. A concern with the treatment of animals appears sporadically in Western thought from the classical period, but a review of Charles Magel's (1981) comprehensive bibliography on animal rights reveals an explosion of interest in the subject in the nineteenth century. Thomas (1983) has documented the fluctuations of European attitudes toward nature and animals in the early modern period. The Victorians inherited a complex set of traditions and attitudes toward animals. Above all, Judeo-Christian tradition emphasized a transcendent God separate from his creation and symbolizing the separation between spirit and nature. But Thomas illuminates a recurrent impulse in European history toward a more ecological view linking humanity to the world of nature. For instance, the biblical treatment of animals has had many interpretations. The Old Testament and Jewish tradition had viewed animals as more or less within the Covenant, and thus, according to Jewish law, animals should also rest on the Sabbath. The Torah prohibited the muzzling of grazing animals, lest they be cruelly prevented from nourishing themselves. Ritual slaughterers were compelled to be humane, and, as mentioned earlier, a deaf man could not be a butcher because he might not hear the cries of animals. Later, Christian interpretation sharply demarcated animal from human, and this heritage of the separation of human and animal on theological grounds has been fundamental to European cosmological categories. Saints Paul, Augustine, and Aquinas stressed that animals were soulless and therefore did not share the rights of humanity. In the dominant Christian theological view, kindness to animals was thus linked to human ends because it would encourage kindness to humans. Still, popular Christianity incorporated the Old Testament themes including animals within the Covenant: "In the Victorian countryside on Christmas Eve, the horses and oxen were rumored to kneel in their stables, and even bees gave out a special buzz" (Thomas 1983, p. 137). So the European gulf between soul and body, and human and animal, proclaimed by Christian dogma was mitigated by various folk traditions. Throughout much of early modern Europe,

> all animals were thought to have religious instincts. Classic authors taught that fowls had "a certain ceremonious religion" and that elephants adored the moon. Such traditions were easily Christianized. Psalm 148 declared that all creatures praised the Lord, even "beasts and all cattle; creeping things and flying fowl." "Let man and beast appear before him and magnify his name together," sang Christopher Smart. Some theologians and many poets regarded bird-songs as a kind of hymn-singing.

> There are also hints of popular beliefs in something very close to the transmigration of souls. The souls of unbaptized children were vulgarly assigned a great number of animal resting-places; they became headless dogs in Devon, wild geese in Lincolnshire, ants in Cornwall, night-jars in Shropshire and Nidderdale. Fishermen sometimes regarded seagulls as the spirits of dead seamen. (Ibid., pp. 137–138)

Nevertheless, the dominant theological teachings of Christian Europe proclaimed that the world had been created by God for human use and that humans were ascendant over all other species. The authority of Genesis was cited to the effect that God had said to humanity:

> The fear of you and the dread of you shall be upon every beast of the earth and upon every fowl of the air, upon all that moveth upon the earth, and upon all the fishes of the sea; into your hand are they delivered. Every moving thing that liveth shall be meat for you. (Genesis, ix: 2–3)

While biblical exegesis claimed human separation from, and ascendence over, animals, it is clear that other themes are woven into the European fabric. Thus, the picture of the human relationship to animals inherited by the nineteenth century was complex, reflecting both doctrinal religious and folk traditions. The Cartesian dualism of the Enlightenment had added scientific arguments to the Christian theological claim of human uniqueness, emphasizing the separation of mind and body, analogous to the doctrinal separation of human soul from animal nature. Victorian natural cosmology had sharply demarcated categories of human and animal, but a motif of the human connection to the natural world has fluctuated with the dominant theme of separation throughout European history. It is within the context of this dialectic in European tradition that humane and antivivisection sentiment must be examined.

Historians of the Victorian period, such as French (1975) and Harwood (1928), identify a growing sentiment against cruelty to animals among the educated classes in England by the mid-eighteenth century, as documented in art, poetry, and philosophical discourse. In art, Hogarth's painting, *Four Stages of Cruelty,* shows some of the common aspects of the brutal treatment of animals in eighteenth-century city life (French 1975). And Cowper, Blake, Burns, and a host of lesser-known poets treated the subject of cruelty to animals extensively (Harwood 1928). Several themes emerged during the eighteenth century concerning the philosophical treatment of animals (Regan and Singer 1976). Catholic theologians continued to argue the utilitarian doctrine first proposed by Aquinas in *Summa Theologica* that kindness to animals encourages kindness among humans. Shaftesbury and his followers proposed that benevolence and sympathy express the highest impulses of humanity and ought to be encouraged toward helpless creatures. Jeremy Bentham, the utilitarian philosopher, included animals within his "Utility Principle of Morals." In *Principles of Morals and Legislation* (1789) he wrote of animals, "The question is not, can they *reason*? Nor can they *talk*? But can they *suffer*?" (Magel 1981, p. 13) Bentham maintained that because animals were capable of suffering, they had the right to life, liberty, and the pursuit of happiness. This last argument became the battle cry for the nineteenth-century animal protection movement and is frequently cited in modern animal rights literature as a signal development.

Several excellent sources document the rise of humanitarian sentiment in British society (Coleman 1924; Fairholme and Pain 1924; Harwood 1928). No organized movement for animal protection existed in Europe until the nineteenth century; the British movement was the first and became the model for less powerful organizations that later developed on the Continent (Dembeck 1965). Before 1800, convictions for animal abuse had sometimes occurred in Great Britain but had always rested on the concept of damage to the animal as property (Harwood 1928). By the late eighteenth century, protests began to center on the concept of cruelty to the animal itself. By the turn of the century, sermons, tracts, and articles railed against "the numerous and accessible cruelties to animals in streets, marketplaces, cockpits and the like, often involving members of the working class" (French 1975, p. 27). It is these activities that became the focus of the early animal protection movement.

A number of key events preceded the formation of the Society for the Prevention of Cruelty to Animals (SPCA), the first humane organization. Between 1809 and 1822, several bills for the prevention of cruelty to animals were submitted to Parliament and were narrowly defeated. In 1822, "Humanities Dick" Martin, M.P. for Galway (1754–1834), submitted Martin's Act, which became the first law against cruelty to animals, and prosecutions took place under this act during much of the nineteenth century. Subsequent revisions broadened its coverage to all domestic animals (French 1975; Harwood 1928). Martin's Act was specifically "an act to prevent the cruel and improper treatment of cattle against those who wantonly and cruelly beat, abuse, or ill-treat any horse, mare, gelding, mule, ass, ox, cow, heifer, steer, sheep, or 'cattle' " (Fairholme and Pain 1924, p. 142). "Cattle" was used here in its nineteenth-century generic sense.

Martin's Act did not include cats, dogs, and other mammals, or birds. However, Martin rose in Parliament before the passage of the act to describe the atrocious practices at Westminster Pit (a working-class gaming arena in London), where monkeys were pitted against dogs and where cocks, bears, and badgers were tormented for the amusement of the audience (Fairholme and Pain 1924). All of these practices had been popular amusements among the wealthy during earlier periods, and upper-class game hunting was ubiquitous, but the early humane movement addressed working people's treatment of animals. The earliest prosecutions under Martin's Act reveal, as does the structure of the legislation itself, the class bias of the early humane movement. The movement was from the start composed of upper-class and middle-class individuals and directed toward working-class sentiments and practices involving animals. The class structure of the nineteenth-century humane movement is one of many differences between that movement and the later struggle against vivisection, in which the justification of the mission to enlighten the lower classes could no longer be invoked, and the target was an educated elite.

Inspired by Martin's Act and the humane bills, a group met in 1824 in London to form the SPCA (Dembeck 1965). Present were Sir Samuel Romilly, known for work in criminal law reform, and Sir William Wilberforce, a leading abolitionist, as well as other socially and politically prominent humanitarians. The society listed as patrons and leaders royalty and titled aristocrats, including Princess Victoria and, later, other members of the royal family. In

1835, Princess Victoria extended patronage to the society, which thus became the Royal Society for the Prevention of Cruelty to Animals. From the beginning, the society's mission, which was successfully achieved, was to broaden its appeal to the middle class. Through an identification with aristocratic leadership, middle-class members could view themselves as the upholders of an aristocratic tradition of noblesse oblige. Although hundreds of societies for animal protection existed in Europe by the end of the century, none ever achieved the degree of power that the RSPCA and the American Society for the Prevention of Cruelty to Animals (ASPCA) enjoyed in the Anglo-American world (Dembeck 1965). The 1824 movement established a system of inspectorship to be employed by the society at markets, slaughterhouses, and on the streets. In 1829, a society tract defined the following targets: sheep driven to market in a cruel way, slaughterhouse conditions, cruel driving of oxen, horses, and donkeys, inhumane slaughter, calve-carting, and bull-baiting (Fairholme and Pain 1924). In the 1830s, the categories of animals on which Society activity focused were broadened to include other domestic animals, birds, cats, and dogs, and the Society began to concentrate on cock and dog fighting and bull-baiting. Pets were not a major concern of the early movement, as the keeping of pets was not widespread among the middle class until later in the century (Turner 1980).

The American humane movement shared many features of the English movement. A leadership made up of individuals who might fairly be called American "aristocrats" and a middle-class membership characterize the U.S. movement. The first state charter for an animal protection society was granted by the New York legislature in 1866 (the first such document in the Western hemisphere) and included as signatories such luminaries as J. J. Astor, Peter Cooper, E. V. S. Roosevelt, and George Bancroft (Coleman 1924). The target of the American movement, like its British antecedent, was working-class cruelty to animals.

An examination of the life of Henry Bergh (1823–1888), founder of the ASPCA, reveals some of the flavor of the early movement. Bergh came from a family of wealthy shipbuilders in New York and was appointed by Lincoln as acting consul to Saint Petersburg in 1862. In Russia, he was horrified by the treatment of animals. He returned to the United States determined to build a movement to correct these abuses in his own society. In 1864, he was able to gain the support of many socially and politically prominent people in New York, including New York City's Mayor Hoffman. In April 1866, the ASPCA was granted its charter. In that year, Bergh successfully submitted a bill to the New York legislature stating that

> every person who shall by his act or neglect maliciously kill, maim, wound, injure, torture, or cruelly beat any horse, mule, cow, cattle, sheep or other animal belonging to himself or another, shall upon conviction, be adjudged guilty of a misdemeanor. (Ibid., p. 39)

Bergh became the first president of the Society and remained in that role until his death in 1888. As Martin had been, earlier in the century in London, Bergh was apparently the first actual defender of his bill:

> That same evening Henry Bergh buttoned his overcoat and went forth to defend the law. . . . He had not long to wait before he found a driver beating his horse. (Ibid., p. 40)

As in Great Britain, the earliest cases of violation of this new law involved the arrest of working-class individuals. In 1866, the first recorded prosecution took place: a Brooklyn butcher was fined ten dollars for cruel carting of calves. Other arrests followed that year for the plucking of live fowl, adulteration of horse and cattle food with marble dust, and leaving cattle on the streets for long periods without food or water. Another major early target was the overloading of horses or the use of unfit horses on street railways and omnibuses (Coleman 1924). In 1867, the society took up the issue of dog- and cockfighting and rat-baiting in the slums of New York and raided and arrested "the notorious Kit Burns, the acknowledged leader of the dogfighting fraternity" (ibid., p. 48).

In 1866, an incident occurred involving a nonmammalian species. This is a rare, perhaps unique, account of protest against the treatment of a cold-blooded animal during the nineteenth century on either continent. Bergh discovered a boat full of live turtles from Florida on their backs with pierced flippers. The captain and crew were arrested under the new law, and Louis Agassiz, the great naturalist and antievolutionist, spoke at the trail, saying that "the great creator, in endowing it (the turtle) with life, gave it feeling and certain rights, as well as to ourselves" (ibid., p. 43). The captain was acquitted, the judge told Bergh to mind his own business, and the event was satirized in *The New York Herald*.

By 1869, Boston, Philadelphia, and San Francisco had incorporated humane societies. The Massachusetts society pioneered the first humane magazine, *Our Dumb Animals*. In the same year, New York's society tried to attack the practice of live pigeon shooting, which was popular with sporting clubs. The shooters themselves and the manufacturers of sporting goods fought Bergh in the legislature and won. They were able to get a law passed which formally legalized the sport (Coleman 1924). As long as the societies confined themselves to addressing the abuse of domestic animals by members of the working class they were overwhelmingly successful. When they infrequently strayed from this formula in identifying victim or abuser, they met with resistance. Later in the century, the movement became concerned with the handling of injured and sick animals, and Bergh designed a fleet of horse ambulances that were later used during the First World War to rescue animals from European battlefields. In the 1890s, the humane societies took up dog licensing and municipal pound work.

The American humane societies, like the British, were always well funded. By the end of its first year, New York's society had raised over seven thousand dollars in bequests and donations. A large bequest of one hundred thousand dollars from a wealthy Frenchman in 1873 allowed the society to purchase permanent headquarters at Fourth Avenue and 22nd Street in New York City (ibid.). Although there is evidence that some of the early humane society leaders were personally against animal experiments, vivisection was not a major issue until the middle to late nineteenth century in Great Britain and never really became one in the United States. In Britain, antivivisection exploded as a volatile issue for the RSPCA and led to a fragmentation of its ranks and the formation of a radical antivivisection society with no formal ties to the rest of the humane movement. In the last decades of the century, the British antivivisection movement came to attack the conservatism of the RSPCA almost as frequently as it did vivisection (Coleridge 1916).

French (1977) has chronicled the rise of the antivivisection movement and noted that it protested much more than animal experiments. Antivivisection arose in Great Britain in response to profound changes in medical practice, changes that signaled the birth of medicine as a technological, research-based science. Only within the last century was Western medical practice based on the experimental method in research. Although animal experiments had been performed sporadically for centuries (Harvey's *De Motu Cordis,* published in 1628, described the circulation of blood based on the use of vivisection) and the philosophical groundwork for explicit animal-human analogies in physiology had been laid in the seventeenth century (Regan 1982), experimental physiology had its real birth in the nineteenth century. Before the nineteenth century, medicine was based largely on clinical observation and deduction of function from anatomical structure gained through the dissection of corpses. This change in medicine began early in the century on the Continent and spread to England in the latter part of the 1800s. It is important to realize that during the nineteenth century, clinicians had been the early experimental physiologists. As the experimentation with living animals became the underlying theoretical basis for clinical practice, the public perception of physicians altered. The image of the sympathetic, intuitive healer began to shift to that of the coldly clinical man of science (French 1975).

An important controversy early in the century illustrates some of the issues that arose when vivisection became the most respected and most used method of experimental physiology in continental Europe (Sechzer 1983). In 1822, the French physiologist Magendie made the first discovery of localization of function in the nervous system based on evidence that sensory and motor signals are carried by different routes. He cut the anterior and posterior roots of spinal cord nerves in living animals and found that loss of sensation, but not loss of movement, resulted from cutting the posterior roots. Conversely, motor paralysis, but not loss of sensation, resulted when the anterior roots were cut. For both loss of sensation and motor paralysis to occur, both roots had to be cut. Magendie's work is a model of the early use of vivisection in the understanding of the functioning of the nervous system. The publication of his results led to a famous confrontation called the

"Bell-Magendie controversy." The English anatomist Sir Charles Bell accused Magendie of copying work he had done eleven years earlier. Bell claimed that injury to the posterior or dorsal roots had no effect, while anterior or ventral root injury produced convulsing of the muscles innervated by the root. He had concluded that anterior roots conduct motion and sensation by way of the cerebrum.

Bell had used the older method of deduction from anatomy because of his revulsion toward vivisection. He had thus failed to understand the function of dorsal roots. Although he had started to experiment on a rabbit, he wrote:

> I was deterred from repeating the experiment by the protracted cruelty of the dissection. I therefore struck a rabbit behind the ear, so as to deprive it of sensibility by the concussion, and then exposed the spinal marrow. (Sechzer 1983, pp. 5–7)

He missed the opportunity to note the way in which sensation is conveyed because the subject was unconscious. Magendie's conclusions proved correct. The modern understanding of nervous system function was based on animal vivisection, which began to replace the older deductive-observational method in continental Europe. According to French (1975, p. 19), "Bell's antipathy to vivisection and his attachment to deductive inference from anatomy characterized the early 19th century British tradition as surely as Magendie's relentless animal experimentation and empiricism . . . presaged the future of French physiology." In the early part of the century, Britain lagged behind France, Germany, Italy, Switzerland, and Austria in experimental physiology. One English medical journal pointed with pride to the fact that English science was "unstigmatized" by what was considered a Continental vice (French 1975).

Despite British misgivings, the experimental method came to England by 1870 from France and Germany. Michael Foster, a student of the pioneering physiologist Claude Bernard, became praelector of physiology at Trinity College, Cambridge, and the first full-time physiology teacher at a British university that year (Turner 1980). After this, a group of experimental physiologists educated on the Continent began to enter new academic positions and to change British education and research. Also in 1880, the

British Royal College of Surgeons started a series of reforms of examining procedures. The result of these reforms was to require more physiological knowledge on the part of clinicians, mandating physiological research experience and training (French 1975). That year, the British Association for the Advancement of Science formed a committee to devise guidelines for physiological experiments. The effect of these changes in British research was great, and after the 1880s, British experimental medicine grew rapidly. By the 1880s, the newly developed disciplines of bacteriology and immunology frequently used animal subjects, and clinical procedures became based increasingly on research results.

Vivisection and opposition to it were rare in nineteenth-century America. In the late 1860s, Bergh had unsuccessfully tried to have an antivivisection clause passed as part of an anticruelty bill. There were some brief battles in 1869 and 1870 between anti- and provivisection spokespersons in Boston and Philadelphia, with both sides borrowing arguments from the developed movements in England (Turner 1980). Although later in time, far less powerful, and fragmented, the American movement had some vivid moments. Keen (1914), an American provivisection physician, describes a 1914 exhibition at Philadelphia in which a horrified public viewed pictures of vivisected animals. At hearings before the Pennsylvania legislature held between 1910 and 1912, physiology laboratories were called "scientific hells," "temples of torment," and "torture houses." There is little doubt that had American physiology been as advanced as that in Britain at the time, there would have been a stronger antivivisection movement in the United States.

In Great Britain, the policy of the RSPCA with regard to vivisection originated in discussions held at an 1862 congress sponsored by the society on the topic of vivisection. The society developed what antivivisectionists viewed as a mildly restrictionist policy condemning all painful experiments performed without anesthesia but not condemning vivisection in general. Despite the wide range of opinions held by members, this has remained the society's position to the present time. The antivivisection movement never forgave the RSPCA for what it considered a capitulation to the interests of scientists. This began a rift between the traditional humane society and the rising antivivisection movement that would explode ten years later.

In 1875, Cobbe, the charismatic founder of the British Anti-vivisection Society, suggested to the RSPCA that it form a sub-committee aimed at restricting vivisection and to testing whether Martin's Act could be applied to that end. If the act were inade-quate, Cobbe suggested new legislation would be necessary. She enlisted the support of some influential figures in the humane movement for this effort. At this time, she was a member of the society, but her confrontation with the RSPCA over this issue was crucial in determining its future position. The society's response was moderate and reflected the diversity of attitudes among its membership, some of whom were not convinced that the society ought to criticize medical research. A fight ensured in which Cobbe accused the society of cowardice, and its president wrote a letter to the *Times* disclaiming any connection between Cobbe's ideas and the RSPCA. Cobbe never forgave the humane move-ment for this betrayal.

On May 4, 1875, deserted by the humane movement, Cobbe presented the first antivivisection bill in history to the House of Lords. The bill was actually somewhat more moderate than plat-forms and demands would be in later years. The RSPCA, many of whose active members were doctors and scientists, withdrew en-tirely from the issue. By the mid-1870s, the lines were drawn be-tween the reform-oriented RSPCA and the increasingly proaboli-tion antivivisectionists. In 1875, Cobbe formed the Victoria Street Society (V.S.S.), dedicated to the protection of animals liable to vivisection. She enlisted the support of a wide group of influential friends, and throughout the century, Cobbe's group led the fight against vivisection. Other antivivisection groups formed and of-ten became involved in bitter internecine fights with Cobbe's soci-ety, but the V.S.S. always maintained its predominance.

During this period experimental medicine mobilized to protect its interests. In 1875, an influential provivisection group formed which later became a lobby to protect experimentation. Although neither practiced vivisection, the evolutionists Darwin and Hux-ley supported a petition and bill to protect the experimentalists' right to use animal subjects. On May 12, 1875, what came to be known as the Scientist's Bill was presented to the House of Com-mons. It was an attempted compromise, based on the principle of regulation of painful experiments only. Painless experiments us-ing anesthesia for purposes of scientific discovery would be legal and not prosecutable under Martin's Act. Scientists would apply to the Home Secretary for a five-year license to perform painful experiments. Pain would be permitted if suffering was kept minimal, if it was for the purpose of new discovery, and if anesthesia would frustrate the purpose of the experiment. Licensees would be registered, and there would be penalties for violation. Arguments ensued over the two competing bills, Cobbe's more sweeping antivivisection legislation and the Scientist's Bill. Ultimately, legislative deliberation on the issue was tabled in favor of the formation of a Royal Commission on Vivisection that sat to consider the issue. It was during the existence of this commission that the first antivivisection group, the Victoria Street Society, was formed.

As opinions became more and more polarized, the humane and antivivisection movements began to define their positions. Medical researchers and antivivisectionists lobbied aggressively. On the recommendation of the Royal Commission, Parliament passed the Cruelty to Animals Act of 1876, which remained the standing act in Great Britain for regulating animal experimentation until its revision in 1986. While the act pleased moderate restrictionists, antivivisectionists bitterly criticized its structure and mode of enforcement as, at best, useless, if not actually evil. Any hope of rapprochement between the two movements was completely obliterated. The Cruelty to Animals Act was moderately restrictionist in approach and set up a system of licensing and registration through the Home Secretary's Office. Penalties were established for infringements. The act did recognize as justified painful experiments to advance new physiological knowledge, save or prolong life, or alleviate human suffering. The antivivisectionists felt completely betrayed and fought the act aggressively for the next decade.

From its inception, the antivivisection movement was sharply demarcated from the moderate, proscience RSPCA. It was a different movement both ideologically and structurally. For instance, women occupied important leadership positions, which was not the case in the traditional humane movement, and the religious affiliation of many leaders was to evangelical groups rather than to the more conservative Church of England. Many of the leaders had strong affiliations with a number of other causes such as feminism and the antivaccination and anti-Contagious Diseases Acts movements. Finally, the antivivisection movement differed from the humane movement in aspects of its class structure. The antivivisection movement could not invoke the "mission to the lower classes" as had the RSPCA. Experimental physiologists were part of the social elite of the medical profession and thus of the society at large.

The movement was led by three London-based societies: the Victoria Street Society, the London Antivivisection Society, and the International Association for the Total Suppression of Vivisection. In addition to these, there were at least seven provincial or specialized societies, such as the Society for United Prayer against Vivisection and the Scottish Society for the Total Suppression of Vivisection. To focus public attention on the issue of vivisection, the movement used methods of protest that had become well established by the last part of the century. Cobbe enlisted the support of people like Herbert Spencer, Lord Chief Justice Coleridge, Lord Shaftesbury, and the evolutionist A. R. Wallace, among other prominent persons. Although she tried to gain the support of the Church of England, she did not meet with early success. Cobbe wrote in the *Zoophilist* (1881), the publication of the Victoria Street Society, that

High Church clergymen have exhibited little interest in the agitation for the suppression of scientific cruelty, and have left the work to be done by Evangelicals, Roman Catholics, Broad Churchmen, Jews, and Unitarians. (Quoted in French 1975)

The movement produced a huge body of literature, including six periodicals published by the major societies. Prominent among these were the *Zoophilist* (1881–1915) and the *Home Chronicler* (1876–1879). There were also numerous tracts, short stories, and novels. Sensational posters were displayed around London. After passage of the 1876 Cruelty to Animals Act, the petition became an important tool in bringing the issue to public scrutiny. The twenty years following passage of the Act of 1876 were the most active period of agitation (Turner 1980; French 1975). In 1876, the House of Commons received 805 petitions for the total abolition of vivisection, with 46,889 signatures. In 1883, there were an average of six antivivisection petitions presented to

Parliament each day, with 1,000 signatories to each (French 1975). Another important resource of support for the antivivisection movement was the electoral pledge. A candidate for Parliament who would pledge support for total abolition of animal experimentation received promises of voting support as well as financial donations and manpower from antivivisectionists. All of these methods had been developed during the fight for the abolition of slavery and were used by numerous reform groups of the period (ibid.). The *Home Chronicler* of 1878 published a list of marginal seats in the House of Commons held by members of Parliament who had voted against an 1877 bill for total abolition, and the *Zoophilist* of 1885 printed a form letter to send to candidates requesting their position on total abolition (ibid.). Any notion that the Victorian movement was composed of politically naive individuals is far from the truth. Its leaders were adept at techniques of protest and political pressure.

Antivivisection had formal ties to two other important movements of the period that shared ideological similarities. These were the antivaccination movement and the anti-Contagious Diseases Acts movement. The same Parliamentary spokespersons were consistent in their support of these three movements, and there is evidence that the constituencies of all three movements had significant overlap (Marmor et al. 1960; French 1975; Coleridge 1916). The movements cooperated, and their literature reveals a perceived mutual affinity based on a common critique of research-oriented scientific and medical practice. The Contagious Diseases Acts of 1864, 1866, and 1869 mandated the apprehension and examination by physicians of working-class women suspected of prostitution. A feminist agitation in the 1870s and 1880s joined women across class lines to protest the acts. The antivivisection and the anti-Contagious Diseases Acts movements shared a nineteenth-century feminist analysis that linked the oppression of animals and women.

Women predominated in the ranks of the antivivisectionists, and the movement was significantly linked to British feminism of the period. Feminism and its opposition were active causes during this period. In the 1870s and 1880s, after a fierce struggle, women began to gain entrance to British colleges like Newnham Hall (created in 1873 to afford women preparation for the Cambridge

Higher Local Examinations) and Girton (a women's college developed on the male model that same year). The debate over women's suffrage was also an important issue at this time. The legal condition of women was often equated to that of animals by proponents of women's rights as well as their enemies. A suffragist of this period wrote that

> those who compare the political status of women to that of criminals, lunatics, and idiots, give too favourable view of the facts. The true comparison is that which was used by Mr. Justice Byles in Court of Queen's bench, when he likened the political condition of women to that of dogs and horses. After indignantly scouting the claims of women to humanity: "I will not" said the Judge, "allow that woman can be man, unless in a zoological treatise, or until she is reduced to the condition of fossil remains," he proceeded to level the political rights of women to those of the domestic animals. (R. M. Pankhurst 1868, quoted in Bauer and Ritt 1979, p. 226)

The universally acknowledged architect of the movement, Frances Power Cobbe, was a feminist who articulated a philosophy of the mission of women to bring about the spiritual regeneration of society. Cobbe was active in many feminist causes, writing widely on the rights of women. She made explicit comparisons between the treatment of animals and women in her arguments for women's rights, as in the following passage from *The Duties of Women* (1888):

> . . . the old hypothesis that the beasts were made chiefly for the use of man is as completely exploded as the parallel notion that the stars exist to add to our winter nights' illumination, and to afford guidance to our ships. Even the animals most completely appropriated by us would hardly be described by anyone now as "made" for our use alone. . . .But, if it be admitted as regards horses and cats that they were made, first, for their own enjoyment, and only second to serve their masters, it is, to say the least, illogical and stupid to suppose that the most stupid of human females has been called into being by the Almighty principally to the end that John or James should have the comfort of a wife; nay, even that Robert or Richard should owe their birth to her as their mother. (P. 50)

The late Victorian popular discourse that compared women to animals was deployed by those on both sides of the "women's question," while the scientific discourse of the period viewed women as closer to animals than men and as exemplars of ancestral forms. The shout of an anonymous street boy, "Votes for women, votes for donkeys, votes for dogs" (Bauer 1973, p. 206) reflected an association that underlies feminist themes in the antivivisection movement. There is much evidence that women identified the vivisection of animals as a metaphor for their own oppression. Sometimes the identification was more explicit; Anna Kingsford and others analogized the physician's treatment of animals in research with his clinical treatment of women, especially poor women.

The movement's chief advocate, Cobbe, had spent her childhood in Dublin studying philosophy, astronomy, history, and Greek. At age fourteen she underwent a religious crisis, after which she became a Kantian and, finally, a Unitarian preacher. In her twenties, she wrote essays on Kant's theory of intuitive morals, which were published anonymously to avoid offending her father. Cobbe lived on an inherited income, never married, and worked for many causes, including the establishment of reformatories for young girls, the defense of women's rights, and antivivisection (Murray 1982). Cobbe was able to use the Victorian image of the morally superior woman in the cause of protest, but the movement was also stigmatized because of the predominance of female leadership, and its leaders were attacked as female hysterics (French 1975). This predominance of women in the movement, as compared to the traditional humane cause, has complex roots. Antivivisection provided an opportunity for leadership by women that they did not find in the more conventional societies for prevention of cruelty to animals. Cobbe's explicit feminism was important in linking feminist values and activism to the antivivisection movement. The remodeled and idealized animal of the Victorian period represented the emotional and spiritual values of the heart and of natural instinct as opposed to the ruthless rationalism and materialism of science and logic. As women were also symbolically linked to these values, it was felt by many that the two formed an appropriate partnership for returning society to an alignment with natural laws. Although not explicitly a feminist movement, antivivisection was symbolically connected to the wider feminist aspirations of the period.

Like Cobbe, many of the leaders of the movement had ties to Victorian Evangelicalism (Stevenson 1956). Evangelicalism, which had arisen in England in the eighteenth century and had become an important force in Victorian life and thought, preached the value of revelation and natural faith and emotion over theological logic. It rested on the sense of innate human sinfulness and the possibility of salvation through the spiritual rebirth of the individual. The movement called for the converted to fight sin in its many manifestations. The early nineteenth-century British evangelical movement was lead by William Wilberforce, the abolitionist, who urged the upper and middle classes toward the moral reform of society. Hannah More, another important Victorian evangelical, proposed that women had a special mission in the reform of society. Within the evangelical groups, women had an exalted spiritual role, although their domestic mission was clearly defined. Evangelical Christianity, feminism, and antivivisection have all had an important resurgence since the 1960s. Although not organizationally entwined, as they once were, these movements still share significant elements in their critique of aspects of the technological dominance of nature, which is seen as the apotheosis of a hyperrational world view. An examination of the ideological basis of antivivisection shows its deep ties to evangelical ideas, particularly the value of emotion over the cold logic of the new medical sciences.

The scientific community organized quickly in response to antivivisection. The British Physiological Society was founded in 1876 and used two journals, *The Nineteenth Century* and *Nature,* as a forum for the defense of research. Important scientists like Darwin, Huxley, Owen, and Romanes were all members, and Darwin published an article in *Nature* in support of experimental medicine (1881). In 1882, the Association for the Advancement of Medicine by Research (AAMR), composed of numerous prestigious medical men, was formed to publicly defend the cause of research. The AAMR developed a program of public education, including pamphlets and lectures. Probably more important was the political strategy it adopted whereby a close relationship was formed with the Home Office. From 1882 to 1913, the AAMR occupied a quasi-official role in reviewing license applications for the Home Office, and important licensees were on the AAMR council. In 1882, 42 licenses were granted, while by 1913, 638 were issued. In fact, with the success of this group, there were few problems in obtaining licenses after the 1880s (French 1975). In 1913, the role of the AAMR was taken over by the advisory committee from the Royal Colleges of Physicians and Surgeons and the Royal Society.

According to historians of the period (French 1975; Turner 1980) and to the antivivisectionists themselves (Coleridge 1916; Cobbe 1894), the scientific-medical community was tremendously successful in gaining political ascendancy over the antivivisectionists. Although the movement brought about the regulation of research using animals and succeeded in preventing outright abuses, the scientific community, in the end, was able to protect its interests. By 1885, the AAMR gave up its public crusade and concentrated on forming politically important ties. Science and medicine were more autonomous and less vulnerable to public opinion in Victorian England than in this country today. According to French's analysis, it was the ability of this prestigious group to quietly use powerful social and political networks that led to the eventual defeat of the call for the strict abolition of vivisection. The Cruelty to Animals Act did have a significant impact on scientific research in Great Britain, however. Although there were only three prosecutions under the act, this does not indicate its influence on scientific practice. Following the legislation, a group of important medical researchers left England to work on the Continent. Important scientists like Joseph Lister, who worked on tissue inflammation, and T. R. Fraser, a famous toxicologist, never worked in England again. G. F. Yeo, who did signal work on cerebral localization, stayed in England but stopped experimenting altogether after being refused certification in 1881.

The overall impact on research was subtle, but it is clear that the act discouraged some experimentation. Cross, the first home secretary to administer the act, refused certification to a significant number of applicants. No good statistics exist on the frequency of license refusal, but French cites at least three instances where refusal effectively terminated a researcher's experimental practice. There were also reports of difficulty in getting the necessary signatures required by the act unless one had a sufficient reputation and was associated with an important center of research, usually in London. The real impact of the act was probably its chilling effect on research. The antivivisectionists published the names of licensees and organized charity boycotts of hospitals with research centers where experimentation was undertaken. Some hospitals, afraid to lose the donations that were an important source of their revenue, discouraged the use of animal subjects.

Antivivisection in Victorian England was a movement addressing trends in society that are richly symbolized by the act of vivisecting an animal but that go far beyond this single issue. As in other important protest movements, the motivations of its participants were diverse, but the underlying critique was of the perceived dominance of nature by impersonal and technologically oriented institutions. For the antivivisectionists, the animal experiment was the key symbol of the oppression of living beings. Antivivisection was a powerful movement because it drew on deeply felt anxieties that found their symbolic focus in vivisection.

Neil Smelser has written about the nineteenth-century humane movement as a "norm-oriented" movement that attempted to support social norms through demands for laws and regulatory agencies designed to control the behavior of individuals (1962, p. 273). The Victorian antivivisection movement was a fundamentally different kind of protest arising from radically different social pressures. Its goal was not only the abolition of animal experiments but also, for many, a vast regeneration of values. This gave the movement a greater kinship with other movements of a revitalistic nature that address much more fundamental issues than the reform of behaviors.

The most pervasive symbol of the nineteenth-century humane movement was the unenlightened workingman beating his horse. The horse remains what it is, a sympathetic victim, but still an animal sharply demarcated from humans. The symbolic target of antivivisection was the educated, dispassionate scientist, probing the living animal with his instruments, and it was no longer clear that this "animal" was an animal. The Victorian antivivisection literature deployed the anthromorphic images of animals current in late Victorian art and literature which endowed them with some of the spiritual qualities of humans.

Ideologically, antivivisection was based on a radical protest of changes in the Victorian cosmology wrought by science and the new research-based medicine. The goal was no less than the "millennium of mercy," of which Cobbe wrote in 1884, "When we think of what earth might become were the tiger passions within our race to be bred out at last" (1884*b,* p. 4). It would be a world purged of the materialism, relentless empiricism, and technological expertise of the new science and medicine.

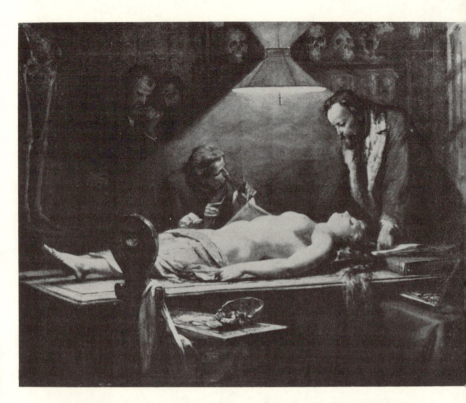

"Professor Johann Lucae leitet eine Sektion," Gemalde von Johann Hasselhorst, 1864/66, plate 285, Wolf-Heidegger and Cetto, 1967 *Die Anatomische Sektion in Billicher Darstellung,* S. Karger, Basel, p. 546.

3

Natural Incursions

Lewis Carroll (1875), creator of a wonderland of real and imagined animals, looked with horror toward a day

> when successive generations of students, trained from their earliest years to the repression of all human sympathies, shall have developed a new and more hideous Frankenstein—a soulless being to whom science shall be all in all. (Quoted in French 1975, p. 303)

For many Victorians, this monster rose as a specter of the new medical sciences in which the older traditions of natural history involving clinical and anatomical observation were rapidly giving way to new technological specialties. These specialties were rooted in an interventive approach to the body. The later Victorian physiologist did not passively observe but cut into the living body of an animal to learn how that body functioned. Armed with this new knowledge of physiological mechanisms, he returned to his patients a different man. No longer perceived as the intuitive healer, with long personal association with the patient, this new doctor was a technological specialist with a medicine kit full of therapeutic interventions. The medical specialist, basing his knowledge and practice on research, and trained in a host of new techniques, had his ontogeny during the late Victorian period. The response of the antivivisectionist predicted with startling clarity the anxieties of the new century: the increasing domination by science and medicine of the body and of nature. The rise of modern physiological research methods and the understanding of the human evolutionary relationship to animals brought about profound alterations in the late Victorian world view. The natural cosmology inherited by the Victorians had sharply demarcated categories of human and animal. The cognitive boundary between human and animal was challenged by new developments in science. By using animal subjects in research, the physiologist made an explicit analogy between the animal body and the human body. There is much evidence that this was deeply upsetting to many Victorians who responded by challenging the propriety of any experimentation with animals.

The antivivisectionists were acutely sensitive to these events in the scientific realm, and their reactions are recorded in their voluminous writings. The new scientific technologies were seen by many Victorians as incursions on nature. There were now many things that could be done to the body in a therapeutic context including vaccination and a variety of new surgical interventions. Experiments with animals had both a practical and a symbolic connection to the new scientific technology. Practically, techniques were developed through the use of animal subjects. Symbolically, the animal represented to the antivivisectionists the "natural" aspects of the human body increasingly besieged by science. Underlying this symbolic meaning of animals as "victims of science" was a deep identification with them. This identification between human and animal was facilitated by the anthropomorphizing of animals in late Victorian society which was expressed through much of their literature and art. This phenomenon has complex roots and is related to the rise in the keeping of pets by the increasingly urban population in Great Britain. The "cult of the pet," which developed at this time, projected, through a vast literature, highly anthropomorphic images of animals that were new to European society. Antivivisection protest, empowered by the widespread anxiety about the new technologies of science and medicine, transformed the anthropomorphized animal of the period into a powerful symbol.

The Victorian cosmology underwent an enormous shift midcentury, brought about by advances in medical research and scientific ideology. The vivisected animal became an important symbol of nature besieged by technological transgressions. The literature of the Victorian movement has frequently been dismissed as sentimental and hyperbolic compared to the efforts of the modern movement. This is a mistake for two reasons. The critique developed by the Victorians was often sophisticated and anticipated every fundamental issue confronted by the modern movement, from philosophical and moral issues, such as the elaboration of the theory of "speciesism" (the domination of other species by humanity as a form of oppression), to practical problems, such as presenting alternatives to vivisection in research. Furthermore, much of the presumably irrational hyperbole of the antivivisection movement makes sense within the framework of its symbolic meaning. For the Victorian antivisectionists, vivisection was symptomatic of pervasive social ills.

The period of the mid-1850s to 1900 was characterized by increasing government involvement in the regulation of public health (Stevenson 1956). Anesthesia, vaccination, and antisepsis—all developed in the nineteenth century—had brought about a vast change in the possibilities for medical intervention. Previously, only the very poor, with no other recourse to medical treatment, had used hospitals, and they used them with well-justified trepidation (Foucault 1975). By the 1870s and 1880s, the middle and upper classes sought physicians with hospital appointments and used hospitals themselves. The early nineteenth-century physician had been strictly a clinician. His role was closer to that of a spiritual comforter, adviser, and family friend. Few aggressive therapies were available for his use. The change in late nineteenth-century European medicine to a research-based science with specialist practitioners, many of whom were researchers as well as clinicians, was unsettling to many accustomed to the old ways (French 1975; Turner 1980; Stevenson 1956).

The Victorian antivivisectionists were part of a wider protest against the perceived threat of the growing power of the medical establishment, and the antivivisection movement was closely aligned with two other causes, the antivaccination and anti-Contagious Diseases Acts movements. All protested against the materialism of science and medicine, which set the concerns of the body above those of the spirit and technological expertise above compassion. In all three movements, physicians were portrayed as dangerously intruding into the realm of nature. The anti-Contagious Diseases Acts movement provides a parallel case to the protest against vivisection. Both movements shared significant themes in their fight against instrumental violations of living beings. Recent feminist historiography of the agitation against the acts, notably the work of Judith Walkowitz (1977; Walkowitz and Walkowitz 1974) reveals its profound affinity with the antivivisection movement.

Between 1870 and 1885, British women crossed class lines to agitate for the repeal of legislation to regulate and examine prostitutes. Countries on the Continent, such as Belgium and France, had legislated systems of police-supervised inspection and licensing of prostitutes. In the 1840s, suggestions for a similar policy in Great Britain began to appear in the British medical journal *Lancet*. A paper by William Acton on the subject of venereal disease in military and civilian populations was read before the Royal Medical and Chirurgical Society in 1846 and became very influential as an argument for the acts (Sigsworth and Wyke 1972). By 1850, *Lancet* and other prestigious journals had called for legislation for the medical control of prostitutes. Fourteen years of debate followed before Parliament enacted the first of three Contagious Diseases Acts in 1864. The debates preceding the acts reveal Victorian attitudes toward prostitutes and venereal disease. Some of those against regulation saw venereal disease as a natural and divinely ordained retribution against unholy activities and claimed that state regulation of vice was itself a degradation. Those in favor of the acts cited the repeated publication in army and navy reports of the high rates of venereal disease among the military and the fact that innocent wives would be affected by their husbands' traffic with prostitutes.

When the 1864 Contagious Diseases Act was passed it affected only naval and military stations within specific towns for an initial three-year period. It provided for a special body of plainclothesmen who would operate under military supervision. If one member of this special force, or a registered physician, should suspect that a woman was a common prostitute (a vague term for reasons to be discussed), the woman would be required to submit to an examination. If found diseased, she would be taken immediately to a special Lock Hospital (a hospital with a venereal ward) and detained there for up to three months. Refusal to submit to the examination carried severe penalties. In 1866, the act was revised to include provisions that extended it to new towns and mandated periodic examinations of women for one year. The period of detention in locked wards was also extended. By 1869, the act was further extended geographically and detention in the Lock Hospitals extended to nine months. Between 1870 and 1885, 17,367 petitions bearing over two million signatures were presented to the House of Commons demanding repeal of the acts. A number of societies formed to protest them, and public meetings on the topic were frequent. Women from the upper classes agitated in poor neighborhoods in the townships of Plymouth and Southampton to encourage women accused of prostitution to resist examination. The anti-Contagious Diseases Acts movement is thus an example of early feminist protest across class lines against the treatment of a specific group of women.

Opponents of the acts condemned them as state interference with civil liberties and cited the statistical inadequacy of evidence for their effectiveness in suppressing venereal disease. Other grounds for protest were tied to the growth of the feminist movement in Great Britain. The acts were viewed as cruel to women and as violations that imposed a double standard on the sexual activity of women. Protestors also cited the possibility of the arrest of innocent women, of infection from unwashed speculums during the examinations, and the difficulty of distinguishing venereal disease from other vaginal lesions. Feminist literature of the period identified the patriarchal role of the examining physician the degrading aspects of these "instrumental violations" of women. Proponents of the acts, many of them physicians, formed their own association and called for extension of control to civilian populations. The upper-class women involved in the protest took large risks, by Victorian standards, in associating themselves with prostitutes, and many were denigrated. Working-class women protesting their own examinations ran even greater risks. The acts were suspended in 1883 and taken off the statute books three years later, probably as much in response to their expense and the unviability of extending them to civilian populations as to the protests.

The acts must be seen within the context of the role of prostitution in Victorian society. Prostitutes were not a professional class at this time, and prostitution provided temporary or seasonal employment for many poor women. Working-class women who were well integrated into their communities might pass through a period during which they worked as prostitutes to supplement meager wages or to save money for marriage. Demographic and economic changes had pushed many women from the countryside to towns, where they met with limited employment opportunities. Rather than the "dehumanized vagabonds" of much of the Victorian literature on prostitution, they were often poor working women struggling to survive. Walkowitz (1977) has looked at the records of arrests under the acts and developed a typical profile of those accused. She presents a picture of prostitution as a rational choice given the alternatives, not as a deviant act. In 1867, following the collapse of the copper mining industry, twenty thousand dependent women and children were left behind after the migration of skilled miners from the area. The closest large city was Plymouth, and Walkowitz gives evidence that this displaced group of women made up a large proportion of the prostitutes in that area. The typical prostitute, caught in the web of restrictions, forced examinations, and incarceration, was an underpaid working woman of about twenty years of age. Once arrested, she might be separated from her family, incarcerated, and sent to a workhouse or rescue mission to be "rehabilitated."

The first to become involved in protesting the acts were socially concerned people from various evangelical denominations who met at the 1869 Social Science Congress at Bristol. Shortly after this, the Ladies National Association organized under the leadership of Josephine Butler (a feminist who was also involved in the fight for higher education for women), and in December 1869, they published a "Women's Manifesto." There were many forms of resistance employed by the women accused of prostitution and their working-class allies: crowds would gather as women were dragged off to be examined; often, neighbors would intervene; there were riots in the Lock Hospitals. During the "Siege of Devonport," in spring 1870, middle-class reformers agitated widely among working-class women in poor neighborhoods, workhouses, and hospitals to persuade them not to sign the voluntary submission. Fliers described the examination as a degradation and affront to all women and admonished women to "reform and resist." Working women and "ladies" met to condemn the acts as class and sex legislation. In Southampton, there were 420 cases of refusal to submit to examination before magistrates and seven years of resistance to the acts (Walkowitz 1977). Almost any working-class woman within the garrison towns under the acts' control was vulnerable to examination and confinement. In testimony to Parliament, a visiting surgeon to one of the Lock Hospitals, who was also a magistrate, gave his working definition of a prostitute:

> A prostitute is any woman who there is fair and reasonable ground to believe is, first of all going to places which are the resorts of prostitutes alone, and at times when immoral persons are usually out. It is more a question of mannerism than anything else. (Ibid., p. 425)

The acts were, among other things, part of the medical establishment's attempts to increase its power. Many physicians saw the acts as a first step in the creation of a state-supported medical system regulating prostitutes which would extend to nonmilitary populations. The Contagious Diseases Acts have also been viewed as an effort to institutionalize prostitution, to separate prostitutes from the ranks of the respectable poor, and to sever prostitutes' associations and identification with working-class communities. "In these Acts one may perceive imperialist compulsions turned toward the domestic colonization of the poor" (ibid., p. 194).

Prostitutes in the late Victorian period in Britain were an obsessive focus of much popular literature that projected contemporary images of female sexuality (Murray 1982). The Victorians had a dense iconography of prostitution metaphorically connecting prostitutes to animals. Prostitutes carried the complicated projections of a society that viewed women, animals, and nature as associated images. Women were linked to nature through a scientific and popular discourse that pointed to their greater emotionality, naturalness, and nurturant proclivities. This positive imagery was associated with Victorian ideals of womanhood. But the linking of women with nature, formalized in the early years of the "scientific revolution" (Jordanova 1980) and solidified by the nineteenth-century scientific study of sex, also contained negative associations of the dark side of nature immanent in European thought. Sometimes described as "dehumanized" victims, prostitutes were also perceived as wild, dissolute, and destructive. It is in the Victorian iconography of prostitution that the negative link between women and animals is seen. The sexually degraded woman is an animal, often a mare, as Lansbury (1985) has shown in her analysis of Victorian pornography and its metaphoric ties to images of vivisection.

Prostitutes were often explicitly portrayed as animals. An examining surgeon at one of the Lock Hospitals described the "dehumanizing influence of the abominable places to which so many of the prostitutes are driven" in a British garrison town. "Several of the women have habituated themselves to a kind of gypsy mode of living, sleeping under horses in stables or large holes dug out of sandbanks" (Walkowitz 1977, p. 192). Prostitutes were women "whose status was quite literally barbarous, and whose treatment by the law was based on conceptions derived from experience with animals: They were prostitutes, and prostitutes, like animals, had no legal personalities" (F. B. Smith in Bauer and Ritt 1979, p. 169).

"The Wrens of the Curragh" (1867), published in *Pall Mall Gazette,* was a report about army prostitutes living in nestlike huts on the edge of a military base in Ireland, in which the women were metaphorically transformed into nesting birds:

> The nests have an inner space of about nine feet long by seven feet broad; and the roof is not more than four and a half feet from the ground. You crouch into them as beasts crouch into cover, and there is no standing upright 'til you crawl out again. They are rough misshapen domes of furze-like big rude birds'-nests, compacted of harsh branches, and turned topsy-turvy upon the ground. . . . I wanted to know how my wretched companion in this lonely, windy, comfortless hovel came from being a woman to be turned into a wren. (Murray 1982, pp. 403–406)

Both upper- and working-class women perceived the genital examinations mandated under the acts as "unnatural and degrading, a form of instrumental rape" (Walkowitz 1977, p. 81). A repeal agent who asked a woman the difference between having intercourse with strangers and being examined by the physician received the following reply:

> I should have thought you'd have known better nor that. Ain't one in the way of natur', and the other ain't natur' at all. Ain't a

different thing what a woman's obliged to do for a living because she has to keep body and soul together, and going up there to be pulled about by a man as if you were cattle and hadn't no feeling, and to have an instrument pushed up you. (Ibid., p. 82)

The anti-Contagious Diseases Acts movement protested, among other things, the instrumental violations of living beings. In this sense, the acts provoked a response similar to that of many women toward vivisection. The male physician's instrumental violations of animals and prostitutes were metaphorically similar, involving manipulation of natural beings by the new medical technocrats. Women, animals, and prostitutes (women who have become animals) formed an associated group of signs in the Victorian cosmology. Both antivivisection and the protest of the acts involved a response by women to the medical manipulations of categories of beings with whom women identified.

The paired structural terms *culture/nature* and *human/animal* have been an important source of meaning and metaphor in Western society. They are part of a series of oppositions that mutually define each other. These dichotomies seem to anchor us, particularly in times of rapid social change (Jordanova 1980). In the Victorian period, the opposition between human and animal, a concept the Victorians had inherited from both Christian cosmology and the scientism of the Enlightenment, was linked to another dichotomy central to Victorian social ideology—the association of women with nature and men with culture. Jordanova has described the historical dimensions of this construct through a study of sexual metaphors and symbols in nineteenth-century biomedical science. The notion of women as natural contained positive and negative connotations. Women were viewed as both superstitious and emotional, or as carriers of a new morality through which civilization's artificiality might be transcended. Nineteenth-century medicine defined male and female sexuality as polar opposites, whereas earlier medical models had constructed sex differences as a continuum: male and female qualities were believed to occur to various degrees in any given individual. Nineteenth-century physicians were very concerned with the problem of how the boundaries of gender might be blurred, about feminized males and masculinized females. Females could be masculinized by too much physical or intellectual labor.

Events in the world beyond the physician's office had created a class of women who worked outside the home, often without the protection of the extended family. The boundaries of gender were contested on the streets of urban townships and in meeting halls where women met to protest their oppression. In many Victorian towns, the increasing numbers of independent, employed, and underemployed working-class women sharply contrasted with the social ideal of the protected "guardian angel" of the home. In the 1880s, British upper-class women began to enter institutions of higher education against fierce opposition. Feminists agitated for women's suffrage and property ownership for married women. At the same time, Victorian medicine created whole categories of pathology based on the most rigid definitions of male and female. Thus, the reification of differences between the sexes occurred in the face of societal changes that questioned the Victorian assumptions about gender roles. Recent feminist historiography has examined the solidification of polarized Victorian medical views on sex differences as a response to changes in women's roles in society.

In the nineteenth century, "science and medicine as activities were associated with sexual metaphors which were clearly expressed in designating nature as a woman to be unveiled, unclothed and penetrated by masculine science" (Jordanova 1980, p. 45). In wax anatomical models and lithographs, women were shown as objects of natural study. Thus, a popular lithograph of the 1860s showed a beautiful young woman who had drowned being dissected by an anatomist interested in the physical basis of female attractiveness. A group of men stand around a table on which the corpse lies, and one man holds up for observation the thin sheet of skin that covers the breast. "The corpse is being undressed scientifically, the constituent parts of the body are being displayed for scrutiny and analysis" (ibid., p. 57). These images were widespread in Victorian culture, and their association with vivisection is striking. The propaganda of the Victorian antivivisection movement makes the same contrast between the passivity of living organism and the active intrusion of the physician with his instruments. Many women responded to these images and metaphors with anger and alarm based in part on the cultural linkage between women and animals as natural categories explored by science.

The antivivisectionists' critique of the new medical sciences raised many questions concerning the efficacy of heroic, interventive medicine. The claims of modern physiology were attacked as false, and clinical procedures based on physiological research were called harmful. Many nineteenth-century surgical interventions involved cures that were as dangerous as the diseases they were designed to treat. Some of the antivivisectionists' criticisms of interventive medicine were based on homeopathic beliefs. Many antivivisectionists believed that disease resulted from disharmony with nature and that only by restoring a balance with nature could health be achieved, not through medical interventions of any kind. The vivisected animal was seen as the symbolic nexus for many issues. On a practical level, vivisection could be eliminated, according to the antivivisectionists, because anatomical and clinical observations would achieve the same results. The antivivisectionists were appalled by the instrumental incursions of physicians into women and animals. Many believed that the ruthless materialism of science and its technological manipulations had to be stopped and a millennium of mercy restored in which humans once again lived in harmony with nature.

Stephen Coleridge attacked the practical benefits of clinical procedures based on vivisectional research:

> I have carefully studied the annual reports of all the large metropolitan hospitals for many years past, but have never discovered any figures which inform the public how many operations are followed by death of the patient. (1916, p. 111)

In a chapter entitled "The Appeal to Utility," Coleridge (1916) includes a table showing the "natural decrease" in various diseases for which vaccination programs had not been instituted and the increase in diseases for which public health programs mandated vaccination.

> Here we see that when improved sanitation and water-supply, the abolition of foul slums, the prevention of over-crowding, and the County Council regulations against infection, are left as the sole protection of the people from these common diseases, those diseases have a marked and universal tendency to disappear, whereas when to these conditions and circumstances there is superimposed the malign activity of the vivisectors and their nostrums, this beneficent tendency in common diseases to disappear

is often checked, and sometimes becomes changed into a sinister tendency to advance upon and overwhelm mankind. (P. 43)

Some of the attacks on science displayed a confusion about how experimental science operates. The Victorian period was strongly influenced by an older natural history tradition of collecting and classifying facts. The application to biology of the scientific method, with its emphasis on repetition of experiments, was confusing to many educated people. George Bernard Shaw was an ardent antivivisectionist and viewed science as an artificially contrived sham:

> I, an artist-biologist, mistrust laboratory methods because what happens in a laboratory is contrived, and dictated by its controllers. The evidence can be manufactured. The cases are what newspaper reports of police cases call frame-ups. If the evidence is unexpected or disappointing it can be remanufactured until it proves what the controllers want it to prove. (Quoted in Bowker 1949, p. 18)

But the overriding criticism of science was directed against its materialism. Coleridge wrote:

> The worship of Science, which has depressed this country for the last fifty years, is a very degrading episode in our history, it has ridiculed a classical education because human letters conferred mind upon mankind instead of money, and it has elevated a sterile materialism to the dignity of a religion. (1916, p. 167)

Turner, among others, has noted the tie between morality and physical health implicit in Victorian sanitarianism, which rejected scientific medicine in favor of cleanliness, moral restraint, and harmony with natural processes:

> The danger to health came as much from the corruption of morals as from the contamination of the environment. To fight against "impurity," "pollution," and "filth" [the standard rhetoric of the movement] did not mean merely to build sewers. (1980, p. 103)

All of the "dirty stuff" discovered through vivisection, through the intense concentration on bodily processes, became identified with the moral impurity that many perceived to be rife in modern life. The concept of "knowing" the animal through vivisection (the biblical connotation lending a sexual subtext to that term) is a frequent theme in Victorian literature. The dual meaning was appropriate to the act itself, the violation of a living body, and to the theory resulting from it—"knowledge" of humanity's animal nature, implicit in the use of physiological analogues. From the doctrinal, evangelical point of view, diseases represented, for some, God's punishment for moral impurity. Practices like compulsory vaccination also were seen as a menace to other traditional values. Coleridge wrote:

> Freedom of the person as established in England for many generations is the peculiar possession of our race and country. . . . The compulsory vaccination act went down before the repugnance of the Englishman as a violation of his right of private judgment and the insufferable claim of Doctors to inject diseased matter into his body. (1916, P. 106–107)

According to one Victorian antivivisectionist physician,

> When man is in harmony with his environment he has Physical Health, but he can never have that socially, or on a large scale, until he is first brought into mental harmony with the ways of his being and the righteous purpose of his Creator. The medicine of the future must largely consist therefore, in trying to bring about this holy adjustment. (Quoted in French 1975, p. 332, from *Animal Guardian* [1898])

By the turn of the century, Caroline White, a leading British antivivisectionist, had become convinced that cleanliness and pure air would end all disease, and antivivisectionist homeopaths lectured on such subjects as "The medicine of the future: Dietotherapy" (Turner 1980, p. 119).

The antivivisectionists tied the moral issue of cruelty to animals to the general decline in ethical values brought about by science.

> The dark and awful abyss into which the lust of cruelty will plunge a mortal Soul is incomprehensible to those [possessed of] wholesome happy natures, and to them the horrors of vivisection will always remain inconceivable. (Coleridge 1916, p. 149)

Some of the antivivisectionists' writings invoke a hyperbolic willingness to be martyred that reflects their passionate conviction that vivisection was a terrible evil. As Robert Browning wrote in a letter to Cobbe, "But this I know, I would rather submit to the worst of the deaths, so far as pain goes, than have a single dog or cat tortured on the pretense of sparing me a twinge or two" (1874; quoted in Coleridge 1918, pp. 18–19). Some stanzas from a poem by Browning convey this aspect of the popular literature on the subject. Browning was writing in response to widespread reports about the experimental drowning of dogs by physiologists.

> Up he comes with the child, see tight
> In mouth, alive too, clutched from quite
> A depth of ten feet—twelve, I bet
> Good dog! What off again? All right!
> John go and catch—or if needs be
> Purchase—that animal for me!
> By vivisection, at expense
> Of half an hour, and eighteen pence
> How brain secretes dog's soul, we'll see!
> (Quoted in Coleridge 1918, p. 19)

Central to the Victorian movement's philosophical and strategic thrust was the assertion that scientists themselves have no particular standing in terms of the moral decisions involved in experiments.

> It is manifest that the whole question of Man's Rights over and duties towards animals is a moral one which has no special relation to science; and therefore distinguished men of science have no more qualification to claim authority to dictate to us about it than have distinguished musicians, painters or lawyers. (Coleridge 1916, p. 29)

Public attitudes toward science are always linked to complex forces in the social, political, and economic spheres. The antivivisectionists were responding to a complex set of factors in the late Victorian cultural milieu. Changes in the Victorian cosmology blurred the boundary between human and animal and lent a symbolic logic to the role of animals as victims of science. At the same time, widespread anxiety about the issue of humans' animality provoked by the public dissemination of, and ideological permeation by, evolutionary theory added momentum to animal symbolism in antivivisection.

During the Victorian period, images of animals underwent important transformations. Animals have a rich iconography throughout European history which reflects aspects of people's attitudes toward nature during different periods. Fables, myths, beastiaries, and heraldic emblems all attest to the symbolic richness of animals in European life. Klingender (1971) writes of "the power of the animal symbol to blend a host of distinct meanings and overtones, distilling their essence, as it were in a single image" (p. 94). Changes occurred in the attitude toward animals as shifts in natural cosmology reflected alterations in the European world view. In the third century A.D., scholars turned to animals for guidance: "Tell me of the hates of wild beasts, sing their friendships, and their bridal chambers of tearless love upon the hills, and the birth which among wild beasts need no midwife" (Oddian, in ibid., p. 91). In the late medieval period, beast fables and religious and moral tales portray animals as aspects of uncontrolled nature transformed by human sanctity. The English language is replete with usages derived from animal names which reflect a projection of negative animal characteristics or attributes onto humans—beast, bitch, swine, ass, sloth, and so forth. All, notably, are pre-Victorian coinages. Saints were frequently believed to have tamed or saved beasts (ibid.). At the same time, allegories stressed the fidelity of dogs and the role of owls and other birds as witnesses both of sacred events, such as Christ's entombment, and human vice and folly, as in the paintings of Bosch.

> Animals have a symbolic function in expressing hidden or secret urges of society as well as serving simultaneously as the companions or servants of man. Whatever the precise relationship between man and beasts which the pleasure principle prompts us to imagine, it clearly transforms the real animal by turning it into a symbol on to which human feelings and wishes may be projected and which is therefore liable to evoke those feelings whenever we encounter either the living prototype or its image in art. (Ibid., p. xxiii)

Harwood (1928) and Turner (1980) have shown the changes in the late eighteenth- and early nineteenth-century view of animals. Concurrent with the rise of romanticism in art and literature, and Evangelicalism in religious life, animals were sentimentalized and anthropomorphized. However, social attitudes toward animals frequently incorporate disparate and sometimes contradictory elements. The Victorian romantic movement projected images of nature that were often chaotic and threatening. A darker symbolism of potential danger also charactrized Victorian nature iconography. Williams (1975) has shown how the opposition be tween country and city in European thought contains rich ambiguities. The country has represented peace, innocence, and simple virtue, and during the same historical periods, backwardness, ignorance, and limitation. The city has represented learning and progress but also worldliness and corruption. Since much else exists beside these polarities of country and city (i.e., suburbs and villages), Williams suggests that these cultural dichotomies provide coherence in the face of threatened social disorganization.

The human/animal dichotomy in Western thought has had similarly complex associations. Animals were profoundly anthropomorphized and sentimentalized during the Victorian era, as reflected in art, poetry, and literature of the period. Land ownership and rural life came increasingly to symbolize the values of an older landed gentry, disappearing in the face of increased urbanization. The British had always kept dogs, but it was during the Victorian period that the cult of the pet developed, based in part on the perception of pets as a surviving link to older rural values. Pet-keeping also reflected a trend toward withdrawal into the small family unit, in contrast to the extended rural family, in the pursuit of emotional satisfaction (Thomas 1983). In this context, it is worth remembering that the humane concern for animal welfare was, from the start, an urban, middle-class, and upper-class phenomenon. The daily rounds of agrarian life in nineteenth-century England involved riding, shearing, butchering, herding of animals, and crude veterinary surgeries. Domestic animals were used in working roles, and the boundary between farmer and domestic animal in the countryside was unambiguous. Unlike the pet in an urban environment, the farm animal was never anthropomorphized. In 1700, over three-fourths of the British population still lived in the countryside; by 1851, the majority of Britons lived in towns and cities (ibid., p. 243). The growth of humane sentiment is related to complex social changes resulting from this rapid urbanization. As animals became marginal to processes of industrial production, ideals of land ownership and rural ways of life were retained as important cultural values. The urban middle class took weekend trips to the countryside, developed elaborate gardening hobbies in small urban plots, and kept pets.

In the sense that the pet is also a family member, it fits into a category of animals studied by anthropologists which act as mediators between the human realm and the nonhuman realm. Thomas (p. 112) points out three features that distinguish the pet from rural domestic animals: it is allowed in the house, it is given a personal name (domestic stock were, in contrast, given semihuman names or names describing attributes of the animal), and it is never eaten. Thus, the social boundary implicit in the agrarian relationship between human and beast is breached in the relationship between master and pet. As an example, Bentham owned a cat named Sir John Langborn which became, with age, Reverend John Langborn, and, at last, Revered Doctor John Langborn (p. 115). In the 1870s, a hostile critic wrote of Cobbe:

> Her dog and cat are a great deal to her; and it is the idea of their suffering which excites her . . . she is not defending a right inherent in sentient things as such; she is doing special pleading for some of them for which she has a special liking. (Quoted in Thomas, p. 120)

In analyzing the role of the pet, some have viewed it as a safe, symbolic acting out of politically oppressive relations between human beings.

> What is it about pets that makes them useful and attractive to human beings. . . . I will suggest that pethood derives its powerful and, at first blush, wholly beneficial aspect from its ability to allow pet owners to experience a relationship ever present in political ideology: the relationship between the distinction of which beings are our familial kin from which are not kin and the distinction of which beings are our species kind from which are not our kind. Pethood allows us as individuals to experience and enjoy that ideologically crucial distinction in a way that is at once comforting and harmless. And indeed, we generally think of pethood as an innocuous and even trivial institution of "consumer society." We will see here, however, that the particular idealized articulation of kinship with kind that the traditional institution of pethood helps

> to perpetuate, conceals even from would-be kindly human beings a brutally inhumane political reality. (Shell 1986, p. 121)

This "political reality" is the domination, exploitation, and sometimes murder of those defined as "other." Extrapolations from this metaphor can be understood in the antivivisection literature, which sometimes analogized the rights of animals with the rights of colonized peoples. Animals were symbolically linked there to several classes of exploited beings, such as women, workers, and colonial subjects. Concern for their treatment is also a symbolic enactment of movements within Victorian society toward decolonization of both the poor in Great Britain and her colonial subjects.

Not surprisingly, most of the nineteenth-century advocates of antivivisection were devoted pet-keepers. In contrast, rural life does not encourage such ambiguities, Berger (1980) notes:

> A peasant becomes fond of his pig and is glad to salt away its pork. What is significant, and is so difficult for the urban stranger to understand, is that the two statements in that sentence are connected by an *and* and not by a *but*. (P. 5)

Or as Seamus Heaney wrote:

> "Prevention of Cruelty" talk cuts ice in town
> Where they consider death unnatural
> But on well-run farms pests have to be kept down.
> (Quoted in Thomas 1983, p. 181)

Cobbe wrote numerous popular articles on dog psychology based on her belief in the almost human cognitive and emotional propensities of dogs (1872*a*, 1872*b*). Animals were anthropomorphized as bearers of the qualities associated with the heart rather than the intellect. A secular romanticism developed which exalted these emotional, intuitive qualities. Stories with horses and dogs as protagonists were extremely popular, while authors such as John Burroughs and J. G. Wood portrayed animals that were human and even nobler than most people. In the popular classic *Black Beauty* (Sewell 1877), animals have "knowledge which did not depend on reason, and which was much more prompt and perfect in its way" (quoted in Turner 1980, p. 75).

Lansbury has explored the anthropomorphic imagery in *Black Beauty* and a number of similar texts that were widely distributed by humane societies and read by generations of British schoolchildren. In *The Old Brown Dog* (1985), she examines the symbolic meaning of the 1907 "Brown Dog riots" in the Battersea District of London, in which trade unionists and feminists (an unlikely partnership; the labor unions had not supported women's suffrage in the nineteenth century because they perceived women as a competitive source of cheap labor) fought medical students from London University over a statue of a brown dog that had been used for vivisection. According to Lansbury, the prescriptive theme of compassion for animals in books like *Black Beauty* overlay another message about the proper relationship between worker and employer. The good horse's loyalty and respect for the master was an admonishment to British working-class people at a time when trade unionism had gained a significant following. The symbolic association was also deployed by labor unionists, who couched their descriptions of workers' oppression in the same "beast of burden" metaphor.

Lansbury contends that there was strong antivivisection sentiment among working-class people for many reasons. Many of the poor felt they were treated like animals by physicians in the charity hospitals who also worked as vivisectors. Kingsford described physicians' callousness toward working people and related it to their training as vivisectors. Antivivisection hospitals, like the "Old Anti" at Battersea, in which the attending staff were pledged not to perform vivisection, were frequented with confidence by many working-class people. Like women, working people identified with vivisected animals for a number of reasons.

Popular art also anthropomorphized animals, showing card-playing dogs and animals engaged in a variety of other human pursuits. Many middle-class homes had hand-colored lithographs of animals. Edwin Landseer (1802–1873) became the most eminent British painter of the period. His dogs are anthropomorphic and often function as allegories of human situations, particularly those based on class differences and other aspects of social life. They are completely deanimalized and seem to be caricatured humans. Similarly, Berger (1980) notes of Grandville, another popular allegorist of this period:

> Here animals are not being used as reminders of origin, or as moral metaphors, they are being used en masse to "people" situations. The movement that ends with the banality of Disney began

as a disturbing, prophetic dream in the work of Grandville. The dogs in Grandville's engraving of the dog pound are in no way canine; they have dog faces, but what they are suffering is imprisonment like men. (P. 17)

By the turn of the century, the English language had been purged of many of its colorful terms for animals; for example, "brute" and "beast," both of which had come to be seen as derogatory.

A concurrent and equally profound shift was taking place in the popular view of human nature. Even as the Victorians repressed the physical and carnal, they suffered from an acute perception of the human as an animal whose immanent brutishness might erupt with terrifying results. The Victorian antivivisection literature made use of this imagery in its portrayal of the bloodthirsty, sensuous, bestial vivisector. The transformations involved in the imagery of the brutish vivisector standing knife in hand over the anthropomorphized animal are complex and serve as rich ground for analysis. A similar theme is expressed in Mary Shelley's Frankenstein (1818). The scientist, full of zeal for the technological conquest of life, takes over God's role with dire consequences. Popular Victorian classics, like Stevenson's *The Strange Case of Dr. Jekyll and Mr. Hyde* (1886) and H. G. Wells's *The Island of Dr. Moreau* (1896), deal with the theme of the transformation of human to "apelike," "insensate" animal, or animal to quasi-human monster. A new form of caricature developed in which the Irish were portrayed as apes. Previous styles of caricature had always used animals to portray human foibles, but the animals had functioned allegorically and generically, without recourse to ethnic stereotyping.

These literary and artistic transformations of human into animal had parallels in the scientific discourse of the period. Cesare Lombroso, an Italian criminologist who was widely read in England, developed a theory in the 1860s which held that natural criminals could be recognized by their resemblance to apes. In his view, certain criminals were actually living representatives of earlier, brutish stages of development (Gould 1981). Similarly, in the work of the early evolutionists, it was proposed that women and the lower classes had not advanced very far in evolutionary terms and represented earlier stages of development (Fee 1974). In

Durkheim's *Suicide* (1897), women's sexuality is akin to that of animals:

> Women's sexual needs have less of a mental character because, generally speaking, her mental life is less developed. These needs are more closely related to the needs of the organism, following rather than leading them. Being a more instinctive creature than man, woman has only to follow her instincts to find calmness and peace. (Quoted in Jordanova 1980, p. 64)

This "animal within" had both positive and negative associations. In 1903, William James wrote in a letter to the *Springfield Republican*:

> The water-tight compartment in which the carnivore within us is confined is artificial and not organic. It never will be organic. The slightest diminution of external pressure, the slightest loophole of licensed exception, will make the whole system leaky, and murder will again grow rampant. (Quoted in Turner 1980, p. 69)

James's words mirror fears expressed in much of the antivivisection literature. The act of vivisection opens up the possibility of humans' worst impulses (and their most "bestial") flooding out. Repression of this bestiality and the striving for the millennium of mercy of which Cobbe spoke are thus symbolically to be achieved through the prohibition of vivisection. In a complex transformation, the animal is anthropomorphized and becomes the chief victim of the worst instincts in human nature.

Victorian attitudes toward nature underwent radical alteration. Uniformitarian geology, paleontology, and evolutionary theory presented a new cosmology of vast time spans and chaotic, teeming variation in the organic world. The responses of the Victorians to these alterations are reflected in popular literature and art. Alfred, Lord Tennyson, who was an active antivivisectionist, wrote the phrase "Nature red in tooth and claw with ravin" after reading Lyell's classic exposition of the new geology, *Principles of Geology* (ibid., p. 66). Ethnology, anthropology, and the study of prehistory developed rapidly from midcentury, and both the American and British societies of ethnology were created in the 1840s. The result was that Victorian society was inundated with information about primates, tribal societies past and present, and human evolution, which also transformed the image of humans as sharply demarcated from animals. The new data of social anthropology challenged many earlier assumptions about human nature.

> Until about 1860, marriage, the family, and sexual roles were assumed to belong to the natural condition of man, institutions beyond and above any mere geographic or historical accident. Between 1860 and 1890, however, social anthropology demonstrated that the idealized family of the Victorian middle class was dictated by no law of nature, that monogamous marriage was only one of various human sexual possibilities and that women were not necessarily born only to domestic and decorative functions. (Fee 1974, p. 87)

Darwinian theory had an enormous impact on late nineteenth-century thinking. The antivivisectionist response to Darwinism was complex and involved a simultaneous rejection of the materialism of evolutionary theory and deployment of the concept of continuity between human and animal in antivivisection arguments. Scientific naturalism treated the human as an animal, and part of the response of the antivivisectionists was to deemphasize the physical relationship yet at the same time to endow animals with the spiritual qualities of humans (French 1975). Cobbe's writings illustrate this complex, sometimes contradictory response to Darwin. The *Descent of Man* inspired her "with the deadliest alarm," but she incorporated evolutionary ideas into her arguments.

> It is the boast of the school of Science to which they belong that it has exploded the old theory that man is unique in creation, with a higher origin than the brutes, and a different destiny. They give us to understand that God—or rather the "unknown and unknowable"—has "made of one blood" at least all the mammalia upon earth. Not merely our corporeal frames, but Thought, Memory, Love, Hate, Hope, Fear, and even some shadowy analogues of Conscience and Religion have been traced by the great thinker at the head of this school, throughout the lower realms of life . . . and, in the eyes of most cultivated and thoughtful persons in these days, the claims of a dog, an elephant, a seal or a chimpanzee to consideration and compassion are at least as high as were those of a negro a century ago in the eyes of a Jamaica planter. (Cobbe 1884*a*, p. 8)

The impact of Darwinian theory on Cobbe's development of antivivisection had a more personal aspect, which is clarified in her 1894 autobiography. Cobbe vacationed near the Darwins' summer residence and initially had a warm friendship with Darwin. They exchanged letters on the emotional and cognitive propensities of dogs and corresponded on their mutual disagreement with John Stuart Mill on the issue of hereditary and environmental influences (both believed that heredity was of primary importance). Cobbe's beliefs about hereditary characters in humans differed significantly from Darwin's, however; she and the other antivivisectionists used the theory of evolution as an effective argument for the relationship, and therefore sanctity, of all living things, but they were deeply disturbed by the implications of the theory as they pertained to the animality of people.

Cobbe was a skillful lobbyist. Because of the importance she perceived in broadening the appeal of antivivisection to include British Catholics, she enlisted the reluctant support of Cardinal Manning, the preeminent Catholic in the realm. In her autobiography, she recounted her grilling of the cardinal before a speech he agreed to make on the subject of vivisection for the Victoria Street Society:

> I spoke of the moral results of Darwinism on the character and remarked how paralyzing was the idea that Conscience was merely an hereditary instinct fixed in the brain by the interests of the tribe. (1984, p. 449)

That antivivisection was in part a response to the anxiety aroused by the new scientific naturalism, which linked all organic life through evolutionary theory, is suggested by Cobbe's statements and those of other antivivisectionists. Cobbe's profound anxiety about those implications reverberates throughout much of her writing. In 1872, she published a large collection of essays entitled *Darwinism in Morals and Other Essays*. Later, reviewing the theory of ethics expounded in *The Descent of Man*, she wrote:

> Man's consciousness is not only *a* fact in the world but the *greatest* of facts; and to overlook it and take our lessons from Beasts and Insects is to repeat the old jest of Hamlet with Hamlet omitted. A philosophy founded solely on the Consciousness of Man, may, and, very likely, will, be imperfect; and certainly it will be

incomplete. But a philosophy which begins with inorganic matter and the lower animals, and only includes the outer facts of anthropology, regardless of human consciousness, *must* be worse than imperfect and incomplete. It resembles a treatise on the solar system which should omit to notice the sun. (1884, p. 446)

In summary, advances in many areas of science—evolutionary theory, paleontology, comparative anatomy, physiology—and the diffusion of knowledge about tribal peoples blurred the early Victorian demarcation between human and animal. The anthropomorphizing of animals and the imagery of the "beast within man," which pervaded Victorian popular literature, reflect adjustments to a changing world view. Once the logic of this ideological transformation is perceived, many of the seemingly hyperbolic or rhetorical statements of the antivivisectionists have new meaning. The new physiology had opened the animal, looked inside it, and made explicit analogies to human bodily functions. This was a profound disruption of Victorian cosmological boundaries. In a world in which cognitive boundaries were increasingly seen as having lost their integrity, people were exposed to a sense of great vulnerability. Vivisection became a central symbolic act. As the physiologist cuts into the animal, he exposes nothing less than the gaping maw of the crisis. The tremendous emotional appeal of antivivisection cannot be understood in terms of compassion alone, although kindness to animals is a very important motive for many adherents. The extreme focus of protest on scientific experimentation to the exclusion of other potentially painful acts involving animals is clarified by examining the symbolic aspects of vivisection. This is why arguments for the ultimate compassion of experiments that yield clinically beneficial results are usually unsuccessful with antivivisectionists.

Animals were richly endowed symbols for the Victorians, and vivisection became a highly emotional issue for large numbers of people. Then and now, the resulting resistance to experimentation has been motivated not by a negative animus toward science per se but rather by the full panoply of symbolic associations that the image of the animal evokes in Western culture. Similarly, hostility toward science and medicine does not alone explain the rise of strong antivivisection sentiment during particular periods. Attention to the symbolic role of animals explains important aspects of the Victorian movement that are usually dismissed as Victorian sentimentality, hyperbole, or even lunacy.

The Victorians lived through complex transformations of a number of their important cosmological categories. The animal/ human border was blurred by events in both the scientific and popular realms. Animals became the carriers of anthropomorphic projections specific to a new urban, industrial society. At the same time, the border between organism and machine was threatened by "instrumental violations," incursions by vivisectors into animals and by physicians into human beings. Those who wept over a vivisected dog also wept over the configuration of the new century.

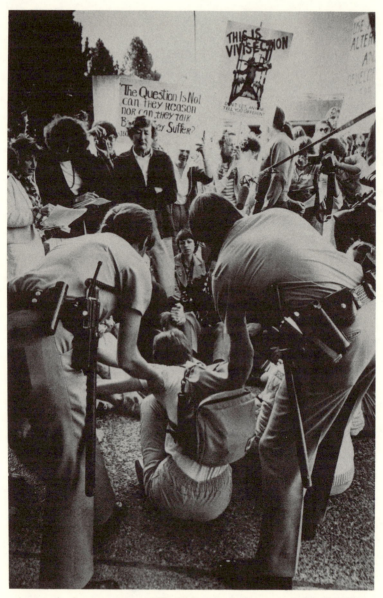

Arrest of a demonstrator at "World Day for Laboratory Animals," University of California, Berkeley, April 1987. Photo by Ron Delany.

4

The Vivisection of our Planet: The Modern Protest of Animal Experimentation

Like its Victorian predecessor, the modern protest against animal research is a distinctly different kind of movement from the traditional animal welfare movement in the contemporary United States. The appearance of grass roots animal rights groups in many urban, university communities during the late 1970s marks a significant departure from the modern social response to the use of animals by science. The American humane movement has always been strongly proscience and largely concerned with encouraging humane treatment of animals, particularly pets, in a variety of nonscientific settings. In fact, the humane societies have rarely addressed the issue of animal experimentation, and then, only reluctantly. By contrast, the new animal rights groups have focused specifically on questioning the morality of science and its practitioners in their use of animal subjects. Although there have been recent divergences from this single-issue approach within the animal rights movement (i.e., the interest of some adherents in factory farming and animals used in the entertainment industries), the signal concern of the modern movement is experimentation.

As was true of Victorian antivivisection, membership in a modern animal rights group does not necessarily imply former involvement with the humane movement. Although some activists have belonged to humane societies, many have not and have come to animal rights through former or concurrent membership in a number of other protest movements. For example, many activists have belonged to the ecology, antiwar, and feminist movements and have found a resonant voice in animal rights.

Andrew Rowan's (1984) balanced book on animal research contains a brief history of humane activity between 1900 and 1960 and a short description of the resurgence of antivivisection sentiment in the modern animal rights movement. The only other account of recent developments in the literature is a short report written by a consultant retained by Harvard University to research the movement (Martin 1982). Martin and Rowan agree that the animal rights movement has benefited from a general upsurge of public interest in the subject in the period since the late 1970s. Griffin and Sechzer (1983), Grodsky (1983), Pratt (1980), and Burghardt and Herzog (1980) briefly discuss aspects of the modern movement without detailing its history or structure.

As an anthropologist, I had the opportunity to record the thoughts and memories of activists in the large, well-organized Bay area movement through a series of informant interviews. Details of membership and historical recollections of my informants confirm the general impression that a significant shift in emphasis in recent years has resulted in the animal rights movement's increasingly sharp divergence from the concerns of the traditional humane organizations. An additional source of information has been the journals and newsletters published by the new groups which reflect developing animal rights ideology. The ephemera of the new movement, in the form of pamphlets and fliers distributed at demonstrations, has been a rich source of material for analysis.

The new movement represents a resurgence of interest in the issue of the use of animals by science unmatched since the British Victorian movement of the 1870s and 1880s. Although antivivisection sentiment has always existed among small groups of people in the United States, it has been a fringe phenomenon receiving little public attention. The emergence of new groups and coalitions in recent years, coupled with vastly increased media attention and legislative activity, all attest to the distinct burst of interest during the period since the late 1970s. In addition to legislative activity, media attention, and protests and demonstrations, several developments within the academic community itself show the recent increase of interest in the subject of animal welfare in research. University administrators find themselves frequently confronting criticism and protest from the animal rights community. A number of universities have held conferences on the ethics of the use of animals in research. The government agencies that fund research have sponsored meetings on this issue in the last several years. The New York Academy of Sciences held a workshop in spring 1983 on the role of animals in research and published papers in a volume of its *Annals* edited by Sechzer. Scientific journals have begun to include articles on the topic. New committees have been formed at all major universities whose charge it is to monitor compliance of animal researchers with various agency guidelines. In 1986, the National Science Foundation funded a large study of ethical issues in the regulation of animal research. That same year, the primary funding source for biomedical research—the National Institutes of Health—withdrew support from a research project at a prestigious eastern university as a result of lack of compliance with NIH guidelines for laboratory animal care. These developments are unique in their impact on the practice of twentieth-century academic research.

From their inception, the traditional humane societies have been proscience in attitude. In 1908, Henry Bergh, nephew of the founder of the American humane movement and treasurer of the ASPCA, said:

> As a member of the committee on vivisection of the ASPCA, I have found every disposition on the part of representative men of the [medical] profession to more than meet us halfway in any intelligent and honest effort to properly restrict the practice. (Quoted in Rowan 1984, p. 50)

Although in some sections of the country, particularly the Northeast, there was moderate antivivisection activity in the late nineteenth and early twentieth centuries, research-oriented science enjoyed rather uncritical support for most of the twentieth century. In each decade before World War II, there were epi-

sodes of attempts at antivivisection legislation, but they were sporadic and unsuccessful. In the period between the wars, scientific
research developed enormous prestige in the United States. The
powerful Hearst Press in California was strongly antivivisectionist, but despite its support, antivivisection initiatives
were defeated by large votes in the California legislature during
that period.

U.S. public support of science in its use of animal subjects continued into the postwar period. In the late 1940s, pound seizure
laws requiring release of unclaimed dogs and cats to medical research institutions passed in several states with little or no protest.
In 1949, antivivisectionists attempted to get the Los Angeles City
Council to pass an ordinance prohibiting pound seizure. Instead,
the medical community persuaded the council to pass an ordinance explicitly authorizing pound seizure. After the antivivisectionists succeeded in scheduling a referendum, both sides
campaigned vigorously, and Los Angeles voters strongly supported pound seizure. Other public referendums in Baltimore and
Illinois also resulted in the support of pound seizure by large margins (Rowan 1984).

The change in public attitudes toward science is related, among
other things, to the increased funding of research by government
agencies. The Public Health Service Act of 1947 provided the legislative basis for a growth in government research funding from
$0.7 million in 1945 to $98 million in 1956 and $930 million in 1963
(Rowan 1984; Burghardt and Herzog 1980; Sechzer 1983). Concomitant with the increase in federal funding and research has
been a huge rise in the numbers of animals used. The International Committee on Research Animals found that the number of
rodents and rabbits used in research in the United States between
1959 and 1965 rose from 17 million annually to 60 million annually.

In the 1950s, following a restructuring of the humane movement, two groups formed which began to address the issue of animals in research: the Animal Welfare Institute (1951) and the Humane Society of the United States (1954). Although issues of
proper care were raised (e.g., the cleaning of cages), the demands
and militancy of these early activist efforts were limited. In the
1960s, as centralized federal legislation became a trend (Rowan

1984; Griffin and Sechzer 1983), the first federal legislation on animal care was adopted. The Laboratory Animal Welfare Act of
1966 was debated in congressional hearings between 1960 and
1966 with discussion focusing on the British Cruelty to Animals
Act (1886), the prototype of all such legislation. Both sides were
debated vigorously. A proresearch antirestrictionist stated:

> The vast majority of advances in surgery since 1876 have come
> from the United States and other free countries, not from En-
> gland. These include open-heart surgery, surgery of the arterial
> system in major measure, development of the pacemaker, meth-
> ods of closed intestinal anastomosis, studies leading to the under-
> standing of the fundamental problems of intestinal obstruction,
> replacement of hopelessly damaged heart valves, kidney trans-
> plants, and many others. This must not be construed as to deni-
> grate British scientists, but rather to stress that the restraints im-
> posed upon them have blocked their progress in humane
> endeavors. (Quoted in Rowan 1984, p. 55)

In contrast, T. Abel, vice president of the Royal College of Surgeons in London, defended the effect of the British act before
Congress:

> We do not commit the atrocities which are reported from time
> to time in some other countries. We do not allow extravagant cru-
> elty committed by some investigators of stress and shock. We
> have proved that the desired results can be obtained by less inhu-
> mane methods. We are convinced that the freedom of all and sun-
> dry to use animals indiscriminately would not improve the value
> of research. (Ibid.)

The arguments presented in the congressional hearings probably had less to do with the passage of the legislation than did two
highly publicized incidents. One, in 1965, involved a family's unsuccessful attempt to recover a lost pet dog from a large New York
animal dealer. The other was an article in *Life* magazine (February 4, 1966) showing abusive treatment of dogs by animal dealers.
After each incident, Congress received enormous quantities of
mail (Rowan 1984). After much debate, the act (now called the
Animal Welfare Act) passed on August 24, 1966. Two amend-
ments (1970, 1976) were subsequently added to the legislation.
This sequence of legislative proposals, exposure of dramatic

abuses of laboratory animals through the media, and increased public support for legislative restriction is a pattern that continues to the present time. As the nineteenth-century antivivisectionists had decried the British act of 1886, so the Animal Welfare Act has been continually criticized by the animal rights movement as ineffective.

There are many indications that a substantial change has occurred since the mid-1970s in both public sentiment toward animal experimentation and activism by the new animal rights groups. My activist informants all date their involvement with the movement to a period during the late 1970s and early 1980s. Most activists cited the publication of Singer's *Animal Liberation* (1975) as an important event that infused the emerging movement with a cohesive moral and philosophical perspective. It has been augmented by a growing body of literature as other moral philosophers take up the issue of the treatment of animals (Fox 1985; Regan 1983; Rollins 1981). The growth in the literature on ethics in the years since 1975 has been concurrent with the development of the militant and radical approach of the grass roots groups. At the same time, there is evidence that science has been steadily losing the kind of overwhelming support it enjoyed for much of the twentieth century from a public disinclined to challenge the perceived agent of progress. This has been noted by people on both sides of the research issue. Patrick Corbett (1972), a philosopher and antivivisectionist, writes:

> The revolt of poetry and art against the formalizations of our culture, the revolt of the young against the roles which technological society requires them to fill, the concern with music, drugs and oriental techniques of meditation, the sudden anxiety to conserve as much as possible of the natural environment—these and innumerable other tendencies show that we are having second thoughts about the idealization of Man the Theorist and Man the Technologist which has dominated Europe for the last three hundred years. (Quoted in Godlovitch and Harris 1972, pp. 236–237)

The experimental psychologists Griffin and Sechzer (1983) also have noted these changes.

> Public attitudes reflect a growing awareness of the social and ethical costs of scientific developments; the increasing role of gov-

ernment in scientific research (one result of which is that scientists are perceived less and less as an independent force and increasingly identified with the power complex of government, the military, corporate industry, and academia); mistrust and misunderstanding of the nature of scientific knowledge; and rejection of the authority of science. (Pp. 188–189)

Public attention to the costs of scientific progress has been acute in the last decades. The perception that we are poisoning the earth and approaching a crisis in this regard is widespread among adherents of animal rights as well as members of the National Academy of Sciences. It is within the context of these changing attitudes toward the authority and morality of science that the rise of the animal rights movement must be examined.

The movement has synthesized both generally accepted and fringe positions in its linkage of animal experimentation with the ecological crisis and issues like iatrogenic problems in medicine. At present, the research community has claimed the terrain of the "rational," and animal rights groups have been burdened with the terrain of the "irrational" and "emotional." This obscures the complexity of interests on both sides of the issue. The animal rights movement incorporates widely accepted ideas with less popular ones such as the contention that the abuse of laboratory animals is of paramount importance in solving the current ecological or nuclear crisis.

There are now numerous grass roots groups in urban areas across the United States which emerged in the late 1970s and early 1980s to protest the use of animals in experimentation. The grass roots groups that have formed over the last five years do not have the monetary resources of the traditional societies for animal welfare, which have always been well funded. The Massachusetts Society for the Prevention of Cruelty to Animals, which is the wealthiest humane society in the nation, has assets of $42 million (Martin 1982). Bequests and donations are the major source of income for the traditional societies, as they have always been in Great Britain. Additional funding has come from investments, services to animals, and membership dues. The new groups have sometimes tried with varying degrees of success to obtain financial help from traditional humane societies. The animal rights movement must depend on resources based on the deep commitment and activism of adherents, and they are rich in these human resources. For example, some of my informants in the movement had left successful professional careers to devote all of their energies to animal rights.

It is extremely difficult to assess the actual membership of the new groups. Data are scarce, and some of my activist informants expressed a lack of specific knowledge of the numerical strength of the movement and, indeed, were interested in gaining such knowledge themselves. Mailing lists, for instance, do not fully reflect the number of people who come to meetings and join demonstrations but do not have any official ties to particular groups. Three of the large national groups with animal rights platforms, Friends of Animals (FOA), the Humane Society of the United States (HSUS), and the Fund for Animals (FA), reported combined membership in 1982 of 446,000 (ibid.). These groups represent only the large, nationwide animal rights organizations; they do not include memberships in the many local and regional groups.

In some instances, a member of one of the traditional humane societies has become involved in animal rights issues, and certainly most animal rights activists are implicitly concerned with traditional issues of humane treatment of animals in all contexts. But the new movement stresses ideas that are not derived from the traditional humane movement, such as "speciesism," the concept that humanity's treatment of animals constitutes illegitimate and immoral domination of other beings in a manner ideologically linked to racism, sexism, and other forms of oppression. Activists often describe their involvement as part of progressive, anti-imperialist political movements for the decolonization of women, the poor, and the Third World. Animals are linked to these categories as victims of the same patriarchal, capitalist forces that have colonized and exploited other groups. The term *animal rights* was first used by Ryder in his *Victims of Science* (1975). It was popularized by Singer in *Animal Liberation* (1975), which many advocates refer to as the "bible" of the movement. There, Singer defines speciesism as "a prejudice or attitude of bias towards the interests of members of one's own species and against those of members of other species" (p. 7).

Although all animal rights groups endorse the concept of protest against speciesism, there are several ideological divisions within the movement. Some groups support total abolition of animal experimentation, while others propose more stringent regulation. In my discussions with activists, I was struck by the degree of pragmatism of most of my informants on this issue. For example, many said that while total abolition was the ultimate goal personally desired, espousing such radical reform was not practical at this time. Activists described submerging personal preferences so as to accentuate common goals and make whatever small gains are practical now. Many informants strove to work peaceably with others with whom they had such ideological differences. Strategic divisions also exist within the new groups. While most groups favor legislative reform, education through literature, and nonviolent demonstrations, some groups such as the Band of Mercy, the Urban Gorillas, and the Animal Liberation Front advocate direct action, including laboratory break-ins and the liberation of animals. In recent years, this strategy has gained in popularity, and such tactics have been employed more frequently. Just as there are strategic and tactical divisions among animal rights organizations, there is a definite heterogeneity of beliefs and life-styles among individual members. For instance, some are vegans, ultrastrict vegetarians who neither eat nor use animal products of any kind, while others believe that vegetarianism is not a necessary concomitant to advocacy of animal rights.

A common misperception is that "antivivisectionist sentiment remains strongest among wealthy and prominent people including writers, actors, and artists" (Martin 1982, p. 4). While it is clear that the modern movement, like its nineteenth-century predecessor, has attracted prominent people, its mainstay is middle-class individuals with no particular social standing. Although reliable membership data on demographic categories such as social class, ethnicity, educational level, and sex are not available, the movement's greatest strength clearly is not concentrated among a social elite. Observation suggests that the new activists are typically white, college educated, from middle-class urban and suburban backgrounds, in their early to middle thirties, and female. My informants proposed that this was an accurate profile of a "typical" animal rights advocate but that all of these characteristics were variable. Several activists commented on the fact that there is a considerable age range at meetings, including a "fair number of gray heads." Although women predominate in the movement, many men are significantly involved. An activist informant suggested that men were actually overrepresented in leadership ranks in the movement because of the sexism inherent in society as a whole. The movement has attracted a number of academics and scientists. For example, in 1982, a group of veterinarians formed the Association for Animal Rights, which has ties to two of the large, national animal rights organizations.

The current attempt to establish legal rights for animals can be traced to two lawsuits brought by Helen Jones of the Society for Animal Rights, the earliest animal rights group. In *Jones v. Butz* (1974), which dealt with kosher slaughter, the U.S. District Court ruled that Jones had legal standing as "next friend and guardian for all livestock animals now and hereafter awaiting slaughter in the United States" (Martin 1982, p. 4). In another case, in which she challenged practices at two New York City zoos, she was also found to have standing as guardian of the animals' welfare. Jones and other early activists made some efforts to unite the movement. In 1973, as founder of the Society for Animal Rights, she led a demonstration at the Pentagon protesting the air force's use of beagles in their testing of poison gas. When the next march was directed to the defense of all animals, many people lost interest (ibid.). In contrast, the 1980 society funded "Animal Liberation from Laboratories" rally in Los Angeles involved the coordination of thirty-nine national and California-based groups. The ability to form such coalitions and work together despite differences of both an ideological and a tactical nature has characterized the recent movement. The strategic commitment to seek consensus was reflected in all my discussions with activists.

Recent events that illustrate the increased ability of heterogeneous groups to work together are the highly publicized demonstrations at the National Institutes of Health-funded regional primate centers which have been held each April since 1983. While the demonstrations were organized by the smaller grass roots groups, the new movement was able to enlist the support of several traditional humane organizations. The choice of the primate centers for these national demonstrations was part of a sophisticated and pragmatic strategic approach. One of my informants, who was involved in organizing the demonstrations, commented that primates elicit a response from the public because they are easy to identify with and because they resemble humans. An article in the *Newsletter* of Buddhists Concerned for Animals explains the reason for choosing the primate centers thus:

> The Mobilization for Animals (MFA) coalition has targeted the Primate Centers based on their brutal history of animal exploitation which typifies the way lab animals are treated throughout the animal experimentation industry. The primate centers have very high mortality rates, not only on account of experiments, but due to conditions in which animals are forced to live. As primate expert Jane Goodall stated, "Research scientists can have no concept or appreciation of what a chimpanzee really is." Which is perhaps why so many scientific laboratories maintain chimpanzees in conditions that are appalling, housed singly for the most part in small, concrete cells with nothing to do day in and day out except to await some new, and often terrifying or painful experiment. (Buddhists Concerned for Animals 1983*a*)

While stressing that concern must be broadened to all animals, the same *Newsletter* goes on to state:

> Why people in the Animal Rights Movement have chosen primate experiments to zero in on, rather than say, rodent research, is not based on Speciesism within the movement, but based on having an animal for which the general public could feel compassion. Monkeys are very much like us and we love them for it.

Another sign of increased organizational sophistication is the fact that a successful national coalition was formed to organize the primate demonstrations. Originally the idea of Richard Morgan, a Tennessee English professor, an ad hoc committee calling itself Mobilization for Animals met in 1983 to develop strategy. Representatives of many local groups attended. At a workshop on demonstrations, the decision was made to target three centers: Madison, Wisconsin, Davis, California, and Southborough, Massachusetts. Two of the large, established antivivisection organizations endorsed the demonstrations; each gave $5,000 and promised an additional $5,000. Mobilization for Animals developed a mailing list of 8,000 names and hired a professional company to handle mailing. They also received tax-exempt status and began to solicit funds from SPCAs and humane societies (Martin 1982). The demonstrations received unprecedented local and national media coverage and were impressive evidence of the movement's ability to unify around a specific issue.

The movement has also tried to work with other issue-based organizations that share some of its basic ideology, for example, large ecology and conservation groups such as Greenpeace, which endorsed the primate center demonstrations. This effort has not been without its problems (a theme touched on by several of my informant activists), and there appears to be a certain amount of bitterness on the part of some activists toward the larger and more entrenched conservation groups. The Sierra Club is one such group that has not been responsive to the movement's solicitations.

A further indication of increased activism and public response can be seen in the repeal of some of the animal procurement bills passed during the 1950s. The recent success in Massachusetts of local referendums against pound seizure illustrates this trend.

> Between 1981–1982, forty-one municipalities passed local resolutions opposing pound seizure, and in 1982, the New England Antivivisection Society and ASPCA led an intense battle in the State legislature to repeal the pound seizure law. This effort ended in defeat in the final moments of the session. However, they came away with the belief that public sentiment was with them, and they decided to switch tactics and take the matter directly to the people. (Attorneys for Animal Rights 1984)

A campaign called Pro Pets was initiated which was directed by the former Massachusetts state senator Samuel Rotundi.

> Rotundi elicited the cooperation of the largest humane societies in the State. Professional advertising experts assisted in the campaign, creating a campaign theme, brochures, posters, buttons, bumper stickers, and advertisements. Pro Pets organized and coordinated a volunteer work force which ultimately had 2,100 participants, a massive volunteer effort. The volunteer work force compiled the names of 150,000 pet owners in Massachusetts in order to complete a mail-out to those persons. Volunteers went out to the communities throughout the State, collecting the signatures of registered voters to present to the legislature.
>
> As the signature drive began, the animal activists continued to pursue the possibility of legislation, and found that the initiative was having a noticeable impact: Harvard University, the major

user of pound animals in Massachusetts, was now willing to end
pound seizure, rather than face the issue on the 1984 ballot.
(Ibid.)

The success of this effort in Massachusetts illustrates not only
the growing public responsiveness to the issue of animal research
but also the increasing strategic sophistication of animal rights activists in organizing such campaigns to crystallize public opinion in
their favor. This increased sophistication is also apparent among
West Coast activists:

> The first workshop, a two hour plenary session, provided an
> overview of the philosophical and moral questions raised by our
> treatment of animals. Professor Bernard Rollins, Colorado State
> University, led off with a discussion of how the animal rights
> movement has progressed. . . . Next Professor Steve Sapontzis,
> California State University, Hayward, spoke about eradicating
> the "logic of prejudice," . . . In the workshop on Representing
> the Animal Rights Activist, Arthur Margolis, of the California
> State Bar, and Leonard Post, Post and Kellman, Oakland, Ca.,
> discussed advising and representing activists in criminal proceed-
> ings, including framing defenses, raising animal rights issues in
> the course of the defense, picking a jury. (Ibid.)

New legislation directed at animal protection has been introduced at the state and federal levels with increased frequency
since the mid-1970s. Congressional representatives have reported
receiving thousands of letters supporting an animal rights bill real-
locating 30 to 50 percent of all funds used for animal research to
the study of the development of alternatives to animal models.
The architect and major lobbying group for this bill and several
other animal rights bills has been United Action for Animals.
During the subcommittee hearings on the bill before the Ninety-
sixth Congress (1979–80), there was a widely publicized incident
that had enormous public impact. Edward Taub's Maryland physiology laboratory was raided on September 11, 1981, after Alex
Pacheco, an activist who was working as a summer volunteer, had
developed a case against the researcher for extreme mistreatment
of his monkey subjects. Taub was found guilty of providing inade-
quate veterinary care, a charge that was later reduced on appeal to
one count of animal cruelty. These events were carried on the

front page of the *Washington Post*. The following day, subcommittee hearings focused on the role of the National Institutes of Health, which funded Taub's laboratory, and the United States Department of Agriculture (USDA), the agency charged with inspection, in overlooking the conditions in which the monkeys were kept. The USDA did not comment, but Raub of NIH admitted a failure of the system in the Taub case (Rowan 1984). Publicity surrounding the event in some ways represents the culmination of the trend toward increased media attention to the issue of laboratory animals, which had been building for at least five years.

The structure of federal and state legislation on animal research is complex. On the federal level, the Constitution has been interpreted as not granting the power to regulate the use of animals in research directly. Thus, all federal legislation had been based on the commerce clause, making funding by federal agencies, such as NIH, contingent on compliance with congressionally established guidelines and conditions. The states are not compelled by the Constitution to seek indirect means of regulation in this area. There have been state laws prohibiting cruelty to animals since 1858 and laws restricting their sale since 1954. The government regulation of animal research is a confusing web of agencies and guidelines. Federal regulation of the use of animals in research is complex and divided among departments in both the legislative and executive branches. The congressional Subcommittee on Science, Research, and Technology makes policy decisions on legislation. The USDA, through its Animal and Plant Health Inspection Service, administers the Animal Welfare Act. The Department of Health and Human Services regulates the use of animal subjects through NIH. Finally, four regulatory agencies, the Environmental Protection Agency, the Food and Drug Administration, the Consumer Product Safety Commission, and the Occupational Safety and Health Administration, are involved in the overall regulatory scheme.

On the federal level, the first confrontation over the issue of research animals occurred in the early 1960s and resulted in the NIH publication *Guide for Laboratory Animal Facilities and Care*. The 1966 Animal Welfare Act mandated the registration of research facilities with the Animal and Plant Health Inspection Service to promulgate standards of treatment and transport for animals by researchers and dealers. These standards include "minimum requirements with respect to housing, feeding, watering, sanitation, ventilation, shelter from extremes of weather or temperature, and adequate veterinary care, including the use of anesthetics, analgesics, or tranquilizing drugs" (Griffin and Sechzer 1983). The act mandates that pain-relieving drugs must be used during experimentation. When a painful experiment is conducted, a report must be filed stating whether drugs were used. As rats and mice were excluded, the original legislation covered only 4 to 5 percent of animals used in research. A 1970 amendment broadened the act to include all warm-blooded animals. In 1976, the scope of the act was again expanded to cover specifications for handling and transport.

Before it will fund projects using animal subjects, NIH imposes more stringent conditions. A written statement from the researcher assuring compliance with the Animal Welfare Act and the "Principles for Use of Animals" and "Guide for the Care and Use of Laboratory Animals" is required. NIH also requires accreditation by the American Association for Accreditation of Laboratory Animal Care (AAALAC) or the operation of an institutional animal care committee that monitors practices and facilities for compliance. As AAALAC requires such a committee, most institutions now submit to inspection and also have a standing committee. This policy covers all researchers and institutions using vertebrates in their studies. But animal rights groups maintain that these regulatory efforts do not effectively control abuses of lab animals and that researchers essentially do as they wish.

The animal rights movement has succeeded in taking antivivisection out of the margins of American political life and into a central position. Over a relatively short period of time, it has focused public attention on experimentation with animals and has proposed, lobbied for, and, in certain instances, won legislation to restrict research practices. There is not an experimental physiologist or scientist in a host of other disciplines who is not acutely aware of the growing power of the movement and its potential impact on his or her work. As the animal rights movement has grown in recent years, it has developed a cohesive ideology, which can be examined through a small, but growing literature. This literature consists of a number of recent books and many newsletters and fliers, passed from hand to hand and floating through the spring sunshine outside the primate centers each year.

Even a superficial reading of the movement's literature reveals its deep disjunction from the traditional humane movement. The themes emerging from it and from the statements of activists form a coherent ideology of protest that is similar in some fundamental aspects to that of the Victorian antivivisectionists, who also protested much more than experiments and contested aspects of the dominant world view of their society. But animal rights deploys meanings that are specific to the late twentieth century and that are quite different from those of the Victorian antivivisectionists.

Since the publication of the first animal rights books in 1975, a small body of literature has developed on the ethics of animal research, aspects of pain and suffering in laboratory animals, and suggestions for the replacement of animals or the reduction of their use by science (Ruesch 1978; Pratt 1976, 1980; Regan and Singer 1976; Diner 1979; M. Fox 1980; M. A. Fox 1985; Roberts 1980; Rollins 1981; Regan 1982, 1983; Rowan 1984; Sechzer 1983). Two earlier volumes were also very important to the development of the movement: *The Principles of Humane Experimental Technique* (Russell and Burch 1959) and *Animals, Men and Morals* (Godlovitch and Harris 1972). The ideas proposed in each were influential. Russell and Burch's "3 Rs" of humane experimental approach—reduction, refinement, and replacement—were an important tool of analysis for the movement in its early stages, and the influence of Godlovitch and Harris's moral philosophy seems to have been crucial to the movement's early development. Singer writes:

> In the fall of 1970 I was a graduate at the University of Oxford. Although I had specialized in moral and social philosophy, it had not occurred to me—any more than it occurs to most people—that our relationship with animals raised a serious moral issue . . . through Richard and his wife Mary, my wife and I became friendly with Roslind and Stanley Godlovitch, also vegetarians studying philosophy at Oxford. In long conversations with these four—and particularly with Roslind Godlovitch, who had worked out her ethical position in considerable detail—I became convinced that by eating animals I was participating in a systemic form of oppression of other species by my own species. The central ideas of this book derive from these conversations. (1975, p. xvii)

Most of the activist-informants with whom I spoke cited the publication of *Animal Liberation* as a signal event in their development as animal rights activists, and references to it are ubiquitous in the popular literature of the movement. Singer bases his analysis on the utilitarian theories of Bentham (1748–1832). Bentham's argument rested on two tenets—that the interests of any one being should be accorded neither more nor less weight than the interests of any other (a proposition termed the universal equality of interests) and that the capacity for suffering and enjoyment is the definitional prerequisite for recognition as a "being" possessing "interests." If one accepts these basic premises, it then follows that since most animals have the capacity for suffering and enjoyment, they therefore have interests that must be accorded equal weight to the interests of other organisms, including humans. Although recent theoretical arguments within the movement reflect an increasingly vigorous exchange between contending philosophies (Regan 1983), Singer's revision of Benthamite utilitarianism remains very influential. Ideological aspects of the movement are illuminated by an examination of Singer's thesis. Singer quotes Bentham on the rights of animals:

> The day may come when the rest of the animal creation may acquire those rights which never could have been withholden from them but by the hand of tyranny. The French have already discovered that the blackness of the skin is no reason why a human being should be abandoned without redress to the caprice of a tormentor. It may one day come to be recognized that the number of the legs, the villosity of the skin, or the termination of the *os sacrum* are reasons equally insufficient for abandoning a sensitive being to the same fate. What else is it that should trace the inseparable line? Is it the faculty of reason, or perhaps the faculty of discourse? But a full-grown horse or dog is beyond comparison a more conversable animal, than an infant of a day or a week or even a month old. But suppose they were otherwise, what would it avail? The question is not, can they *reason*? Nor can they *talk*? But can they *suffer*? (Bentham 1789, in Singer 1975, pp. 7–8)

The capacity for suffering, and therefore enjoyment, is the utilitarian basis for the claim that animals have interests and, therefore, share with humans the right to equal consideration. Singer also builds the case, suggested by Bentham's statement, for an analogy between speciesism and other forms of discrimination such as racism or sexism. This has become an important tenet of the new movement, and activists view their struggle as a logical extension of the movements against racism and sexism. Singer defines speciesism in the following way:

> Speciesism—the word is not an attractive one, but I can think of no better term—is a prejudice or attitude of bias toward the interests of members of one's own species and against those of members of other species. It should be obvious that the fundamental objections made to racism by Thomas Jefferson and Sojournor Truth apply equally to speciesism. If possessing a higher degree of intelligence does not entitle one human to use another for his own ends, how can it entitle humans to exploit nonhumans for the same purpose? (Ibid., p. 7)

The influence of popular animal ethologies on animal rights ideology can be seen in Singer's manifesto. He cites work from the 1960s by Lorenz, Tinbergen, Eibl-Eibesfeldt, Goodall, and Schaller and concludes that "in keeping with our picture of the world of animals as a bloody scene of combat, we ignore the extent to which other species exhibit a complex social life, recognizing and relating to other members of their species as individuals" (p. 236). Understanding the ways in which animal ethology and its popularizations have influenced animal rights is crucial to an understanding of the development of the movement's ideology.

Another theme of Singer's is that animal experiments are largely unnecessary because the world's major health problems can be eliminated with good nutrition, sanitation, and health care based on techniques already developed.

> Finally, it is important to realize that the major health problems of the world largely continue to exist, not because we do not know how to prevent disease and keep people healthy, but because no one is putting the manpower and money into doing what we already know how to do. The diseases that ravage Asia, Africa, and Latin America, and the pockets of poverty in the industrialized West are diseases that, by and large, we know how to cure. They have been eliminated in communities which have adequate nutrition, sanitation, and health care. Those who are genuinely concerned about improving health and have medical qualifications would probably make a more effective contribution to human health if they left the laboratories and saw to it that our existing

stock of medical knowledge reaches those who need it most. (P. 81)

Most public health officials worldwide would agree with much of what Singer says here. But how salient this argument is to the issue of laboratory research on specific diseases is not addressed in *Animal Liberation*. This critique of biomedicine, based on its underemphasis on nutrition and sanitation and its unequal distribution, is a recurrent theme of the modern animal rights movement.

Another theme in movement philosophy, which Singer discusses, is the danger posed by science and the view of scientists as agents of harm to the natural environment. Animal rights ideology contests the privileged status of the scientist in modern culture:

> As well as the general attitude of speciesism which researchers share with other citizens there are some special factors operating to make possible the experiments I have described. Foremost among these is the immense respect that we still have for scientists. Although the advent of nuclear weapons and environmental pollution have made us realize that science and technology need to be controlled to some extent, we still tend to be in awe of anyone who wears a white coat and has a Ph.D. (P. 63)

Singer elaborated many of what would become the major themes of the animal rights movement: the right of other species to equal consideration, the disharmony of the human relationship with nature in modern industrial society as reflected in our treatment of other animals, the view of science as an agent of nature's destruction, and the goal of increased human health through a realignment of the human organism with nature and more equitable distribution of resources.

Fox's *Returning to Eden* (1980) also offers insights into the developing ideology of the new movement. Fox, an animal rights advocate, is a veterinarian and animal psychologist who has written extensively on the behavior of dogs and wolves. He has also been involved in the human potential movement and has worked at the movement's center, Esalen, in northern California. In 1976 HSUS named him director of the Institute for the Study of Animal Problems. Fox forcefully suggests the revitalistic nature of the new movement. "The dawning of a new Eden" depends on the recognition of animal rights. Fox proposes that the imbalance on earth caused by scientific and technological dominance of nature is mirrored by imbalances within the body, which he views as a microcosmic, yet nonautonomous, ecology. In his view, most sickness is caused by ubiquitous problems of modern urban life:

> Much human sickness and suffering are caused by stress, social problems, anxiety, overcrowding, psychosomatic factors, work pressures, family problems, improper diet . . . and pollutants and adulterants in food, water, and air. (P. 175)

In his critique of medical practice and its fundamentally misguided reliance on animal research, he notes what he perceives as the actual dangers to patients posed by modern medicine, citing the "increased" incidence of physician- and treatment-caused problems. He departs from these widely accepted "rational" attitudes in his view of biomedicine as iatrogenic by its very nature and in his indictment of laboratory research with animal models as an important cause. In Fox's view, science and technology are the perpetrators of nature's exploitation. "Good" nature is contrasted to "bad" science:

> While today we may glorify the scientific, technological, and cultural achievements of our species, many people still find greater satisfaction with the wonders of nature; most human creations pale into insignificance before those of natural creation. (P. 21)

Nonindustrial societies are viewed by Fox, and many adherents, as spiritual examples or guides toward a more balanced relationship with nature viewed as characteristic of non-Western culture.

> Many Amerindians . . . have long contended that the white man does not respect the nonhuman spirit world and that he relates to the world as something separate from himself. He acts on the basis of his own laws, but not within the framework of a broader ethic which includes all creation. (P. 33)

Although books like Singer's and Fox's have been influential, the ephemera of the current movement, its newsletters, leaflets, and appeals for funds, which are distributed on campuses and at demonstrations, are the richest source of written material on the developing ideology of the new groups. Because the movement is in its nascent stage, and because most of its literature consists of fliers and newsletters, an examination of this material is essential to understanding animal rights ideas. Underlying the criticism of animal research is an indictment of oppressive relations in modern culture as represented by the scientific exploitation of animal models. Thus, universities and researchers are seen as the institutional representatives of a materialistic, impersonal, and destructive society that seeks total domination over the world of nature. They are viewed as using people as callously as they use animals and as part of the technological "vivisection" of the earth. Finally, all these perceptions are linked to a revitalistic, millennarian, and radical realignment of the human relationship to nature through the elimination of the exploitation of animals.

In much of the literature of the movement, the profit motive is implicated as the ultimate cause of animal experimentation. Research is identified as part of "the animal experimentation industry," which is in turn connected to a conspiracy or collaboration among medicine, drug companies, and universities, as illustrated in a Mobilization for Animals flier distributed in 1982 which refers to the regional primate centers as representatives of "all the greed and savagery of the animal experimentation industry." Scientists are often viewed as tied to experimental methodology by their need for money; they have a vested interest in colluding with institutions in the support of research.

> Unfortunately, decision-making committees at the primate centers are composed of people with a vested interest in the continuation of animal experimentation. One of the current researchers at the Davis Primate Center is also President of the International Primatological Society, which exists for the purpose of encouraging international and national trade in primate exports, breeding programs, and primate research in general. Animal experimentation is a multi-million dollar industry, and there are people involved who are less than anxious to see research progress into alternatives to live animal testing. (Buddhists Concerned for Animals 1983c)

> The truth is that animal experimentation is a highly profitable enterprise. There is no money in preventive medicine, which con-

sists of a return to a simple, natural diet, exercise, and control of anxiety and stress by awareness. (Animal Rights Connection, n.d.)

The profit motive of the "animal research industry" and the fundamentally flawed approach of a technology-dominated, interventive medicine are criticized in the context of conservative cutbacks in funding for social programs.

> The biomedical research industry, not the public, benefits from huge expenditures of tax-payer money on experiments which are rooted in interventive rather than preventive medicine. This obscene waste of lives and dollars, at a time when funds for essential social programs are being cut, impoverishes us both ethically and socially. (Mobilization for Animals 1983)

In the literature of the movement, biomedicine is implicated as dangerous and uncaring. Animal rights locates the source of iatrogenesis in animal experimentation, as did the Victorian anti-vivisectionists.

> The accumulation of damaging side effects in the newly developed pharmaceuticals should give rise to an investigation whether or not this accumulation is due to the employment of animal experiments.
> Critics of the sciences have warned for decades of the consequences of organ-related animal experimental medicine. For this kind of medicine leads into an inhuman impasse which leaves the patient alone with his suffering and makes a true doctor-patient relationship impossible. (Stiller, n.d., pp. 6, 7)

In a similar vein, *Agenda,* the news magazine of the Animal Rights Network, quotes one commentator as saying that

> for the past two centuries, scientists and researchers have been inducing cancer in billions—not millions—of animals, in hopes of finding a cure (or are they? this book [*The Cancer Syndrome*] asks) and the results have remained the same . . . the only humans benefiting from cancer research, Moss declares, are the people who are paid to do the experimenting and their constituents—the hospitals, medical associations, government agencies, foundations, and large corporations (Moretti 1983, p. 26)

Science and scientists are often portrayed as corrupt. (Some activists with whom I spoke voiced a modification of this view: scientists were corrupted by their economic dependence on a system that rewarded animal research; they were, in this sense, also victims of the system. No one felt that scientists might do their work with a strong sense of moral conviction.) This is a distinct contrast to the historically careful, approving tone of the traditional humane societies' public utterances.

> Scientists are less responsible than businessmen . . . the problem with science at the moment is there are just as many corrupt people as there are in business, but the structures of science are so anonymous and so protective of individuals' names that a corrupt person in science can go on forever without ever being exposed and even having to face the consequences of his actions. (Horrobin 1982)

Another important theme in the new literature is the perceived link between the government, the corporate war industry, and animal research. These institutions are sometimes viewed as literally aligned with each other in conspiratorial fashion and sometimes as metaphorically linked in their analogous exploitation of humans, animals, and nature.

> The rising consciousness of millions of people is caused by the realization that as they look around them, government and multinational companies are busily destroying our future. Profits and the next election are very short term goals after all, unlike the lifetime of our children and their children. Now millions are marching against nuclear weapons and thousands more also reject our treatment of animals (who are used to test those weapons). The rejection is often channeled through the new action groups like the Animal Liberation Front. (Windeatt 1983, p. 22)

In addition to its explicit ideological links to the holistic health critique of interventive technological medicine, the antiwar movement, and the ecology movement, many see animal rights as having a natural affinity to feminism, specifically, to themes in modern radical feminism which link the patriarchal oppression of women to the exploitation of nature. This "essentialist" vision of women as aligned to nature and sharing its historical "victimization" by Western culture is by no means the only current perspective in modern feminism; it recently has been analyzed from other feminist perspectives (Haraway 1985). A flier put out by Feminists for Animal Rights juxtaposes a pornographic photograph of a woman tied to a chair and a photograph of a cat in a restraining device. The text is as follows:

> Animal rights is a feminist issue. In patriarchal society, women and animals are considered inferior, cute, evil, uncontrollable, emotional, impulsive, instinctive, childish, irrational, property, objects.
>
> In patriarchal society women and animals are referred to as: chicks, bitches, pussies, foxes, dogs, cows, beavers, birds, bunnies, sows. . . .
>
> Why have women abandoned animals to the crimes of the patriarchy?
>
> We are a group of feminist, vegetarian women, with a vegan orientation (Veganism refers to the renunciation of all animal products, including leather, wool, etc.), who are dedicated to ending all forms of animal abuse. Since exploitation of animals and women derives from the same patriarchal mentality, our struggle is for women as well. (Feminists for Animal Rights, n.d.)

The ideological ties to these other causes are developed explicitly by many of the new activists. Many informants saw their involvement in animal rights as part of a wider interest in decolonization or anti-imperialism. Connections between people of color in and out of the Third World, white women in our society, the poor, and animals were stated by many activist-informants. For many informants, membership in animal rights groups overlapped with membership in other issue-based organizations dedicated to ecology, antinuclear protest, feminism, and antiracism. *Agenda* frequently has articles, interviews, and book reviews pointing out the ties between these concerns and animal rights. The following interview with the activist Karen Urtnowski in 1983 is an example.

> *Agenda*: How do you see human and animal causes as related?
> *KU*: Environmental destruction and war affect all living things in similar ways. Women's rights are the most clearly related to animals' rights because our exploitation is justified on the same basis, that we are useful and/or aesthetically pleasing. We are both ma-

nipulated for men's ends, and the profit motive is the same. Men have women to manage their homes, they use dogs to protect them. They like both to be pretty and obliging.

There is an equal lack of animal consciousness in the women's rights movement, which I also oppose. Last year, I asked that cheese not be served at a feminist anti-pornography meeting, because it is a product of the exploitation of the femaleness of animals. (Schleifer 1983, p. 6)

In the San Francisco Bay area, Buddhists Concerned for Animals produces a newsletter that cites the links between these concerns and Eastern religious ideas.

As Buddhist monks and lay people, we are finding ourselves able to reach people who may otherwise not be involved in the effort to liberate animals from suffering. We aim to point out the relationship of the current animal rights movement to the traditional Buddhist path, and to a sometimes overlooked but present aspect of other religions. (Buddhists Concerned for Animals 1983a)

The interrelationship of these different causes is an important, and frequently cited, point in the recent literature of the movement. The newsletter of Buddhists Concerned for Animals will mention animal experimentation by the military, and a vegan animal rights activist will discuss feminism in *Agenda.* Concern for animals is seen by many as the nexus for a number of related issues. Sally Gearhart, an activist who is chair of the Speech and Communications Department at San Francisco State University, stresses these relationships:

Animals are part of the environment, they are endangered species, they are being used in exploitative ways that are bad for the environment. And certainly, along with us, they will be victims in any nuclear holocaust. All those things make the connections between the overall environmental and antinuclear movements pretty obvious. The ones that are not so obvious, but where I think we must make the liaison, is with the consciousness about racism and the woman's movement and the gay movement. (Mills 1983)

A reading of the rhetoric of the new movement reveals its ideological disjunction from the norm-oriented, reformist humane groups of previous periods. It envisions an entire redefinition of the relationship between humans and animals rather than mere reform of their treatment. As one animal rights flier expresses this theme:

> The problems of the world cannot be completely solved until all the "rights of life" issues are dealt with. Rights for animals is one of the final pieces in the puzzle that will achieve a humane world— peace. The animal rights movement is one of the final links that will unite all causes. (Hamilton, n.d.)

It is this goal, among others, that makes productive dialogue between adherents and nonadherents of animal rights in the arena of reform so difficult. As it is not a movement primarily directed toward reform, discussions of reform alone fall short of addressing underlying issues. These issues have to do with some of the basic values and practices of Western culture and with the perceived power relations between oppressor and oppressed, of which the use of animals by science is both a manifestation and a symbol for movement adherents.

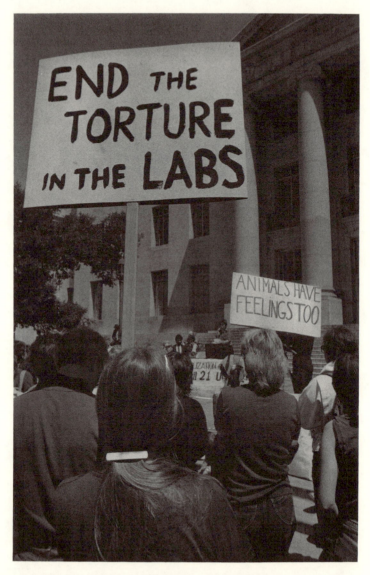

Animal Rights Activists at "World Day for Laboratory Animals," University of California, Berkeley, April 1987, Photo by Ron Delany.

5

Animal Rights Activists

I began to meet and talk with activists in the blossoming Bay area animal rights movement in summer 1984. My informants were not difficult to find. For an anthropologist, choosing a population to study and then finding people within that population to act as informants often involves complex problems and considerations. In my case, the process was simplified by two factors. First, the architects of the Bay area movement constitute a well-defined population of individuals who are, by the very nature of their endeavor, highly visible and vocal. Second, I was interested in learning about the developing ideology of a protest movement from those in the process of constructing the movement. I had no interest in establishing statistically significant correlations of mean yearly income, education, and interest in animal rights or any similar questions mandating sophisticated sampling techniques. I wanted to know what these people thought about their work, about animals, science, and medicine, and about living in twentieth-century technological culture. I wanted to ask them why and how they became activists. Above all, I wanted to listen to their ideas and learn as much as I could about how they felt they had developed these ideas.

I constructed a list of names of activists through several sources. The grass roots groups in the area had recently launched a number of highly publicized and successful campaigns against laboratory practices at the University of California at Berkeley. Many university administrators and researchers with whom I spoke felt quite suddenly besieged. There was very little mystery about the source of the siege. My first list was drawn up with the help of Nikki Simpson, the administrative assistant of Berkeley's Committee for the Protection of Animal Subjects. The committee, whose charge it is to oversee the university's compliance with the complex web of agency guidelines for the care of animal subjects, was in frequent contact with members of the animal rights community. It was from the committee that I first obtained the names of informant-activists who represented the Bay area groups protesting and demonstrating against university policies regarding animals.

As soon as I entered the informal network of activists in the area, other names began to come up consistently in conversations. A second list emerged which was given to me by the first group of activists with whom I spoke. Together, these lists constituted representatives of the grass roots groups in the area. Between June and September 1984, I met with nine activists for extended conversations that took place in a variety of places.

Ethnographic description is, by its very nature, nonobjective; it is a process of cultural translation. This issue is no less salient for the worker in his or her own culture who examines particular world views or belief systems. My informants were not exotic "others," and most came from cultural experiences similar to my own. Our discussions had the familiarity of habit: the conversational style of urban, college-educated Americans. But, although my informants and I may be said to share the same culture, we had past and present allegiances to ideologies with different visions of the relationship between humans and animals. As a primatologist, I was, by professional socialization and training, a product of what might be called the subculture of animal research. There is little doubt that my informants and I came to our discussions with somewhat different perspectives. Thus, the issues of ethnographic authority and objectivity are comparable to those facing informant and ethnographer from different cultures.

Having formerly studied non-language-bearing animals, I now found myself entwined in the intricacies of human discourse. Before long, I saw that my choice of research topic involved, among other things, an attraction to the rebellious stance of the activists. As was true for many of them, animals had been an important part of my life from early childhood. I envied my informants their certainty and avowed anger. At the same time, I sometimes found a particular remark annoying and even laughable. In short, the interviews contained the same kind of emotional ambiguities experienced in conversations that are not part of research. To what extent do these biases influence the framing and presentation of informants' ideas? These issues of ethnographic authority are much discussed by anthropologists at the present time and are largely unresolved (Clifford and Marcus 1985). In the face of unavoidable subjectivity, I have tried to leave the voices of my informants intact as much as possible.

My meetings with informants took place in kitchens, living rooms, and offices and often lasted many hours. The informants range in age from their late twenties to late forties. Six are female; three are male. All are white, college-educated, and, with one exception, from urban backgrounds. Three hold degrees in law and are practicing attorneys, one is a filmmaker, one is a clinical psychologist, and one is enrolled as a student in an MBA program. Three devote their energies full-time to work in the animal rights movement, surviving economically on part-time work that supports their involvement in the movement.

My informants represent the grass roots animal rights groups in the area, for example, Action for Animals, the Animal Rights Connection, Buddhists Concerned for Animals, and Psychologists for the Ethical Treatment of Animals. With one exception, all of the groups originated in the late 1970s and early 1980s. One of the groups whose representative I interviewed is an older humane and conservation-oriented society founded in the mid-1960s which shares some of the concerns of the animal rights movement and has in recent years provided speakers at animal rights events and sponsored rallies, such as Mobilization for Animals Days. Its participation in protest against animal experimentation is exceptional. The more established humane groups have not been involved in animal rights protest, and the involvement of this organization is probably due to the particular interest of some of its leadership in the issue of experimentation.

Before the interviews, I had developed an "interview schedule" with a list of questions I thought would open up the conversation. What folly! My activist-informants directed their comments to those aspects of their involvement which they thought were most important. If they did not like a question, or the way it was phrased, they talked about something they considered more relevant, or rephrased the question. I do not mean to imply by this that my informants were rude, as this is far from the case. But each wanted to clarify her or his particular vision. And all are people who are used to disputing the dominant norms of Western culture as they relate to animals. To believe in the concept of speciesism, that the human treatment of animals constitutes a form of immoral oppression, like racism, mandates such a critique. They are also people with strong verbal skills and the other cultural tools of a middle-class background and higher education.

The interviews with activists illuminated some of the ideological, organizational, and operational aspects of the groups that have recently formed in the San Francisco Bay area. The area has an extremely active movement and is typical demographically of the other urban areas with large university communities, such as Boston and Washington, D.C., where animal rights is strongest. The informants' ideas about their own involvement in the movement supported my hypothesis that animal rights has far wider implications and other roots and goals than a renewed humane response to animal suffering. The interviews also illustrate the heterogeneity of life-styles and opinions of adherents of animal rights. At the same time, certain beliefs form a cohesive ideology for all of the informants. Two activists with whom I spoke indicate the range of different life-styles of activists in the movement. Each is an attorney and each commits substantial time to the movement, but the way in which they live out their adherence to animal rights is certainly very different.

I interviewed Judith Green in her apartment in a working-class neighborhood on the periphery of Berkeley. Her name had been mentioned frequently by other activists in the movement, and she was, indeed, the co-founder with several others of one of the local grass-roots groups. The evening of our interview, I parked my car in front of her building, which presented the rather drab, gray exterior of many of the other buildings on the block. Tape recorder in hand, I pressed the doorbell, which after a minute was answered by a small, tense, angry-looking woman in her midthirties, wearing the ubiquitous workclothes of students in our generation—jeans and a T-shirt. Standing silently by her side was a large dog that appeared to be a German shepherd-wolf mix. The apartment we entered was small and furnished with secondhand furniture and books, a style I associated with my many years as a graduate student. Papers and books covered all the surfaces in the room. The electronic typewriter stood out as the only expensive object in the otherwise austere environment. Work was piled high next to the typewriter, which she told me later was a book on conflict mediation, her compelling professional interest. As we talked, the dog lay on a couch in the corner; I felt his eyes on me throughout the interview, a kind of silent, canine witness to my nervousness.

Judith was angry at the many oppressions of humans and animals. When I asked her how she had become an animal rights activist, she gave me the following account:

> "I was born. It goes back that far. I have been concerned about the underdog, underperson, under-what-ever, since I have any recollection. Animal rights went in the closet for me for a period of time because I got trashed pretty badly for it in my teens. I felt alone and isolated, like I came from a different planet, a different consciousness. I became a vegetarian for ethical reasons, but I didn't feel that I had anywhere to go with that other than in my own life-style. I've been a vegetarian for thirteen years and a vegan for two.

> "At Antioch College, a friend said, 'You'll have to choose between animals and people,' and I said, 'You're wrong, it's going to have to be both. I can't live my life with that kind of distinction.' For a number of years, my energy focused on the oppression, exploitation, and domination of the human species: war, rape, discrimination, institutionalization. I was heavily involved with rape crises intervention and the women's health care movement. About four years ago, I found out about Attorneys for Animal Rights. I was appalled that I didn't know about it. Then I got connected with filmmaker Angela Leonardi and her film *Victims of Science*. I also met Dr. Terri Murphy and Elizabeth Howard. Elizabeth, Terri, Jack Hill, and I started the Animal Rights Connection and things took off from there."

Judith is a feminist, animal rights advocate, and vegan. For her, these philosophies and practices are a completely whole and

consistent protest of what she considers to be the patriarchal oppressions of our society. She told me that patriarchal violence
against women and animals has resulted in their abuse by science
and clinical medicine. She views technological medicine as one expression of the violence of our society:

> "Western medicine is violent in its approach to the human body
> and to other living beings. The emphasis on external substances
> instead of internal regeneration perpetuates the thinking which
> violates sentient beings and promotes the big business in animal
> research."

Judith sees herself as working in all areas toward the evolution of
feminist consciousness. As part of her protest of speciesism, she
has chosen to live as a vegan, one who uses no animal products of
any kind. I came to learn from a number of vegan informants
about the severity of this discipline. Many products in everyday
use contain something from an animal. Indeed, it was surprising
to me to learn how much in our synthetic and technological society
still comes from animals. Thus, it takes many hours each day to
prepare meals and find other kinds of products that contain no animal parts. The asceticism of veganism can go beyond mere incon-
venience and may involve a painful or life-threatening martyr-
dom. For example, Judith described writhing in agony for hours
on the floor during an acute kidney infection, unwilling to use a
pharmaceutical derived through animal experimentation. As Judith spoke, I was suddenly horribly self-conscious about the different parts of animals that I had carried on my body to the interview. Under the steady gaze of the dog on the couch, I slid my
leather pocketbook under my chair and looked dolefully down at
my leather shoes.

  In distinct contrast to the austerity of Judith Green's life is that
of Steven Schwartz, another one of my activist-informants. I
made a formal appointment to interview Steven in his office on
the third floor of a prestigious office building in San Francisco.
The firm in which he is a partner, a large corporate practice, represents many of the big hospitals in the area, and in a very real sense,
he works for the interests of corporate medicine. I was early,
which gave me an opportunity to look around the high-tech,
chrome and glass waiting room of an enormous suite of offices.

Elegantly dressed young women secretaries walked back and forth carrying files. Once again, I thought about my own clothes, not to mention my own run-down, graduate-student dwelling across the bay, which I had come to inhabit as a kind of rabbit hutch, dug in the hole of my research on animal rights. An immaculately groomed young secretary came to usher me into the interview. Steven, a small man a few years older than Judith and I, stood to greet me. Behind him, an enormous window framed a view of the Bay. He was clearly not a vegan and wore expensive-looking leather shoes with brass buckles and an elegant three-piece suit.

I was fascinated by the contrast between Steven Schwartz and Judith Green. Judith described herself as in every sense an outsider, fighting a system that abuses women, minorities, and animals. Steven presented himself as very much an insider, as indeed he is. When our interview was interrupted by a phone call, he described its contents to me. One of his law partners had given the introduction to the keynote speech at the Democratic National Convention, which convened the previous week in San Francisco, and had arranged tickets for Steven on the floor of the convention. When I interviewed Judith, my cheap and somewhat inefficient tape recorder whirred on unnoticed by either of us. As I fumbled with my creaky little machine, Steven had his secretary bring in an impressive dictaphone, which he controlled by turning it on and off during the interview. Steven gave me the following account of how he became an activist in the animal rights movement:

"How did I come to the movement? I just stumbled into it. In fact, it was about 1978, and I went on a whale walk. This was a long ten-mile walk—I don't even know why I got involved in it—but whales seemed like kind of a nice thing to protest for on a Sunday afternoon. After the walk was over, there were a number of booths that had been set up by different animal-concerned organizations. One of them was Fund for Animals in San Francisco, and that was how I met Virginia Handley and some other people. I liked these individuals, and it was my first introduction to the fact that there even was such a movement, and it was a good time in my life because I wanted something beyond my career. I wanted a different dimension to my life at that stage. This seemed very attractive to me, and still does, because it's an area in which,

relative to so many other movements in our society, there is a tremendous need. There's a need for lawyers, there's also a need for
people who are educated, for people who are thoughtful, and you
feel immediately wanted and needed in the movement, and I enjoyed that."

I was curious and asked Steven if he had experiences in the past
with other reform movements:

"Very remote in time. I was in the Peace Corps in 1964. Before
that I was in college, and I was, by the standards of those days, a
liberal, a white liberal who felt guilty that he wasn't black. And so
I spent a lot of time registering black voters and doing things of
that type. But after the Peace Corps, I essentially sort of buckled
down. I went to law school and then I got a job in a law firm, and I
spent my career essentially in a very traditional practice."

Like most of my other activist-informants, Steven had never been
involved in the old humane movement and drew a sharp distinction between it and animal rights:

"I think the current movement asks far more questions than the
old one ever did and is beginning to really focus on whether animals, by virtue of the relationship we create for them and us,
should be permitted to exercise certain rights."

In addition to litigating suits that revolve around aspects of animal
treatment, Steven helped put together one of the new animal
rights groups in the area and a political action committee to lobby
the state legislature. He shares with Judith Green advocacy of
antispeciesism, but in contrast to Judith, he works within an arena
of money and power in which the pragmatics of such committees
are second nature.

"The appeal of the movement traditionally has been emotional, 'How dare you do something to hurt all those dolphins out
there?' rather than just bringing the same kind of hard, economic
influences to bear that the opposition always is there with. So
what I was influential in doing was to try to get a political action
committee off the ground.

"The difficulty that I found is that there was no single grass-
roots organization to really give it a base, so that it could reflect
the strength of the movement. The animal rights movement by

numbers is enormous. It could be the largest movement in the United States. The size and number of people in this country that are—perhaps not at Singer's philosophical level—but very concerned about animals and how they are treated is enormous. There is an enormous population out there that really hasn't been tapped. No one has tried to turn this kind of concern into grass roots, and that's what a political action committee needs. Otherwise it tends to be rather parochial, and it tends to be a low-budget affair, and it makes it difficult to be effective. But nevertheless, we have a PAC, and it has made the animal rights movement more visible with the legislators."

The very different approaches of Judith Green and Steven Schwartz—Judith's idealism and Steven's pragmatism—are characteristic of the heterogeneity of the other activists I spoke with. Some of my informants thought this diversity was healthy, while others believed that it was an obstacle to the successful accomplishment of movement goals. For instance, several informants are vegans like Judith and believe that it is inconsistent to fight speciesism while personally using animal products. I had long discussions with such informants about the many problems involved in finding replacements for common objects ordinarily made out of animal parts like leather or animal fats that are used in furniture oils. However, one of the key activists in the San Francisco Bay area movement is not a vegetarian and believes this to be consistent with his philosophy.

Mariela Gordon, a down-to-earth young woman, is not a vegan and is practical in her approach to the issue of achieving animal rights. I visited Mariela one afternoon in the apartment she shares with her husband and a large tabby cat. She sat down with me at the dining room table, after making a pot of coffee for us to share. Mariela has an engaging smile and long dark hair, is in her late twenties, and in recent years helped to organize one of the new groups in the area. She has been very active in protesting university laboratory animal policies and came to animal rights while an anthropology major at Berkeley. She was, at the time, in an MBA program in preparation for a business career. Mariela described some of the differences among activists in the movement:

"I don't know how much you know about the diversity of animal rights people. We're united in one thing, but we're all very

different, and we're always fighting all the time. In the most extreme cases, they call themselves abolitionists. There's a particular group of people who want to get animal products out of their
lives altogether. They're vegan vegetarians. Some even believe
that keeping pets is animal exploitation. They come off very hostile. I don't think they mean to, but they do. And then there's the
more moderate abolitionist types like me, who think you ought to
stop it, but you ought to do it with diplomacy."

Mariela was very pragmatic about how the movement would
achieve its goals:

"In general, what we want to do is make it easier not to use animals . . . the whole idea is to make the organization do what you
want it to do. In the end, economics is going to come into force,
legal hassles, you know—one day legal experts will be advising
the university to shy away from animals because they're nothing
but trouble. That's my prediction for the future."

Angela Leonardi, another activist, probably represents one of
Mariela's "extreme cases." A quiet, wary-looking woman in her
late forties, she lives alone in a small brown-shingle house in a
middle-class neighborhood in San Francisco which she was able to
buy after her mother's death. It is difficult to recall the precise
number of animals in her house when I visited, but there was a
great commotion involved in putting the dogs in one place while I
entered through a back gate. Several cats ate from small dishes on
the kitchen table. Angela at first appeared to be made uncomfor-
table by my intrusion into her life, an impression that was later
dispelled by her treatment of me, for she was a deeply gracious
woman. She simply had a lot to manage in her animal family and
entertaining a guest in the midst of their needs was no minor feat.
One small dog approached and withdrew throughout our time together, running to me to solicit petting and then drawing back its
upper lip and crawling backward. Angela told me that he had
been abused by a former owner.

The room we sat in had the quality of a Victorian parlor, with
late afternoon light filtering through delicate lace curtains. My
anxiety about the interview and the excessive stimulation of the
animals running back and forth had mysteriously combined to in-
duce a kind of torpor. A lovely piano sat in the corner of the room,

and near it was a pile of music. Edward Maitland's biography of Anna Kingsford, the nineteenth-century feminist and anti-vivisectionist who had attained a medical degree and once offered herself as a vivisectional subject to spare animals, sat on the shelf. I had recently finished Ved Mehta's eloquent biography of Gandhi, which revealed that while a young Indian student on the quirky fringes of late Victorian London society, Gandhi had corresponded with Maitland about his philosophy of Christian Evangelicalism and vegetarianism. Maitland was a mystic, anti-vivisectionist, and cultishly devoted to Anna Kingsford.

Angela is one of two informants who had had some contact with the humane movement before becoming an animal rights activist, but she found that it did not address her deepest convictions and feelings. She became an animal rights activist through direct contact with biomedicine:

> "I was teaching part-time at City College, and three days a week I was in the clerical pool at U.C. Med Center. I was radicalized first as far as human patients were concerned, because even with my feminist background and the good work the feminist movement has done criticizing Western medicine, I still pooh-poohed it. At first I thought 'this doctor is an exception,' and then I realized that the medical industry treats women abominably. After a few months of being shipped around to all these departments, I saw the animals. This was at the Veterans Administration Hospital, which actually is the University of California Medical Center.
>
> "I knew I couldn't do anything for these animals, only the public could, and the only way to inform the public was to make a film. I made my own little market research. I went on television in a free speech announcement, and the response was incredible. I did not believe it, this was in 1978."

Angela is a total abolitionist and vegan, and she talked at length about her struggle to be a vegan and to prepare vegetarian foods for her animal companions:

> "I try to be a vegan, which means not using any animal products at all. It's impossible. I've got a piano and it's got felt. This is rubber, and vulcanization includes some kind of animal products. A lovely desk that has some kind of polish uses oil from an animal. I use rennetless cottage cheese for my animals. Rennet is an en-

zyme from the stomach of a calf which is used to cure cheese. So this is rennetless, but it's from cow's milk. It's hard, and you argue with yourself. You could be a total vegan, but it takes up so much of your time, and you should be spending your time doing other things, right?"

It is quite difficult to derive a typical profile for membership in the new grass roots groups. While several of the activists with whom I spoke are men, my lists of names strongly suggest a predominance of women, and my informants agreed that this seems an accurate reflection of group membership. Jeannie Kant is a lawyer in her midthirties who has recently devoted herself to working exclusively for animal rights. She gives the impression of being anything but an extremist. A very lively and attractive woman with short, dark, curly hair, she agreed to meet me at my house, a small and slightly decaying California stucco cottage that I had rented since my early years as a graduate student at Berkeley. She and her husband had recently bought a home in Marin County, but she agreed to stop by to be interviewed. During the period of my research on the animal rights movement, I worked at an old formica table in the kitchen of my house which was always piled with paper, animal rights fliers, and books. The walls were covered with various artifacts of my obsession—lists of phone numbers of committees and groups. Like many graduate students, I often sat for long periods over my makeshift desk and sometimes forgot to eat.

Jeannie looked to me like the image of glowing health, mental and physical balance, and harmony. My own small dog barked outside the back door, and Jeannie asked to see him. She sat on the kitchen floor while the dog jumped all over her in exuberant canine greeting. She took a photograph of her own dog from her wallet to show me. Jeannie had the following comments on the predominance of women in the movement and on people concerned with human issues:

> "It's interesting; I think in the animal rights movement there are more women than men. Not surprising, since there is a strong tie between women and nature in terms of being close to their own natures and in terms of their strivings toward preserving nature in general. The men in the movement are definite assets, and we work well together. Yet, even with a lot of women in the move-

ment, we have to keep them [the men] on their toes and make sure that all the speakers at a certain rally or conference are not men.

"People in the movement are varied; they come from all walks. Most of them, I would say about 95 percent—and that's a safe and conservative guess—are very concerned about humans and are quite liberal; you know: antiwar, antinuclear weapons, antiracism, and so forth. We are very concerned about human rights; we are focusing on animal rights. These movements are all related because there's the same basic underlying attitude of supremacy that permits and perpetuates the racist, sexist, speciesist attitudes and concomitant crimes against creatures."

Mariela Gordon had commented about the urban makeup of the movement and, like Jeannie, felt that women predominated:

"I understand, you know, we're basically an urban movement anyway. The people in the country think we're a bunch of nuts. . . . It's an urban kind of middle-class movement. I don't like to generalize but it's basically kind of young people, who really don't know a lot about actually dealing with animals. They just deal with them on a philosophical level. . . . My guess would be that in major urban areas, which is where the real action is going on, it's probably the same kind of thing. I don't know if there's an average age for members. I know mostly women, and they're mostly in their early thirties."

Accounts of the ways in which informants became involved in the movement show that in most cases official membership in a group had occurred since 1980. Most informants did not come from a background in humane societies, although many said that their feelings about animals went back to childhood. They had found a focus for these feelings only when animal rights groups emerged over the last few years. Many informants expressed a sense of excitement and surprise at finding that a movement existed which provided an arena for expressing their deeply held beliefs. It particularly fascinated me that Mariela had come to animal rights through contact with physical anthropology and evolutionary studies:

"I've always cared about animals, but I think it was more than anything else, anthropology. I was a very naive person, and when I took anthropology I saw evolution the way, I think, most people see it, as a road to the ultimate being, which is man. And when I took anthropology I realized that each animal is fully evolved. They weren't put here for us. I saw something about the diversity of life, and in my first quarter at the university I experienced this revelation: that we are only one of many animals on earth, and it's not our earth. The logical extension of this is to look around and see what we're doing to animals and to the earth and just to be appalled by it."

Mariela described her growing commitment to the issue of animal rights, which led to her membership in one of the new groups, and her participation as an activist:

"I knew there was a problem with strays. . . . And then I started to give money to organizations, and once you start to give money, you start getting all kinds of stuff in the mail, and I joined a group up in Sacramento which sent out a really nice glossy quarterly. I started reading about some real heavy-duty stuff. I was walking on campus one day, and Jack Hill of Animal Rights Connection said, 'Hey, would you like to read this?' And out of guilt I stopped, and I signed something, and I promised to go to a meeting. I went and I went, and I never stopped going. The more I hung around, the more I realized I could never stop. You know, I can't go on vacation without—at Christmas they're still in the cages. It's like a cloud that you carry always, and it will always be there.

"The group I belong to is called Action for Animals. It was one-half of a split-off of another group that was called Animal Rights Connection. One group still bears the name Animal Rights Connection, and one is Action for Animals. When we split in two we negotiated for the name. . . . I guess it was about 1981 that I joined Animal Rights Connection, and I understand that they'd been pooping around for some time before that, so I'm not sure when they started. But it was some people who were pretty tight friends, and I don't know when their friendship suddenly became an organization."

I visited Terri Murphy, another activist in the East Bay movement, at her house, which, like Angela's, seemed to be full of pets. Terri is a forty-year-old clinical psychologist with a deep, penetrating gaze that gives her the impression of great receptivity as she listens. Unlike any of the other activists who spoke with me, she had been involved in the past with some of the traditional anti-vivisection groups. She, like Angela and Judith, is a vegan.

"I was teaching at West Virginia University. There was a student who went around wearing a T-shirt that said 'Love animals. Don't eat them.' That kind of settled somewhere in my consciousness. I was a closet kind of animal rights person then. My mate and I split up and I decided it was time for another big change, so I came back to California where I once lived. I got custody of the animals and brought them with me.

"I had been a vegetarian for a while while living in the East. This animal rights business was still fuzzy to me; it was not clear in my head, but on some level something was going on. When I got here, I met Angela Leonardi, and then the door opened. And I read Peter Singer's book and met people in the movement and talked about issues, and I knew I was home. I changed my lifestyle overnight."

I was curious about the preceptions of my informants about the question of why the movement was developing in the late 1970s and early 1980s. They are all, to varying degrees, people who think deeply about their choices. Yet no one had any clear idea about why the movement had suddenly appeared in their imaginations or on the American scene at this particular time. Their responses show that as individuals caught up in social processes, we may not have clear ideas about the larger historical context of our own activities. Thus, all of the informants have been instrumental in the formation and activities of the new movement in the San Francisco Bay area, yet many expressed perplexity about why a movement had developed at this time. Several informants said that they hoped I would tell them the answer to this question. Several informants believed that the animal rights movement had links to other social trends that might help explain its growth in the late 1970s. Mariela answered this question in the following way:

"I have no idea [why this is happening now]. I know something has happened, but I'm not a shrewd enough analyst of what's going on in the world to know what's happened. Some people who are more spiritually minded talk about a book, *The Hundredth Monkey*. I'm not really clear on it because I haven't read it, but I know the story. It's kind of a spiritualized yen, and yet it could be a social phenomenon too, the idea that one tells another and tells another, and then there's a threshold when it stops being a one-to-one thing, and then all of a sudden everybody knows. It seems like we're on the verge of that."

Angela Leonardi related the appearance of the movement to human spiritual development and the current awareness of the potential destruction of the earth.

"It has to do with our development, our own consciousness and spiritual development, our own empathetic development toward all other creatures and toward the universe, a recognition that we are all on the same level of equality, that we are kin. . . . When I discovered the movement, I suddenly had an arena to grow in, without being ridiculed, and with support.

"I think its growth also has to do with the fact that there is so much destruction in the world and that people are realizing that we can, in fact, destroy the earth and ourselves in the process. Of course, the antinuclear movement is addressing that very directly. I believe that's the arena that was available for the animal rights movement to come forth."

John Marler, one of the three male activists with whom I spoke, also mentioned *The Hundredth Monkey* when I asked him why he thought the movement had recently arisen. John is an American Buddhist, in his midthirties. I had seen him at animal rights demonstrations on the Berkeley campus. With his glasses, suit, and careful grooming, he looked like a clean-cut young executive from the 1950s. He has been extremely active in the protest against Berkeley's lab animal care policies. He answered my question about why the movement has developed now in this way:

"Critical mass—have you heard of the book *The Hundredth Monkey*? More people are now aware that the state of mind that would permit the testing of radioactive weapons on monkeys also permits the vivisection of our planet for the same purpose. It involves a fundamental disrespect for living systems, an inquisitive mind that is willing to kill what it studies."

Judith Green talked about the "alienation, passivity, and numbing in this society," about people being "shocked out of their stupor":

"The antiwar movement, the civil rights movement, the women's movement, the environmental movement, the antinuclear movement, the peace movement, Watergate, Vietnam, Love Canal, Agent Orange, Cointelpro, the lesbian and gay rights movement, liberation struggles in South Africa, Central America—all contribute to increased awareness, sensitivity, involvement, and connection.

"The specter of a nuclear holocaust, the reality of toxic dumps, of deformed babies, dead rivers, extinct species, have pierced the shroud of numbness and paved the way for questioning authority and wanting to see for oneself. The horrors of the labs and factory farms are no longer hidden."

Several informants commented on what seemed to them to be an increased responsiveness on the part of the media in recent years to animal rights issues. Everyone agreed that the media was extremely important to the movement. Mariela said:

"I've noticed newspapers have more stories about animals, and there's more stuff on TV than there ever used to be. I ask other people, 'Is it just that I'm noticing it, or is it there?' I'm beginning to say it's really there. So it has something to do with the fact that the media has caught on. It's getting to be a popular thing."

However, Angela viewed the media as largely hostile to the movement and in the pocket of the medical industry:

"When one of the heart-lung transplant patients does die, after so many months, if it's published at all, it's on the back page. But every time they do one of those operations, it's on the front page, and the implication is that the other transplant patients lived that long too."

Almost without exception, the activists I spoke with have been involved in other socially ambitious protest movements in the past, particularly the ecology movement, the antinuclear movement, and the women's movement. Most articulated the belief that there were implicit ties between the ideologies of these causes and animal rights, as all reflect a related critique of certain aspects of Western society. Judith Green put it this way:

"The threat of nuclear annihilation and ecological catastrophe have brought home to a lot of people that Western military-industrial policies, practices, and attitudes are pathological and aberrant. 'Might makes right' and the objectification of living beings are wrong. Western society violates the natural world and distorts human animals' role on earth.

"In general, there is a growing and evolving sensitization to all oppression. Animal rights is on the horizontal continuum of movements fighting for liberation and against domination and exploitation."

Several informants believed that "people-related" issues were always complex and ambiguous, whereas animal rights had a kind of moral purity that made involvement extremely rewarding. Jeannie Kant related the despair she experienced years before, while working as an attorney in the prison reform movement, when she realized that her main function had probably been as "an object of sexual fantasy for prisoners." She contrasted the re-inforcements available through her work in animal rights to the inevitable ambiguities involved in the reform of human problems. Angela Leonardi spoke about the connection between animal rights and human oppression and felt that there was a special purity in the plight of animals:

"I think what moves me so much as far as the animals are concerned is that, like children, they are very, very natural. They are really innocent. They are totally victimized. With adults there's always some element of responsibility. You know, with battered women, there's some amount of responsibility. I don't care how poor the woman's self-image, how dependent economically she is on the man, she can still physically leave. An animal in a lab cannot leave."

Activists frequently spoke of their involvement in the movement as work within the human realm which was tied to a revolution in human attitudes toward life and nature. Judith Green said:

"We need to make nonviolent options available to vivisectors too. They are invested in animal research because of concerns about career, competition, ego, income, security. It is a habit. Animal research is familiar. We can work together to find ways for them to have economic and career security but not by depriving other sentient beings of their rightful existence. Again, the emphasis is on life-enhancing, not life-destroying."

The emphasis that my informants placed on the profit motive and career concerns of their scientist adversaries puzzled me. I would sometimes suggest that there were many researchers who did their work with the conviction that it was good and humane and who did not make a great deal of money doing research. I could never get informants to address this issue, because conversation would inevitably revert to my informants' theory that researchers were at best unconscious dupes, if not cynical cruel, or insensitive. It was always assumed that they had lucrative careers.

Informants' attitudes toward Western science and medicine were overwhelmingly critical, with the exception of Steven Schwartz, who works in an area of law in which he represents large medical corporations. I spent a lot of time wondering about how he resolved the problem of believing in animal rights and yet representing an institution that is so intimately associated with animal research. By contrast, the criticism articulated by the other informants was consistent with what I had read in the literature of the new movement. I have come to view it as a very coherent set of beliefs about science and medicine, which are viewed as the institutional representatives of an exploitative system. According to this view, science and medicine are seen as suppressing ethical and spiritual values for materialistic goals, and both are perceived by adherents as deeply implicated in the domination of nature. It is this domination that my activist-informants believe has brought the earth to the point of impending destruction. Most of my informants view the use of animals in research as symbolic of a widespread corruption that will ultimately destroy life on earth. Judith Green taught classes about health law and talked about Western medicine as "violent in its approach to the human body and to other living beings." She said:

> "Western medicine deals with the body as if it were this passive thing to be *done to,* instead of respecting and revitalizing our own self-healing abilities, as acupuncture and homeopathy do. Patients are generally not told about acupuncture, homeopathy, visualization, hypnotherapy, raw juice fasting, vegetarian diets, meditation, and so forth. That's because alleopathic practitioners have a monopoly on the practice of medicine. In their narrow and biased training, they learn that treatment usually means drugs (which they don't know much about, except what the drug companies submit) and surgery. There is so much iatrogenic injury and death. The emphasis on external substances instead of internal regeneration perpetuates the thinking that violates sentient beings and promotes the big business in animal research."

Mariela Gordon also spoke of her perception of science's immoral approach:

> "It's a kind of manipulation in order to perfect a technique, and it doesn't matter what kind of destructiveness occurs as a result. If a real kitten has to be tortured, if an old person in severe pain has to be kept alive another six months, if the possibility that Fresno gets to be destroyed by an atom bomb are taken into consideration, they are low priority."

Terri Murphy characterized the attitude of scientists in the following way:

> "It's called by different names. The euphemisms are 'academic freedom,' 'pushing back the frontiers of knowledge.' It's a kind of intellectual quest without morality."

Some informants did not implicate Western culture but rather human nature as the root cause of these problems. Angela felt that all cultures committed immoral acts against animals.

> "For some reason, we are a very violent species, much more violent than other animals. We seem to enjoy warfare, torture, and we have all sorts of subtle, highly defined, insanely clever ways of torturing political prisoners, animals, our own children."

Other informants believed that our society could be contrasted to tribal groups or to a matriarchal period in history when people were integrated with the natural world instead of ascendant over it. When I visited Judith Green, I noticed that she had on her shelf many recent books that present a perspective that is sometimes called ecofeminism, tying ecology to feminist issues. In this literature, the technological destruction of nature and the oppression of women are tied to patriarchal values, and the preservation of nature to historical matriarchal values. This perspective, a form of essentialism, stresses qualities of women that are fundamentally different from those of men. Much debate in academic and popular feminism has centered on this question of the existence of essential psychological differences between the sexes. Judith's and the other feminist informants' belief that women were in special harmony with nature is not universal among modern feminists.

During our discussion, Judith referred to a period in prehistory during which feminist, ecological values had prevailed:

> "Since I know Western culture best, I would say that it [our alienation from ourselves] is a function of our culture. If you go back tens of thousands of years, to what I consider matriarchal herstory, from things that I've read, those cultures were predominantly nonviolent, peaceful, vegetarian communities. They were very integrated and saw themselves as part of all nature, rather than separate and apart. Native American culture was and is in tremendous harmony with nature, even though they were not necessarily in harmony with each other."

She also felt that other cultures held different views of the human relationship to nature:

> "Also Buddhism . . . and some of the other Eastern religions are based on harmony, nonviolence, and coexistence. So I believe there are cultures all around that have not been so alienated from nature. I think the whole basis of Western culture is domination and exploitation of all living beings, human, nonhuman, the environment . . . that mentality sets up a whole series of attitudes and behaviors that become the mainstay of what this society is about."

Like the Victorian antivivisectionists, many of the activists questioned the validity of modern medical practices in their arguments against animal experimentation. Most were interested in alternative forms of health treatment, such as homeopathy and acupuncture, or special diets as alternatives to conventional medical treatment. They frequently invoked the criticism that medicine and physicians treated human beings as "things" and that according to Western medical theory, the patient was considered passive with no endogenous abilities to heal. For most of my informants, the road to health lay in an integration of the human organism with natural rhythms. There was a pronounced emphasis on nutrition and avoidance of chemical additives, all of which were viewed as more effective than the interventive and potentially dangerous practices of technological medicine in our society. Western medicine was also believed to be based fundamentally on the exploitation of animals. Several informants, in fact, used homeopaths themselves and had begun to use homeopathic veterinarians for their animals.

Jack Hill, another activist-informant, came to talk with me in my paper-strewn kitchen one summer afternoon. Jack had helped to put together the movement in the Berkeley area and is probably an essential element in its health and functioning. He is a tireless worker for the cause, a pragmatic, humorous, self-identified gay man, with a Southern drawl. He was my sole informant from a rural or Southern background. Before our interview, I had self-consciously covered a small roast that sat marinating on the kitchen counter, in preparation for a dinner with some carnivorous friends that evening. Jack informed me early in our discussion that he was somewhat unique in the local movement by virtue of his nonvegetarian diet. While he devotes his energies full-time to animal rights, he views his nonvegetarian life-style as somewhere on an evolutionary continuum in the development of his animal rights consciousness.

Jack's opinions about biomedicine were consistent with those of most of my other informants:

> "Our own bad habits are responsible for most of our ill health. If you look around, the kinds of sickness we have today are largely environmental and diet-related. The health care industry is big business, it's on the stock market, and there are many economic priorities that are not based on health. The industry prefers cures to prevention and the gathering of information to the use of wisdom."

Judith Green spoke about this issue frequently in our conversation:

> "It's frustrating to me. People's lives are being lost as a result of the attitudes of Western medicine and its focus. People are paying for it with their lives out on the street, and nonhuman animals are paying for it with their lives in research laboratories and slaughterhouses. If the focus shifted to really honoring our ability to heal, on wellness instead of the disease model, we would save human and nonhuman animal lives.
>
> "There's an expectation that Western medicine will save us from mortality, from unhealthy habits such as consumption of animal flesh and products, refined sugars and starches, cigarettes, coffee, alcohol, other drugs. . . . People are not encouraged to

take responsibility for their health—Western medicine relies on sickness for its existence."

Terri Murphy uses a homeopath for her animal family but cannot afford one for herself:

> "If I had the money, I would see a homeopath myself. I don't see physicians very much. I have Kaiser insurance, which I keep for emergencies, because I see conventional medicine as very valuable for certain acute problems, mostly emergencies. I don't think it's very valuable otherwise. My animals see a homeopath, an acupuncturist, and a conventional veterinarian. Terri McGinnis is the latter; she's in Albany and she's wonderful. . . .Terri has begun to talk of how conventional Western medicine treats the symptom only; doesn't really get to the basic problem. . . . If we can heal ourselves, then we don't need to have animals in research."

Because of my interest in the influence that popular ethology, particularly primate studies, have had in remodeling people's ideas about animals, I asked my informants if they felt their attitudes had been influenced by the popular studies of animal behavior. Most agreed that they had been influenced by contact with animal behavior studies and mentioned particular books and people that had been important to their thinking about animals. Terri Murphy had come into personal contact with Harry Harlow's famous studies of mother deprivation in rhesus monkey infants:

> "When I was a student at the University of Wisconsin, I walked through Harry Harlow's Primate Center. I was just curious and totally unconscious regarding nonhuman animal needs and rights. I thought, 'this is interesting.' I remember the baby rhesus monkeys with their security blankets, sucking their thumbs, with their heads down, their little rumps in the air, all by themselves, not even a companion. That reached me, and the image haunts me still."

John Marler, my Buddhist informant, said:

> "I read *Conversations with a Gorilla* and was really impressed. I think there's a moral problem bringing a gorilla to this level of consciousness and then keeping it captive. I also remember some comments Patterson makes about other researchers and how they

mistreat primates by keeping them caged, which makes it impossible to do valid research."

Most of my informants believe that our society is in a grave state of decay and disorder and that the recognition of animal rights will herald changes that transcend the issue of animals. Many expressed their desire for, and belief in, a future purged of cruelty, in which humans and animals live at peace with nature. Thus, Angela Leonardi talked about her dream of the Beautiful City, which she had found in the writings of several feminist authors:

> "It's amazing how similar themes can be in good and great feminist writers. One theme is the dream of the Beautiful City. Sometimes it's a dream, sometimes it's not. For Maya Angelou, it's San Francisco as compared to St. Louis. She always wanted to come here. For Doris Lessing, it's the Four-Gated City, sometime in the distant future. It's really the dream of, not the ideal society, but the peaceful society, which is in tune with the world."

My discussions with activists helped me to understand the world view of the movement. My informants' goal is, ultimately, the restoration of harmony between humans and nature through the achievement of animal rights. Like many other Americans, they believe in a potential ecological apocalypse, which, if not stemmed, will destroy all species on earth. Many in our society feel that pollution poses a serious threat and believe that poor health habits are responsible for disease. Thus, the movement synthesizes a number of generally accepted ideas and fringe positions. It is the linking of commonly felt anxieties and beliefs to the abuse of laboratory animals which gives the movement its distinctive and radical quality and which takes it out of the political mainstream.

Cover of *Photo,* #235, a French photography magazine, April 1987.

6

Humans, Animals, and Machines

Antivivisection foresaw the cold, barren alienation of a future dominated by the imperatives of technique and expertise. It was not experiments on animals they were protesting, it was the shape of the century to come.

—R. D. French

The cultural marginalization of animals is, of course, a more complex process than their physical marginalization. The animals of the mind cannot be so easily dispensed. Sayings, dreams, games, stories, superstitions, the language itself recall them.

—J. Berger

Why have powerful movements for the abolition of animal research arisen at certain times, and what are their historical and ideological roots? The answer to these questions lie in changing perceptions during the last century of the human relationship to animals and to nature. Natural cosmology is not static, and important aspects of the relationship between humanity and the natural world have been contested and redefined in modern industrial society. Antivivisection and animal rights have both developed at moments of broad cultural debate about the boundaries between human and animal and organism and machine.

Both movements have responded to these cosmological transformations through a critique of science that attacks the use of animals in research. Each movement has made symbolic use of the remodeled animal immanent in the popular imagination. The roots of opposition to research with animals go far deeper than heightened humane responses to animal suffering.

What are the symbolic roles of animals in urban, industrialized culture? As animals have become marginal to urban life and work, they have assumed new meanings, which overlay older ones. The educated late Victorian lived during a period in which the animality of people and the human qualities of animals were much debated. Both concerns are reflected in the popular art and literature of the period. Animals, especially dogs and horses, were anthropomorphized as carriers of human sentiments and emotions. At the same time, evolutionary theory emphasized the animality of people by showing the human connection to other forms of organic life. The anthropomorphized dogs of Victorian popular art had a parallel transformation in caricatures that showed the apelike characteristics of people. The sharp demarcations between animal and human that the Victorians had inherited from the previous century was blurred by late Victorian romanticism, which idealized and anthropomorphized animals. At the same time, science showed that humans were tied to the animal kingdom through evolution.

These changes in Victorian ideas about animals and their relationship to humans occurred in the context of widespread social anxiety about the human relationship to technology. Underlying the protest of vivisection in the Victorian period was a critique of the domination of nature by increasingly impersonal forces perceived as antithetical to life. New techniques had vastly changed the practices of research and clinical medicine. These incursions of organisms were viewed by the antivivisectionists as dangerous, and science was accused of disordering nature. The vivisection of animals by physiologists became the focus of protest by antivivisectionists, not only because they viewed it as morally corrupt but because they saw it as representing a dangerous social tendency. As one antivivisectionist said of scientists:

> They have seen the moral chaos which in great measure their own work was producing, and old landmarks and rules of life dis-

appearing. They have heard on all sides the cries of bewilderment from men and women, and they have scarcely lifted a finger to lighten the burden or given an hour's thought to the question of how men should face the old fact called life in the new world which had sprung into existence. (A. Herbert in *Times* [London], 1876, quoted in French 1975, p. 8)

Like their ideological heirs in the modern animal rights movement, most antivivisectionists believed that health could be achieved only by living in harmony with nature. Disease was believed to be the result of a state of disharmony, of which poor sanitation or improper nutrition were manifestations.

Like the Victorians, we are inundated with information about animals and about the animality of people. As modern ethological studies have made their way into popular culture through television shows, magazine articles, and books, they have transformed the images we have of animals and thus affected the conscious and subconscious levels of meaning that animals evoke. From the mid-1960s to the present, the border between human and animal has been contested by developments in many of the scientific disciplines that deal with animal behavior. At the same time that both academic and popular studies have revolutionized our ideas about the primates, concurrent trends in the study of human sociobiology have stressed the fundamental animality of people. Basic human drives, such as sexuality and aggression, have been attributed to genetic, evolutionary mechanisms; this biological reduction of human nature has achieved tremendous appeal in many disciplines over the last decade (Kitcher 1985). Many of these ideas have been widely popularized in journals and magazines that are read by nonspecialists interested in understanding the "roots" of human behavior.

Many proponents of the biological view of human behavior have developed evolutionary stories in which the role formerly played by primitive human groups is now occupied by the nonhuman primates. Interpretations of primate behavior (and accounts of the complex behaviors of other kinds of animals like whales, dolphins, and wolves) have increasingly made their way into the public forum since the 1960s and have influenced popular thinking. Studies of the apes, particularly chimpanzees and gorillas, have greatly changed our concept of the cognitive and communicative abilities of higher animals (Kevles 1980). This scientific and popular discourse about the human qualities of animals such as baboons and chimpanzees (their complex social and cognitive abilities) and the animality of humans (the similarities in our social behavior to that of other animals) has pervaded popular culture and influenced attitudes toward research with primates:

> To many, the nonhuman primate is the symbol of man's ultimate exploitation of a species so similar to his own in need, capabilities, and social structure as to be virtually indistinguishable in moral terms. (Rowan 1982, p. 22)

Burghardt and Herzog (1980), in a paper exploring some components of attitudes toward animals in research, note the role of primate studies in the animal rights debate:

> New evidence of the higher cognitive faculties in some animals including reason, language, and emotional sensitivity have resonated throughout the scientific and lay press . . . ethological work on animal and human behavior has thus eroded the key foundation for the age-old rigid distinction between human and nonhuman.
>
> Many primatologists view their clientele as behaviorally closer to humans than to other mammals; circus trainers and their audiences share this view. The evolutionary relatedness of primates to humans often does make them the most appropriate nonhuman animals for use in medical research. This leads to intense conflict, for the critics of primate research equate the production of mentally disturbed abnormal monkeys (e.g., by social deprivation) with actual physiological intervention in medical laboratories. (P. 763)

Animal rights activists, aware of the publicity value of remarks on research made by scientists themselves, have been able to capitalize on the criticisms of primatological researchers. The Action for Animals *Calendar* for June 1984 includes a statement made by Roger Fouts, a researcher involved in ape language studies, about the use of chimpanzees in AIDS research: "I find it highly unethical that an already over-populated species should use an endangered species for medical research" ([Mills] 1984).

The criticism of animal research in the modern period has also arisen in the context of widespread anxieties about the incursions of technologies into nature; the last decade has seen this reflected in the growth of a popular literature on the ecological crisis of Western society. The criticism of technology can be found in popular philosophy, poetry, and fiction (Snyder 1969; Berry 1977; Illich 1977*a*, 1977*b*) and in social movements attempting to preserve the environment and endangered species. The "back-to-the-earth" communes of the last fifteen years reflect aspects of this response. The anxiety about the technological manipulation of nature is also expressed in the protests against genetic engineering and in the antiabortion movement.

The antiabortion movement deploys many of the same meanings as animal rights but is notably missing in the alignment of ecology, antinuclear, and feminist groups at animal rights demonstrations. Like animal rights, it addresses the destruction of living organisms through technological incursions. Its sensational propaganda presents images of aborted fetuses that are strikingly similar to animal rights' depictions of vivisection. The assertions that fetuses and animals have the same categorical status as people are structurally alike: both pose radical solutions to contested cosmological borders. However, the movements appeal to people with different kinds of political identifications. Antiabortion may be the movement most parallel to animal rights for Americans persuaded by the apocalyptic visions of the new right. The antiabortion and animal rights movements differ in other important ways, including the explicitly religious dimension of the right-to-life movement. But both movements are responses to similar anxieties widely experienced in our culture at present.

Many within our society oppose the increasing role of machines (and those who control them) in their lives. The poet Wendell Berry has been an influential proponent of this position. I was referred to one of Berry's books on the technological domination of American agriculture (*The Unsettling of America* [1977]) by Jack Hill, for whom Berry is a kind of folk hero. Berry writes about the spiritual, social, and ethical implications of modern techniques of machine farming. He urges a return to traditional small-scale farming methods and contrasts this to the social and ecological damage wrought by large-scale agribusiness. Berry (1977) connects modern agricultural practices to wider social trends, in particular, what he calls the "specialist system":

> Perhaps the fundamental damage of the specialist system—the damage from which all other damages issue—has been the isola-

tion of the body. At some point we began to assume that the life of the body would be the business of grocers and medical doctors, who need take no interest in the spirit, whereas the life of the spirit would be the business of churches, which would have at best only a negative interest in the body . . . and we began to find it easier then ever to prefer our own bodies to the bodies of other creatures and to abuse, exploit, and otherwise hold in contempt those other bodies for the greater good or comfort of our own. (P. 104)

Berry implicates the trend toward specialization as the cause of alienation between body and spirit, an alienation manifested in the abuse of animal bodies. The animal rights movement has applied a similar criticism to technological, specialist-controlled science. The popular imagery of right-brain versus left-brain influences on human behavior reflects an internalization of this perceived tension with which our culture is much concerned at present. The left brain has come to symbolize the linear and "cold" intellectuality of science; the right brain, intuitive, emotional, and "warm" qualities. Seminars and courses are now available to the public purporting to enhance right-brain abilities in the face of a "left-brain dominated" culture. The common thread is the view held by many today that modern culture and its institutions dominate and suppress the world of "nature," "human nature," and the body.

In the period since the late 1960s, nature has come increasingly to stand in symbolic opposition to those social institutions that are perceived to deprive people of a natural existence. Advertising reflects this, with products in technological society being marketed on the basis of their alleged "naturalness." Cereals, clothing, and cosmetics are routinely advertised as being offered in a close-to-natural state. In many cases, individuals are willing to expend extra time and money in an effort to protect themselves and family members from unnatural additives in foods. While it is clear that many of these attitudes have a pragmatic basis (i.e., people have been poisoned by pesticides), the indictment of the "unnatural" often admits no mitigating factors, such as the concept that some good has been achieved by technology. In his book of essays *About Looking* (1980), John Berger writes about the perceived opposition between the "bad" products of modern society and the "good" embodied in nature:

> As Lukacs pointed out in *History and Class Consciousness,* nature is also a value concept. A value opposed to the social institutions which strip man of his natural essence and imprison him. "Nature thereby acquires the meaning of what has grown organically, what was not created by man, in contrast to the artificial structures of human civilization. At the same time, it can be understood as that aspect of human inwardness which has remained natural, or at least tends or longs to become natural once more." The life of a wild animal becomes an ideal, an ideal internalized as a feeling surrounding a repressed desire. (P. 15)

The ecology movement, the emphasis on "naturalness" in advertising, organic gardening, and the debates about animal rights and abortion each reflect different aspects of the popular concern with this conflict. Berger has noticed the role of animals in this social drama by alerting us to their function as foci for a "repressed desire" implicit in the opposition of nature and society.

An example of these relationships appears in the writings of John Aspinall, an eccentric Englishman whose words can be found quoted on animal rights fliers. Aspinall maintains a large collection of great apes and other exotic wild animals on his family estate in Great Britain. His private zoo has been featured several times on television in the United States. On a flier distributed by Bay Area Action for Animals, one of the new grass roots groups, some of Aspinall's thoughts about modern society are quoted as follows:

> Homo sapiens is in uncontrollable, cancerous growth and medical research has merely exacerbated this condition. . . . The choice before us is a qualitative life for 200,000,000 humans in perpetuity in a partially restored paradise, or a quantitative countdown to Armageddon on a raped planet gutted of most of its resources. (Aspinall 1976, quoted in [Mills] 1976)

I was inspired by the flier to seek out more of Aspinall's writings and found in them a kind of rambling discourse about modern technology, people, and animals which reflects many of the associations made by animal rights advocates. He makes extensive reference to the ethological studies of animals published over the last twenty years, particularly those of nonhuman primates:

> Man's contempt for animals precludes him from accepting the validity of primate studies in relation to himself, and he shies at any inferences that can be drawn from them. . . . I have spent many months in jungles and have always been impressed by the beauty and justice of the forest regimen. . . ."Nature, whose sweet rains fall on just and unjust alike" has much to teach those who are willing to learn. But will they ever be enough to force a shift in opinion large enough to deflect the present collision course of our culture? (Aspinall 1976, p. 151)

> Over a hundred years ago when Darwin asserted that we were related to the apes, the majority of educated men of the time, including Wilberforce and Professor Owen, decried him. Today, when at our disposal we have the recent behavioral studies or ethograms of Carpenter, Schaller, Goodall, Reynolds, Kortland, and others on various social primates, we have either ignored them or failed to draw from them the conclusions that lie embedded like gemstones in their work. (P. 146)

Aspinall links salvation from ecological disaster to recognition of the human-animal bond and animal rights. He exclaims, "I believe in 'Jus Animalium,' the Rights of Beasts . . . I believe in the Buddhist concept of Ahimsa—justice for all living things" (P. 155). The vision of impending ecological disaster brought about by human technology, emphasis on animals as exemplars of the human natural state, and advocacy of animal rights are all tied together in Aspinall's writings. His apocalyptic ecology and "Jus Animalium" are a concise statement of a world view found in movement literature and in the statements of many adherents of modern animal rights.

It is within the context of anxieties about the technological control of nature that the animal rights movement has emerged. Could the poet find a better metaphor for society's subjugation of nature than that of the scientist experimenting with an animal? As the imagined animal, the animal of the mind, has come to resemble us, animal symbols have acquired great resonance. This has not been a simple projection for protesters in the past or present. For the Victorians, vivisection represented the technological invasions of the body. In the nineteenth century, the human body was the perceived focus of medicine's assault, as the animal body was the focus of assault by experimental physiologists. Physiological research, the discovery of pathogeneity, and vaccination were part of a medical revolution that would enable physicians to intervene with surgeries, pharmaceuticals, and vaccines in ways that had never before been possible. Much of the research on which these theories and techniques were based involved the use of animal subjects. In the late Victorian period, vaccines were a target of active protest, and organized sentiment against vaccination was closely aligned with antivivisection. Hygiene, proper nutrition, and morality were believed to be crucial in helping to align the body with nature. The physiologists' cruelty is identified as part of a dangerous trend.

> Truly this mournful spectacle of the perpetration of cruelty by those who best understand what is cruel, and of the contemptuous disregard of the claims of the brutes by those who have taught us that the brutes are only undeveloped men, is one to fill us with sorrowful forebodings for the future of our race. (Cobbe 1884*a*, p. 9)

In the modern period, the technological invasion is of the whole of nature—the vivisection of our planet. In a series of complex transformations, the animal as victim has become a symbol of both humanity and nature besieged. The modern animal rights movement has expanded the Victorian focus, which was almost exclusively on the scientific domination of the body, to include the manipulation and domination of nature as a whole. These two issues are explicitly linked in the literature of the modern movement. As Fox (1980) writes:

> Science through its technology has been used to dominate and exploit nature, including even inner human nature. It was once thought that science and technology would remedy the social ills of humanity by mastering nature. Instead they have only compounded and increased those ills. (P. 136)

To the activists of both periods, it has been scientific researchers, opening and probing the bodies of animals, who are perceived as the agents of harm. Modern research directed at behavioral manipulations of the "psychological nature" of animals are seen as analogous to actual physical manipulations.

My discussions with activists in the animal rights movement raised many questions for me about the phenomenology of beliefs about animals, technology, and nature in industrial society. As a participant in the same culture as my informants, I share with them exposure to a constellation of facts and theories about science, nature, and animals. Yet in our constructions of these "facts" into theories, and our adherence to particular ideas and social movements, we differ in some ways. How do we construct theories about nature and the human relationship to nature in technological culture? As different ideologies contest meanings in a cacophony of voices in American society, these questions take on increasing importance.

It is critical to an understanding of these protests to acknowledge their deep ties to other important themes in industrial society of the last century. Neither movement has arisen as an accidental or eccentric event (nonadherents with whom I spoke frequently expressed the opinion that the animal rights movement was "just a bunch of kooks who will go on to something else when they get tired of animals"), and both are profoundly connected to other ideologies that criticize aspects of Western science and society. Both radical feminism and philosophies of personal revelation are important aspects of protest in both periods. Cobbe was a feminist who developed a philosophy linking the greater moral consciousness of women with the mission to abolish vivisection. In the modern period, the connection between the radical feminist critique of patriarchal society and the animal rights movement is explicitly stated in the movement's literature, and many modern adherents have been active in the cause of women's rights. An article in *Ms.* magazine emphasizes the links between the two issues.

> The destruction of hundreds of animal nations and the killing and maiming of individual animals have their parallel in gynocyde, the murder of women. Examples of gynocide, numerous in history, include the burning of an estimated nine million women as witches in the Middle Ages in Europe. Significantly, animals were often executed at the same time, as witches' "familiars." (Cantor 1983, p. 28)

According to Cobbe, it was the special mission of women to bring out the qualities of the heart in human society. Women were seen as sharing these emotional qualities with animals, with the result that both had the same emblematic meaning. Thus, in her view, women shared a crucial role with the highly romanticized animal of the period in the potential revitalization of society. A frequent analogy in the modern feminist animal rights literature is made between the patriarchal treatment of women and pet-keeping.

> The pet-woman is trained to be dependent and helpless, accommodating, incapable of distinguishing or striving to fulfill her own needs, fixated on her master as provider, protector, rescuer. . . . Woman-as-pet supplants Woman-as-slave in situations where the uselessness of household members is proof of the master's wealth and power. (Ibid., pp. 29–30)

Patriarchal dominance over animals and women is also related in the literature to the dominance by technology of all of nature. One feminist animal rights adherent writes:

> I identified with the air, suffocating in industrial waste. Like the air, the earth and the water, like the animals, woman is seen as an object to be controlled and manipulated for the ends of man. (Corea 1984, p. 37)

Thus, a gay male informant spoke of the "white male mentality": "The white male mentality is a strange animal. I don't understand it. I see the nuclear weapon as just an extension of the male penis. We're going to rape the world."

Some anthropologists have made universal claims for this association between women and nature, describing the subjugation of women cross-culturally as linked to the identification of women with nature and animals because of women's reproductive functions (Ortner 1974). Over the last decade, feminist scholarship has examined the implicit connection made between women and nature in the Western cosmology, asserting the cultural specificity of this construct and its lack of universality (MacCormack and Strathern 1980). The Western perception of women's link to culture emerged as a focus of feminist ecology in the late 1970s and 1980s, which connected male domination of women with the human dominance of nature. Susan Griffin's (1982) critique of pornography as a symbolic domination of nature by patriarchal consciousness and Carolyn Merchant's (1980) *The Death of Nature: Women, Ecology, and the Scientific Revolution* are both examples of the ecofeminist approach. This radical feminism with its essentialism and universal claims about women's relationships to technology has been criticized recently by feminists with very different perspectives. In shocking contrast to ecofeminism, which speaks of "matriarchal integration" with nature, Donna Haraway's *Cyborg manifesto* (1984) suggests an ironic embrace by women of the loss of boundaries between animal, human, and machine:

> American radical feminists like Susan Griffin, Audre Lorde, and Adrienne Rich have profoundly affected our political imaginations—and perhaps restricted too much what we allow as a friendly body and political language. They insist on the organic, opposing it to the technological. But their symbolic systems and the related positions of ecofeminism and feminist paganism, replete with organicisms, can only be understood . . . as oppositional ideologies fitting the late twentieth century. They would simply bewilder anyone not preoccupied with the machines and consciousness of late capitalism. In that sense they are part of the cyborg world. But there are also great riches for feminists in explicitly embracing the possibilities inherent in the breakdown of clean distinctions between organism and machine and similar distinctions structuring the Western self. . . .What might be learned from personal and political "technological" pollution? (Pp. 92, 93)

Such critiques are important in current feminist discourse, but the ecofeminism of the animal rights movement attests to the profound popular influence of radical feminism on American culture. For many women in the movement, medical technology represents the patriarchal domination of women, animals, and nature. My point here is not to debate the radical feminist critique of science and medicine but rather to indicate its pervasive influence on feminist animal rights. While it has been suggested by some historians that nineteenth-century medicine was as dangerous for men as it was for women, these images of technologically mutilated women are important icons for radical feminists. My question is not "Were these problems limited to women?" or "Are these problems universal aspects of women's experience?" but rather "What meanings are derived from these associations by the animal rights movement?"

Feminist historiography has linked the growth of technological, invasive medical practices in the nineteenth century to the exploitation of women, particularly in the field of gynecology (Ehrenreich and English 1973; Barker-Benfield 1976). A vivid example of this critique is found in Mary Daly's *Gyn-Ecology: The Meta-Ethics of Radical Feminism* (1978). In a chapter entitled "American Gynecology: Gynocide by the Holy Ghosts of Medicine and Therapy," she writes:

> The nineteenth century witnessed the erection of gynecology over women's dead bodies. By 1883—the year of the death of J. Marion Sims, the "father of gynecology" (known as the "architect of the vagina")—gynecologists could apply their knives at will to the whole range of woman's being, reduced as it was to sex.
>
> As G. J. Barker-Benfield shows, the more notorious midnineteenth-century gynecologists were bent upon reducing women to their sex organs. Sexual surgery became the Man's means of restraining women. (Pp. 224–225)

Many of my informants suggested that this trend continues in the present and that the way Western medicine treated women was analogous to the way animals are exploited by science. Daly's indictment of Sims and the comments of an activist-informant are examples of the resonance between popular and scholarly radical feminist ideology:

> "Dr. Sims, there's a statue of him in New York, in Central Park, because he corrected vaginal fistulas. He operated on black slave women to perfect his techniques, and he did it at a time when there was no anesthesia. His work was immoral, even if a technique came out of it."

Sims was one of the most famous and influential American gynecologists of the midnineteenth century. His early work consisted of "vivisections" on the bodies of female slaves who were kept in a small building in his yard. Through his sexual surgeries on black women, he explored the structure of the female reproductive organs and produced new techniques for surgical intervention. As his career gained momentum, he associated himself with the Woman's Hospital in New York. Here, he was provided with a surgical theater in which other male physicians watched the sexual surgeries he performed on indigent female subjects, used as models for the development of surgical techniques. A black slave, Anarcha, had endured thirty of Sims's operations in his backyard stable. In New York, Mary Smith, an indigent Irish woman, suffered a similar number between 1856 and 1859. The data gained through Sims's mutilations of black female slaves and indigent women were applied to his growing clinical practice in which he treated rich women. In the end, he had established an international reputation and was highly regarded at Harvard Medical School, where he is reported to have been worshiped as something of a divinity (Daly 1978). Strong evidence suggests that Sims's approach was only unique in its monomania and that it characterized in theory and method much gynecological work of the period.

As Daly writes of the DES daughters (daughters of women who were given the chemical DES as an antiabortant in the 1950s and who later developed reproductive anomalies and some cancers), "Such gynecological 'holy Ghosts' as Sims now haunt the history of women from generation to generation. The seeds of such ghostly/ghastly presences are iatrogenic diseases, and the daughters of women infected by such 'divine' doctors carry in their bodies and minds the cancerous cells hidden there by these 'helpers' " (p. 226). This radical feminist historiography has provided a nightmarish chronicle of bizarre nineteenth-century atrocities against women by the doctors who had recently come to specialize in treating them. It evokes horrifying images of female passivity under the knife of invasive male physicians. Its metaphoric resemblance to animal vivisection is very powerful and difficult to ignore.

According to some feminist historians, the rise of the male gynecological specialty in medicine is related to the first wave of feminism. The year of the first Women's Rights Convention, 1848, also marked the year that another famous early gynecologist, Charles Meigs, described the new science as a way of understanding and controlling women's bodies and souls, which were widely perceived as aspects of uncontrolled nature. A decade later, an English gynecologist, Isaac Baker Brown, invented female clitoridectomy as a cure for female masturbation and other "unruly pathologies" of female sexuality. In 1873, Dr. Robert Battey perfected female castration, or removal of the ovaries, as a cure for female "insanity" (Daly 1978). Ovariotomy was widely practiced for decades and was believed to cure the disordered natures of many women and to return them to husbands and families more tractable and orderly. According to Ehrenreich and English (1973), modern psychoanalysis has continued the metaphoric control of disordered "hysterical" women.

> Under Freud's influence, the scalpel for the dissection of female nature eventually passed from the gynecologist to the psychiatrist. . . . It [Freudian theory] held that the female personality was inherently defective, this time due to the absence of a penis, rather than to the presence of the domineering uterus. (P. 43)

Normal aspects of female sexuality were treated by nineteenth-century medicine in both America and Great Britain as diseases whose cure involved various interventions. Ehrenreich and English quote Dr. Engelmann, president of the American Gynecological Society at the turn of the century, on the issue of the treacherous nature of normal female sexuality:

> Many a young life is battered and forever crippled on the breakers of puberty; if it crosses these unharmed and is not dashed to pieces on the rocks of childbirth, it may still ground on the ever-recurring shallows of menstruation, and lastly upon the final bar of the menopause ere protection is found in the unruffled waters of the harbor beyond reach of sexual storms. (P. 110)

Focusing on the theme of dangerous disorder, Mary Midgley (*Animals and Why They Matter* [1983]) connects patriarchal attitudes toward animals and women and writes about the symbolic meaning of both as projections of human fears of uncontrolled nature.

> The fear of women is a fear of the impulses they arouse and the forces they stand for. They are not seen as actual, limited beings in the world with their own wishes and problems, but as fantasy figures, angels or witches, elements with all the spiritual power of

whatever emotions they represent. . . . The resulting terror is that of the Frankenstein when the monster first peers through his curtain. . . . Female suffrage did not make much difference politically, but its symbolic importance was enormous.

Women, however, are not our main topic here; let us look at other sorts of symbolism. Here is Jung discussing how in dreams animals represent the passions: "This manner or representation is very familiar to the analyst, through the dreams and fantasies of neurotics (and of normal men). The impulse is readily represented as an animal, as a bull, horse, dog, etc. One of my patients, who had questionable relations with women, and who had begun his treatment with the fear that I would surely forbid him his sexual adventures, dreamed that I very skillfully speared to the wall a strange animal, half pig, half crocodile. Dreams swarm with such theriomorphic representations of the libido." (P. 80)

According to Midgley and other feminist animal rights theorists, the medical abuse of women and animals stems from a widespread fear of them. This fear is a response to projections onto animals and women as symbols of uncontrolled nature. Midgley points out that this imagery of nature as chaotic and dangerous is the flip side to the sentimental and romantic view of nature and its symbolic representation in women and animals. Women are thus angels and witches, and animals are romanticized pets or dangerous brutes.

Some of these themes have been examined in the nineteenth-century debate over the use of anesthesia in childbirth (Poovey 1986). In the late 1840s, British physicians began to experiment with chloroform as an anesthesia for obstetrics. In the 1860s, in fact, as the debate about the use of animals by physiologists began to take shape, the British Royal Medical and Chirurgical Society of London was appointing a committee to study chloroform's effects during labor in response to widespread debate in the medical community about its efficacy. The anesthesia question was part of the Victorian debate about female gender.

The issues in this debate center around two, related, questions, although they were never given precisely in this form. First, does the woman in labor properly belong to the realm of nature, which is governed by God, or to culture, where nature submits to man? Second, how can a man know—so as to master—the female body, which is always other to his own? And what does he know when he has mastered it? (P. 139)

Poovey, a professor of English, uses the anesthesia debate as an illustration of the production of knowledge in support of specific patriarchal interests (such as those of the specialist consultant as against the general practitioner in the nineteenth century). She shows that the silenced body of the anesthetized woman in labor fulfilled some of the purposes of the Victorian medical specialist (to control the patient and make her more accessible to the physician) but finally proved problematic. The debate was filled with allusions to the explosive sexuality released in women by anesthesia. As a woman lapsed into unconsciousness, she was released from the bonds of civilization and what emerged was her *animal* nature. Thus, the anesthetized parturant is described as losing her normal modesty, making sexual gestures and sounds; in fact, becoming an animal.

According to these feminist critiques, both women and animals represent projections about nature; their phenomena belong in the realm of nature, which is studied by science and ultimately mastered through scientific and medical technologies. Daly (1978) asserts the continuity of these themes in the twentieth-century patriarchal oppression of women:

> As we shall see, the patter has not changed. Rather, the doctored diseases have spread. The seeds which Sims and his colleagues sowed in the minds of their simian sons, the professional cultivators of that field, have ripened in a rich harvest of medicinally manufactured carcinomas, "cured" by the cutting edge of advanced sexual surgery. The mutilations and mutations masterminded by the modern man-midwives represent an advanced stage in the patriarchal program of gynocide. The supremely sterile, infinitely impotent "immortals" have brewed their final solution. Unable to create life, they are performing the most potent act possible to them: the manufacture of death. This production is a last attempt by these holy ghosts and hospital hosts to erect a fitting temple/tumor for themselves, an appropriate embodiment for their word-made-flesh, a womb-tomb dedicated to the worship of Nothing. (P. 277)

The imagery is once again of pollution and the transgression of boundaries—the consistent theme of antivivisection and animal rights protests of human transgressions of nature in the form of animal experiments. Here the theme is used in an identical metaphor for the incursions of medicine into the bodies of women, polluting them and destroying them as natural entities. It is the same critique of science and medicine applied by the animal rights movement to the issue of man's exploitation of life embodied in an animal. As scholarly feminist analysis claims these meanings, so a concurrent folk analysis links women to animals and criticizes science's manipulations of them in its quest to "know" and dominate nature. This radical feminist analysis elaborating a connection between women and nature, counterposing matriarchal integration with nature to patriarchal dominance of women and of nature, is an important theme in modern animal rights.

In the Victorian period, feminist antivivisectionists symbolically linked women to animals through their presumably shared qualities of emotionality, spirituality, and intuition. This was a complex and many-layered association in nineteenth-century constructions of gender. Late Victorian science proposed an evolutionary sequence in which women occupied a category between animal, primitive, and modern European male. Thus, in Herbert Spencer's *Principles of Sociology,* serialized in the *Popular Science Monthly,* he suggested an evolutionary continuum in which the traits of women were adaptations to primitive conditions. In *The Descent of Man,* Darwin viewed women as closer to the primitive, to nature and to animals, and quoted Vogt, a professor of natural history at the University of Geneva, to the effect that "the grownup Negro partakes, as regards his intellectual faculties, of the nature of the child, the female, and the senile White" (1864). The new scientific construction of the category "primitive" included women and formalized older meanings implicit in the Victorian ideology of gender.

The preponderance of women in both the antivivisection and animal rights movements makes sense in light of these connections. By contrast, there exists a folk theory of why women seem to be attracted to these movements in greater numbers than men. It is a common assumption that childless older women are drawn to the cause because of their identification with pets as surrogate children. My research illuminated very different kinds of correlations, and my informants were anything but the popular stereotype. Many of the women with whom I spoke in the movement were active critics of what they considered to be the patriarchal values dominating modern science and medicine. Symbolic associations are important to our construction of reality, and the feminist critique of biomedicine has emphasized certain symbolic relationships between the treatment of women and of animals. These kinds of associations are social determinants of adherence to animal rights which cannot be examined through neat correlations that reduce the complexity of human motivation to a simple story. One important reason women are attracted to animal rights ideology is because of complex symbolic meanings that can be explored by attending to these discourses about animals and women in our society.

There are also structural aspects to the movements that have made them attractive to women. In the Victorian period, many women worked in the humane movement without acknowledged leadership roles. French (1975) suggests that antivivisection was a more accessible arena for women disenchanted with the conservatism of the humane societies and their insistence on the Victorian norm of male leadership. As most of the modern women activists I interviewed had histories of involvement and "burnout" in other causes, it seems possible that a similar opportunity has been part of the modern movement's attraction for women. However, several activists complained that as the animal rights movement has gained momentum and formal structure, men were increasingly taking public leadership roles.

Another important association exists between the protests of animal experimentation and philosophies of personal revelation such as evangelical Christianity and some currently popular forms of mysticism. In both protests, scientific empiricism has been seen as opposed to emotion and revelation. In the Victorian period, antivivisection had a preponderance of evangelicals, and Cobbe's writings reflect the evangelical rejection of intellectual categories and clerical and medical specialization in favor of emotional, intuitive, revelatory experience. Her anecdotal psychologies of dogs stressed the spiritual bond between animal and human. This theme emerged in some of my discussions with informant-activists, in comments such as "I think of the relationship between humans and other animals as a very spiritual one." One of my informants recounted the following story about an elderly woman which conveys a sense of revelation through interaction with an animal:

> "She was in Yosemite hiking, and something said to her, 'Turn around,' and she turned around and there was a mountain lion, and she was very quiet. She looked straight at the mountain lion and said, 'Good morning.' The lion sniffed the air, looked right at her, turned around, and walked away. That's a profound experience and communication that happened."

This anecdote reminded me of a passage in Berger (1980) contrasting the different experiences of looking at an animal in nature who returns our gaze and the passivity of viewing animals marginalized by the zoo environment:

> What were the secrets of the animal's likeness with, and unlikeness from, man? The secrets whose existence man recognized as soon as he intercepted an animal's look? In one sense the whole of anthropology, concerned with the passage from nature to culture, is an answer to that question. But there is also a general answer. All the secrets were about animals as an intercession between man and his origin. (P. 4)

The sense of a revelatory vision through animals was connected to another theme in my conversations with activists, that of conversion. As one informant put it, once the revelation of the equality of all animals is received, "there's no going back." The perception of speciesism as a form of oppression analogous to racism or sexism was often described as a revelation; one understood it suddenly in a flash of insight that changed one's life. I often felt that my activist-informants held the hope, and sometimes conviction, that my own conversion was soon to come. In the literature of the new movement, the conversion of scientists is an important event often involving the scientist's rejection of empiricism in favor of one or several of a variety of popular mystical, transcendental, and Eastern philosophies. Thus, experimental psychologist Roger Ulrich's conversion is described:

> This animal behaviorist whose experiments admittedly subjected animals to torture now speaks of "my animal friends from rats to monkeys," and has been influenced by the pantheistic philosophy of the American Indian mystic Rolling Thunder, a man who felt

that the earth was an organism and that he himself, and the "deer, snakes, bees, mosquitoes, and pinyon trees were one being." (Pratt 1980, p. 45)

Ulrich says,

I don't consider myself as doing research anymore but rather, consider Roger Ulrich a subject and part of the experiment. Under those circumstances, I hardly know who to thank other than the Great Spirit of Life that is responsible for all. (Ibid.)

The dichotomy between thought and feeling (associated with the polarizations of nature/culture and human/animal) is another set of important constructs in Western society. These mutually defining oppositional categories are projected onto scientists and animal rights activists not only by nonadherents but also by activists in the movement who claim the terrain of what is coded as "emotion." Thus, the researcher is viewed as "cold" and "intellectual" and the activist as "emotional" and "extremist." This obscures the ambiguity and complexity of all human enterprises that are not mediated by discrete neural controls separating thought from feeling. The performance of important aspects of science involves intuition, emotion, and sometimes "extremism" and mystical strivings. There are strong "irrational" elements in research as there are "rational" aspects in advocacy of animal rights (the recent philosophical discourses by animal rights adherents ([Regan 1982; Rollins 1981; Singer 1975] illustrate this last point).

The dissonance I perceived between some of the beliefs of my informants, and my own led me inexorably to questions of how individuals come to construct theories about nature and the human relationship to nature. The phenomenology of attitudes about the ecology of the body and the environment, and, in a sense, the nature of reality itself, was ultimately implicated in my study of the protests in both periods. The potential bases for a variety of attitudes regarding the relationship of science to nature are available to members of technological societies. The very fact that some people will be relatively unconcerned about ecological issues, some moderately concerned about controlling damage to the environment, and some passionately concerned about what is perceived as an impending ecological apocalypse attests to the phenomenological problems associated with beliefs about nature. (There is every reason to believe that belief systems are heterogeneous among members of "traditional" societies as well [MacCormack and Strathern 1980]). We are all exposed to a wide range of facts and theories about the natural ecology, and our responses involve discriminations of a subtle nature.

The literature of both Victorian and modern protests reflects an anxiety about transgressions of the boundary between technology and the body and new attitudes toward the relationship between humans and animals. At present, for many, the line between humans and animals is very thin. The diffusion of modern theories of ecology has contributed to a general sense that humans and the rest of the organic world are only separated by highly fluid boundaries. We increasingly view ourselves as vulnerable organisms within nature, along with other animal species, and thus as potentially sharing a tragic fate. The alarm of protestors over these disappearing boundaries is reflected in much of the literature of the animal rights movement.

Antivivisection and animal rights have appealed to people sensitive to these issues concerning the boundary between technology and organism. In the Victorian period, many perceived the human body as polluted and disordered by new scientific technologies. In the words of one antivivisectionist:

> Mr. Fleming indites a psalm of triumph over the prospect of a boundless field of innoculations just opening to the activity of medical men and veterinary surgeons, who will go forth like so many sowers to scratch the people and cattle instead of the ground, and drop cultivated virus by way of seed, or possibly trees, as the case may prove. Are we then, our oxen, our sheep, our pigs, our fowls—all to be vaccinated, porcinated, equinated, caninised, felinised, and bovinated, once, twice, twenty times in our lives, or every year? Are we to be converted into so many living nests for the comfortable incubation of disease germ? Is our meat to be saturated with "virus," our milk drawn from innoculated cows, our eggs laid by diseased hens,—in short, are we to breakfast, dine, and sup upon disease by way of securing the perfection of health? (Unnamed physician, quoted in Taylor-Bell, 1884b, p. 19)

The modern animal rights movement replies to the passionate queries of this anonymous antivivisectionist with a resounding

"Yes." Medicine's therapeutic incursions into the human body would far surpass the early and, to some, shocking use of animal-derived vaccines. One can imagine the Victorian anti-vivisectionists' outrage at the recent development of techniques of organ transplantation from animals such as pigs and monkeys into the human body or the implantation of machines, such as the artificial heart.

The modern animal rights movement has expanded the focus of the Victorian protest from the invasion and pollution of the human body to the invasion of all of nature by machines. For many today, there is a deep tie between aspects of inner and outer nature; the body and the ecosystem and what happens in the environment may have drastic repercussions within the body. The products of out-of-control technology in the environment now affect the body in a way that individuals often cannot resist or control. This is a frequent point made by animal rights advocates. As Jack Hill said to me:

> "I'm concerned with the subtherapeutic doses of drugs that we're feeding animals. They're all in such crowded conditions that they're susceptible to all these diseases. And the research has shown that the use of these antibiotics builds up resistance to antibiotics in their systems, and we are building up resistance to these things. Some of these folks think that within two or three decades we're going to be in very serious trouble."

Or as an animal rights flier states:

> Animal tests are not the final step. Testing continues on humans when drugs are marketed. Drugs that are removed from the shelves in countries such as North America [sic] and Great Britain are sold to third world countries. The final abuse is inflicted upon the ecological systems of the world when chemical wastes (including drugs) are "dumped," polluting our water, land, and air. (Hamilton, n.d.)

In a vivid passage in *Animal Liberation* (1975), Singer expands this sense of pollution to meat itself in a description that would take away the appetite of even the most confirmed steak-eater:

> Vegetarianism brings with it a new relationship to food, plants, and nature. Flesh taints our meals. Disguise it as we may, the fact remains that the centerpiece of our dinner has come to us from the

slaughterhouse, dripping blood. Untreated and unrefrigerated, it soon begins to putrify and stink. When we eat it, it sits heavily in our stomachs, blocking our digestive processes until, days later, we struggle to excrete it. When we eat plants, food takes on a different quality. We take from the earth food that is ready for us and does not fight against us as we take it in. (P. 183)

According to Singer, an animal's body does not belong inside ours. The flesh of the dead animal "stinks" and "putrefies" and resists incorporation into our own.

Another major element in the literature and ideology of both movements is the attribution of a particular moral incapacity to scientists. In conversations with activists, I was often struck by the importance of this point. Researchers were characterized on a kind of continuum of immorality. Some were pictured as cruel, while others were viewed as being under the influence of certain delusions or as having compromised themselves for economic security. It was really never considered that some animal researchers choose the work that they do because they believe it to be valid, moral, and humane. When I suggested this possibility in conversation, it was always rejected, and I often felt implicated in the "researcher's mentality." One informant said it was amazing to her that people could delude themselves into such a state of denial in order to keep doing research.

The scientist as invader of nature has some interesting resemblances to the symbolism of witches and witchcraft in a number of societies. It seems likely that some of the emotional meaning of vivisection, its revolting and fearsome nature, derives from its resemblance to universal aspects of witchcraft.

> A closer look at the symbolism of witchcraft shows the dominance of symbols of inside and outside. The witch himself is someone whose inside is corrupt; he works harm on his victims by attacking their pure, innocent insides. Sometimes he sucks out their souls and leaves them with empty husks, sometimes he poisons their food, sometimes he throws darts which pierce their bodies. And then again, sometimes he needs access to their inner bodily juices. (Douglas 1973, p. 139)

The Victorian literature deployed images of the bloodthirsty vivisector who, in a frenzy of lust, tortured an innocent animal.

This aspect of vivisection—its nightmarish resemblance to old images associated with witchcraft—may partly explain why many modern adherents, disturbed by contact with accounts of animal research, cannot sleep properly. One activist reported that she could no longer enjoy vacations or Christmas since finding out about laboratory animals. Another became suicidal for some time after reading Singer's book, which details numerous vivisections.

Both animal rights and antivivisection have shared an apocalyptic vision of the destructive potential of technology and have suggested redemption through a realignment of the entire relationship between our species and the world of nature. For protesters in both periods, vivisection is the symbolic nexus for the all the damage wrought by the forces of technology and its specialist-practitioners. Both literally and symbolically, it embodies all of the elements involved in the scientific manipulation of the body and of nature. It is thus a perfect symbol for the modern dominance of technology over life.

Male Chimpanzee, Gombe, Tanzania. Photo by Phyllis Dolhinow.

7

Primate Iconography: Modern Primatology and the Remodeling of Natural Categories

> Writing strictly from the point of view of religious symbolism it is not relevant to ask how accurate is Lele observation of animal behaviour. A symbol based on mistaken information can be fully effective as a symbol, as long as the fable in question is well known.
>
> —Mary Douglas, *Implicit Meanings*

The late Victorian period saw a vast remodeling of images of animals and of ideas about the relationship between humans and the world of nature. Evolutionary science was widely disseminated in Victorian popular literature, and the idea of the human descent from apes became a routine topic for jest in the latter part of the nineteenth century. As one commentator noted in the British journal *Galaxy Magazine* of May 1873:

> The Taine of the Twentieth Century who shall study the literature of the Nineteenth will note an epochal earmark. He will dis-

cover a universal drenching of belles lettres with science and sociology, while the ultimate dominant tinge in our era he will observe to be Darwinism. Not only does all physical research take color from the new theory, but the doctrine sends its pervasive lines through poetry, novels, and history. Journalism is dyed so deep with it that the favorite logic of the leading article is 'survival of the fittest' and the favorite jest is 'sexual selection.' (Pond 1873, p. 68)

The Victorian antivivisectionists responded to these changing cosmological categories of human and animal in complex ways. They denied the animality of humans and at the same time incorporated evolutionary arguments into their antivivisection tracts.

Like the Victorians, our society has undergone a recent period of heightened attention to categories of human and animal and a renewed popular interest in evolutionary thought. The postwar period in the United States and several other industrialized countries has seen an important scientific and popular discourse about the animality of people and the complex cognitive and social characteristics of animals. Nowhere has this been more evident than in the field of primate studies. Modern primatology, which developed in the decade following World War II, is central to the debate about humans and animals at the present time. It has had an important role in influencing popular attitudes toward animals and the human relationship to animals. This is not surprising; as members of the same order, we share many characteristics with other primates, and because of this relationship primates serve better than any other group of animals as emblems of the boundary between human and nature. Social scientists hypothesizing about human behavior have frequently used primatological data in their reconstructions of human evolution. The popular diffusion of these models through the media has been a common trend of the last decade and reveals many basic problems of integration and analysis of the primate behavioral data on which they are based.

An examination of the relationship of modern primate studies, social science interpretations of these studies, and their popularizations is basic to an understanding of current ideas about animals and the human relationship to animals. Several important themes have dominated the popular studies of primates and have significantly contributed to the delegitimization of the boundary between human and animal. The popularizations of modern primate studies have remodeled images of primates both through the anthropomorphizing of monkeys and apes and the animalizing of humans. Concurrent with these trends, nonhuman primates have often been used in evolutionary models to replace the "primitive" human groups of the early years of cultural anthropology. Cultural evolutionism, an important theory in the period when anthropology was a young science, posited several different stages of development through which societies were believed to have passed on the road to modern Western culture. According to the cultural evolutionists of the late nineteenth and early twentieth centuries, "primitive" tribal groups represented living examples of earlier stages of culture. This was, of course, a thoroughly ethnocentric view, and modern anthropology came to recognize the folly of the early evolutionary schemas. Cultural relativism made it untenable to stack living cultures into evolutionary totem poles with Europeans on top. It became a common theme in introductory anthropology classes to stress the complexity of all societies, whether technologically simple or advanced. But a fascinating and analogous process to early cultural evolutionism has occurred in the field of primate studies. In the decades since the 1960s, nonhuman primates have come to replace human "primitives" in many widely popularized evolutionary reconstructions, and these reconstructions have had an enormous influence on popular thinking about animals. Nonhuman primates are, in many respects, our new "primitives," occupying a role that is very similar to the one formerly occupied by the Trobriand Islanders or Crow Indians in the minds of many American and European readers of popular anthropology.

Haraway (1987) analyzes the relationship between the popularizations of modern primate field studies of the apes in the historical context of decolonization and exploitation of the Third World during the postwar period:

> In all of these stories, humans are placed in "nature" in gestures that absolve the reader and viewer of unspoken transgressions, that relieve anxieties of separation and solitary isolation on a threatened planet and for a culture threatened by the consequences of its own history. But the films and articles rigorously

exclude the contextualizing politics of decolonization and exploitation of the emergent Third World, heterosexual marriage in advanced capitalism, masculine dominance of a war-based scientific enterprise in industrial civilization, and the racial organization of scientific research. Instead, the dramas of communication, origins, extinction, and reproduction are played out in a nature that seems innocent of history. It is precisely to renaturalize "man" after the calamities of industrialism, and especially after the bomb, that apes and people are placed together in both the "natural" world of the forest and the "cultural" world of language-users and pet-keepers. This scene is a crucial part of the ideology of relief of "stress," a failure of communication, that has been constructed since World War II. The nature-culture myth is restored by the lush, filmic mediation of tropical animals and white women. The myth appears universal, not the story of any one people addressed to members of that same group. (Pp. 47–48)

We are at a crucial juncture in the debate about the relationship of humans to animals, and an examination of the history of primatology's redefinition of the nonhuman primate is important to an understanding of the modern view of animals. In modern Western culture, science has an important role in the construction of categories of human and animal. Clearly, primatology is at the heart of the scientific transformation of natural cosmological categories in our own society. As Haraway has noted, nonhuman primates are crucial icons in the contested visions of the human place in nature in our period. They have reflected popular concerns about animals, and about human animality, and primate studies have proposed certain constructions of the problem of the human relationship to animals. The animal rights movement is in part a social response to these changing visions of human and animal.

The following passage by Carol McGuinness and Karl Pribram illustrates a pervasive phenomenon that occurs when primatological data are fit into models for the evolution of important human institutions.

In all primate societies the division of labor by gender creates a highly stable social system, the dominant males controlling territorial boundaries and maintaining order among lesser males by containing and preventing their aggression, the females tending the young and forming alliances with other females. Human primates follow this same pattern so remarkably that it is not difficult

to argue for biological bases for the type of social order that chan-
nels aggression to guard the territory which in turn maintains an
equable environment for the young. (Quoted in Goldman 1978,
p. 56)

This is typical of a kind of social science analysis that has appeared widely in popular journals since the early 1970s, and this
interest on the part of social scientists in primate behavior has
yielded important hypotheses about human evolution. However,
the ways in which primatological data from fieldwork are taken up
by scholars from a variety of theoretical backgrounds dealing with
human behavior require close scrutiny if the whole relationship of
animal to human behavior is to be understood. Because of the increased public interest in animal behavior since the early 1960s,
ideas about monkey and ape behavior, and its relationship to human behavior, have received a wide popular audience. McGuinness and Pribram's interpretation appeared in one of many popular journals publishing articles on human nature and its biological
roots. These social science interpretations of primate behavior
have increasingly made their way into the public forum, and this
discourse has significant implications for the recent increase in interest in animal rights. Because no animals serve better as emblems of the boundary between humans and the natural world
than nonhuman primates, it is not surprising that the current animal rights movement has focused so much attention on research
using nonhuman primate subjects.

Primatology has always shared a relationship with social science and the primatological field-worker is anything but a theoretical tabula rasa. He or she leaves for the field with a set of problems that are part of an intellectual tradition. For the anthropological primatologist, this tradition is influenced by social theory, because as part of a shared discipline studying human
beings, anthropological primatology has implicit roots in social
theory. But the process of relating human and nonhuman primate
data that has frequently occurred involves many problems of integration and analysis. These occur when primatologists use social
science constructs and when data from field studies are interpreted by social scientists. In the latter category, and most disturbing to the primatologist, is the concept of "the monkey" im-
plied in McGuinness and Pribram's phrase "all primate

societies," which is, in fact, a conglomeration of bits and pieces of behavior of many species with widely varied phylogenetic relationships to each other and to humans. This highly anthropomorphized "primate" ancestor has appeared all too frequently in popularizations of human evolution.

One problem with this "primate ancestor" is that primate species are all very different from each other, and these differences are not easily codified or understood. Thus, cross-phylum generalizations are not easy to make. For instance, sexual behavior among monkeys and apes exhibits a wide variety of patterns that defy neat phylogenetic analysis. Monkeys display a variety of mating patterns (Rowell 1972), but the most telling data in this regard are from the apes (Nadler 1981). There are significant differences in the sexual behavior of chimpanzee, gorilla, and orangutan which in no way relate to their phylogenetic closeness to humans. Thus, their sexual patterns and our own cannot be fit into a neat or satisfying phylogenetic scale. For instance, hormonal and behavioral states appear closely correlated in gorilla reproductive behavior, somewhat less so in chimps, and least of all in orangutans. Thus, all three of the great apes display different mating patterns that in no way relate to their phylogenetic closeness to humans. This contradicts the popular view that the more advanced the phylogenetic relationship to humans, the less hormonal control of sexual behavior and greater resemblance to human reproductive behavior will be found in a species of animal. The tendency to lump together primate species and to anthropomorphize them is a very common trend of the last decade.

In the McGuinness and Pribram article, monkeys and apes are used as exemplars of earlier stages of human evolution. Thus, according to the authors, the ubiquitous primate ancestor occupies a position similar to that of traditional societies in the evolutionary schemas of the nineteenth-century anthropologists. The diffusion of cultural relativism into all branches of modern social science had made it embarrassing and untenable to fit tribal groups into this slot. In the late twentieth century, it is no longer possible to use tribal societies as analogues for earlier stages of the evolution of modern society. But monkeys and apes have provided the new early ancestral group from which human institutions are supposed to derive. The replacement of human "primitives" by nonhuman

primates also relates to global political events of the postwar period. "With the progressive disappearance of human 'primitives' as
legitimate objects of knowledge and colonial rule, and with the
discrediting of pre-war eugenics, Western anthropologists had to
rethink the meaning and processes of the formation of 'man' "
(Haraway 1987, p. 7). There are many serious misconceptions
about humans and animals that follow from this simplistic replacement of "tribal human" by nonhuman primate in the cosmological
category of "the primitive."

One consequence of this substitution is a basic definitional im-
precision that obliterates the border between human and nonhuman. The passage by McGuinness and Pribram, for instance, is a
morass of terminological ambiguity. What is meant by terms such
as "division of labor," "highly stable social systems," "maintaining order," "containing and preventing aggression," and "lesser
males" when referring to nonhuman primates? Do these terms
mean the same thing when applied to animal societies as they do
when they are applied to human cultures? Clearly they do not, for
the division of labor in human societies is at least in part of a cultural phenomenon and embroidered with symbolic meanings that
are unavailable to nonhumans. Similarly, stability and instability
in human society are complexly bound to sociopolitical and economic factors that do not exist for nonhuman primates. Yet the
popularizations of modern primatology give an impression of extreme similarity between human and nonhuman social behavior
which delegitimizes the cognitive boundary between human and
animal and the recognition that human culture is not simply an
elaboration of basic primate behavioral adaptations.

The problem is complicated by the fact that primatologists are
as guilty of perpetuating this kind of confusion as are their social
science interpreters. Errors in the cross-discipline application of
terminology have frequently occurred in the search for the integrating factors of group life, which has been an important trend in
postwar primate studies. It is interesting, and pertinent to the issue of animal rights, to examine how the concept of the primate
social group as an anthropomorphic political entity structured the
questions primatologists took with them to the field through the
1960s and 1970s. Some of the frequent mistakes made by social
scientists in evaluating nonhuman primate data have resulted

from the way in which many primatologists have described their own data. The following passage by Sarah Hrdy illustrates this problem. Hrdy was a graduate student studying with the anthropologist Irven DeVore at Harvard in the 1970s when she went to India to research the behavior of the Indian langur monkey at Abu, a pilgrimage site. Her accounts of langur social behavior became an influential argument in the burgeoning debate over sociobiology. According to the sociobiologists, human and animal behavior could be reduced to reproductive strategies whereby individuals seek to maximize their future contribution to the gene pool. Humans and animals were pictured as competing for reproductive success and as attempting to foil the strategies of other conspecifics. According to Hrdy's account, langur life was full of violence, political strife, and infanticide. Her work on langur monkeys received wide public attention, and she has written a number of important books and articles for a popular audience. In one such account, she describes langur social structure in the following terms:

> The stable core of langur social organization is overlapping generations of close female relatives who spend their entire lives in the same matrilineally inherited 40 hectare plot of land. (1977a, p. 40)

Here, as in the article cited earlier, terminological ambiguities blur the boundary between human and nonhuman primates. For example, does the term "matrilineal inheritance" have the same meaning to a primatologist that it does to a social anthropologist? What of the terms "uterine kinship," "alliance," and "descent," which have also frequently been used by primatologists to describe monkeys and apes? In many ways, this recycling of social science concepts and terminology through primate studies and then back to social science, where they become incorporated into models for the evolution of human behavior, resembles the party game "telephone." One person whispers a phrase to another, and so on, until its initial meaning has become completely obscured. Thus, the primatologist may go to the field with a melange of models and terms, some of which come from social theories of human behavior and culture. The data applied to these models, and described in highly anthropomorphic terms, are then taken up by social scientists interested in discussing evolutionary hypotheses. By the time these accounts reach the public, the lines between human and nonhuman primate are imperceptible. The popularizations of these models in magazines like *Psychology Today* and in the numerous television documentaries about primates and human evolution are an important source of ideas and feelings about animals. These popularizations of primate behavior and the behavior of other social species like wolves, whales, and dolphins are important events in the growth of current sentiment about animals and their relationship to humans. Although animal behavior specialists often decry the popular abuses of their data, a careful scrutiny of our own assumptions and descriptions of animal behavior is also necessary. The diffusion of a lexicon of confused descriptive terms into social science and into the public forum has had profound implications for public attitudes toward animals.

In the postwar period, during which modern primate studies grew as a discipline, two themes emerged in the popular treatment of primatological data: the anthropomorphizing of the animal and the animalizing of the human being. This first theme is illustrated in some of the early studies of baboons by the anthropologists DeVore and Hall (1965) in the late 1950s and early 1960s. The influence of functionalism in social anthropology is apparent in their description of troop structure, which became central to the model building of many popularizers of primatology such as Robert Ardrey (1961, 1966). Functionalism stresses the ways in which human societies are organized around functionally integrated institutions such as kinship. An almost exclusive focus on the search for the "integrating factors" of group life came to characterize the early baboon studies and indeed many of the early studies of nonhuman primates. The monkey troop was viewed as a kind of functionalist's microcosm of human culture. This makes great sense when viewed in historical perspective. It was a surprise to find that monkeys had such complex and highly organized social structure as the early baboon researchers observed. Thus, the focus on political hierarchy was intense in these interpretations undertaken by anthropologists and others who used the baboon model in evolutionary schemata for human evolution. An implicit analogy was always present between the dominance system of male baboons and human political institutions. Not only did social scientists frequently use the baboon studies in this way but the assumptions that informed the research itself were bound to hypotheses about human society that elaborated models of social structure based on the interlocking "functions" of various institutions. The male hierarchy in baboons was portrayed as holding the troop together. This was then described as the evolutionary "function" of male hierarchy.

When DeVore and Hall wrote, "The baboon group is organized around the dominance hierarchy of adult males" (1965, p. 54), they meant it both literally and figuratively. Dominant males were seen as binding together a loose, potentially chaotic aggregate of females and young. At the same time, the troop was spatially schematized as concentric circles with the most dominant animals in the center and the least dominant on the periphery. In her analysis of American primate studies, Haraway (1978) has pointed out the organismic analogy underlying some of this early work, in which the dominant males are the figurative head without which the body cannot survive. This idea can be traced back in time to the signal work of the American primatologist Clarence Ray Carpenter in the prewar period. Male dominance was visualized as the cement of primate social organization, as human political structures functioned cohesively to maintain stability.

Robin Fox, the social anthropologist, among many others, recognized the usefulness of the baboon data for evolutionary model building and wrote of it in *The New York Times Magazine* as "the area where evolutionary studies, primatology, and social anthropology meet in earnest" (1968, p. 82). About the baboon model, he wrote:

> If this kind of social system was, in fact, typical of man's ancestors, then it provides some powerful clues concerning the evolution of the brain. Clearly it was those animals with the best brains who were going to do the breeding and each generation would see a ruthless selection of the best-brained males, with the dumbest and weakest going to the wall. (Ibid., p. 87)

This view of baboon society was highly anthropomorphic, and the whole question of the lack of close phylogenetic relationship between human and baboon was uncritically ignored. The animals were described as politically organized in a human, albeit totalitarian, fashion (the baboon troop is, according to Fox, "anything but democratic" [p. 82]). Their leaders had many of the idealized attributes of human male leadership in Western culture. The use of the baboon troop as a model for ancestral human populations was very influential in forming an anthropomorphized view of monkeys in popular treatments.

During the same period, studies of apes often encouraged an extreme anthropomorphizing of nonhuman primates. In Jane Goodall's popular *National Geographic* articles and in her book *In the Shadow of Man* (1971), chimpanzees were portrayed as sharing many basic human attributes and were described in highly anthropomorphic language. For instance, all of Goodall's subjects were given human names, and their personalities were described in human terms. Later, through the collaboration at Stanford between Goodall and the psychiatrist David Hamburg, chimpanzee behavioral modeling exemplified the trend in primate studies to animalize humans. Hamburg, an influential and politically astute academic, was extremely concerned with the roots of human aggression in the wake of the Kennedy assassinations. Thus, in a series of articles, he seeks the causes of human aggression in the comparison of human violence to chimpanzee agonistic behavior. This emphasis in Hamburg's work during the 1970s was part of a widespread interest in the primatological origins of human behavior. Like the baboon model for human social organization, these studies were widely popularized.

Popularizations of the early attempts to teach apes language and to raise them with human families also illustrate the modern tendency to anthropomorphize nonhuman primates. Whatever the specific goals of each project, the overall public image was one of talking animals. By the late 1970s, this view had become so pervasive that when researcher Penny Patterson and Stanford University became involved in a dispute over ownership of the gorilla Koko, which Patterson had attempted to teach American Sign Language (ASL), attorney and animal rights activist T. S. Meth could argue that Koko's legal status was directly analogous to that of a foster child. Meth wrote that Koko deserved to be granted

apparatus for the beginning of a historical sense, for the contemplation of self. Her right to remain in a meaningful relationship with the people she has known is greater than the zoo's property rights. (Quoted in Desmond 1979, p. 22)

By the mid-1970s, a shift occurred: primates were less frequently anthropomorphized and humans increasingly portrayed as "like animals." Imagery of the dark side of nature, including human nature, began to dominate discussions within the academic and popular realms. Historians such as Keith Thomas and Richard Turner have noted this ongoing dialectic about nature in Western culture in which periods of romanticization about nature fluctuate with projections of chaos and danger onto the natural world. This is reflected in modern primate studies that romanticized nonhuman primates during the the 1960s and early 1970s and that have more recently developed a much darker vision of our nonhuman primate relatives as well as of human nature.

Many of the same individuals influential in the anthropomorphizing of primates were influential in the later trend. For example, in an article tracing the origins of human kinship to nonhuman primate troop structure, R. Fox writes, "The real question is do the [human] rules represent more than a labeling procedure for behavior that would occur anyway" (1975b, p. 10). Thus, in Fox's analysis, alliance and descent in human kinship are explained as derived from a kind of merging of nonhuman primate characteristics at the biological level in human evolution. In a similar fashion, Hrdy and other sociobiological primatologists talk about human culture as merely a veneer over genetically controlled mechanisms universal to sexually reproducing organisms, including humans. By the midseventies, these mechanisms were posited as reproductive strategies of a "selfish" nature, often involving aggression and infanticide. Stephen Jay Gould (1980) identifies as zoocentric this attempt to build general principles from animal behavior and then subsume humans on the rationale that, after all, we are animals, too (p. 16).

The scientific image of nonhuman primates as violent and infanticidal has been promulgated during a period of political ascendancy for conservatives in the United States. The social policies of the 1960s are regarded by idealogues of the New Right as having failed, among other reasons, because they were policies based on naively liberal attitudes toward human potential. According to many current conservative thinkers, criminals are not created by social problems but by biological and genetic propensities. Sociobiology's emphasis on genetic causes of behavior, on competition in a grim marketplace of limited goods, perfectly fits the neoconservative model of human nature. The sociobiologist's story of genetically controlled violence is often reported in the popular press. (Oyama [1985] and Kitcher [1985] examine the flaws inherent in this genetic reductionism.)

In the 1960s and early 1970s, popular studies of nonhuman primates, particularly of apes, created the impression of an almost human animal. Interestingly, as the romantic aspects of the 1960s anthropomorphic projections onto animals began to shift to a more Hobbesian view of all social life, the formerly gentle chimpanzee would also come to be described as aggressive and infanticidal. In Goodall's accounts of her early work with chimpanzees at Gombe, her subjects were portrayed in highly anthropomorphic terms. *In the Shadow of Man* (1971) was a landmark publication in what would become a vast literature of popular books on animals. In it, she wrote:

> Sexual relationships between male and female chimpanzees are in large part similar to those that can be observed among many young people in England and America today. In other words, chimpanzees are very promiscuous, but this does not mean that every female will accept every male who courts her. (P. 186)

Goodall (p. 236) analyzed the behavioral problems of Flint, a young male chimpanzee whose development she traced as if he were a human child: "What went wrong with Flint's upbringing? Had he been 'spoiled' by too much attention from his mother, sister, and two big brothers?" The image of the chimpanzee in the early Goodall accounts was of an almost human creature living in a state of nature, a being toward whom one could feel a comfortable identification, if not actual affection. Through her collaboration with Hamburg, chimpanzee behavior was used as an explicit analogue of human behavior, particularly human aggression. Hamburg and Goodall compared fighting, tantrums, and rough-and-tumble play in chimpanzees and humans. The function of the chimpanzee-human comparison was ultimately prescriptive and motivated by Hamburg's deep involvement with the causes of human aggression. Goodall's early anthropomorphizing, Hamburg's biologizing of complex human behaviors, and the use of the chimp as a missing link exemplify a pattern in much of the modern social science appropriation of primatological data.

On the heels of the publicity surrounding Goodall's work, experimenters began to attempt to teach apes human language (the language studies by the psychologists Hayes and Hayes in the 1950s were an exception in that they preceded Goodall's popularization). Desmond's *The Ape's Reflexion* (1979) reviews the history of the ape language experiments and the attempts to raise apes with human families. Desmond, a social scientist, was deeply influenced by the ape language material. He is critical of some of the ape language studies' blatant anthropomorphisms, arguing that

> by flagrantly crediting the gorilla with the entire gamut of human mental states—discerned with exquisite distinction: "imagine," "think" and "idea" for example—we effectively enslave the gorilla, robbing it of psychic independence and reducing it to human status. (P. 57)

Nevertheless, for Desmond and many others, the studies were perceived as effectively challenging the whole concept of human uniqueness. Rather than showing that apes can effectively use language, the language studies displayed their remarkably complex cognitive abilities. He writes:

> To be able creatively to exploit object names requires an immense cognitive substructure, a rearrangement of the mechanics of the mind to throw open a profoundly new window on the world. No longer can we reassuringly imagine dumb brutes tied to the immediate present, tyrannized by nature, at her instant beck and call. It is even hazardous to deny the ape an imaginary world, where reason can run through its strategies, devising the right course of action before committing itself to the real world. (P. 109)

The language studies aroused much interest and were highly publicized in popular formats. In 1969, the Gardners announced Project Washoe, their attempt, begun in 1966, to teach ASL to a chimpanzee. The initial motivation for the project was to argue against Noam Chomsky's deep structure of innate language construction. Chomsky had asserted that human language was based on a neural template evolved through uniquely human evolution. The Gardners' behaviorist stance was part of a debate that continued for years. If Washoe could be taught the fundamentals of a human grammar, then the learning theorist's argument that language was acquired through simple learning chains of stimulus and response would be substantiated. In 1966, the psychologist David Premack began work with the chimpanzee Sarah using a plastic-word "language" chiefly as a means of getting at cognitive processes (Premack and Premack 1972). Premack's approach was considerably less anthropomorphizing than that of the Gardners, and Sarah was kept caged. In contrast, photographs of the Gardners and Washoe always presented the chimpanzee within a human setting, and Washoe signed "Doctor" and "Mrs." Gardner (although the significance of this formal address to the chimpanzee subject was never explained). In 1972, Duane Rumbaugh began to use a computer-run language trainer with a chimp named Lana at Yerkes Research Center, and that same year, Patterson began to teach the gorilla Koko ASL. All over the country, people were engaged in attempts at cross-species communication. In 1973, a research group at Columbia started Project Nim using a chimp subject to repudiate the Gardners' behaviorism and to empirically support Chomsky's psycholinguistic, deep-structure approach to language. The debate over whether or not chimpanzees and gorillas are actually communicating linguistically continues to be important in academic circles, but the disagreements have diffused into the popular arena far less than have the stories of talking apes.

In 1975, Maurice Temerlin, a psychiatrist, published *Lucy: Growing Up Human,* his account of the rearing of a female chimpanzee as a family member. Desmond (1979) calls Lucy

> a chimpanzee who lives literally as one of the family. She is analyzed according to Freud but not treated according to Darwin, by which I mean that whenever possible she is interpreted as a primal human. (P. 59)

A photograph from the book shows Lucy and her human "foster mother" avidly looking at an issue of *Playgirl* magazine with expressions of great enjoyment. Patterson's research with Koko continued through the mid-1970s and had a wide popular following. In the October 1978 issue of *National Geographic* ("Conversations with a Gorilla"), she credited Koko with the use of the expletive "damn," and she later appeared with Koko on the Johnny Carson show for fund raising purposes.

Concurrent with, and fueled by, the scholarly debate surrounding the ape language studies was the diffusion of an image of apes as highly anthropomorphized creatures. In 1977, the psychologist Gordon Gallup, reviewing the change in attitudes toward apes, wrote, "Perhaps some day, in order to be logically consistent, man may have to seriously consider the applicability of his political, ethical and moral philosophy to chimpanzees" (p. 13). In a similar vein, Harold Hayes, writing in *The Sunday New York Times*, quotes Meth:

> The gorilla doesn't exist anymore. Under normal circumstances, the only thing this animal doesn't have that we do is language. Now you have changed it. When you give it the conceptual apparatus for conscious reasoning, for mobilizing thought, you have radically altered it. You have given it the pernicious gift of language. If it has never been one before, it is an individual now. It has the apparatus for the beginning of a historical sense, for the contemplation of the self. Her [Koko's] right to remain in a meaningful relationship with the people she has known is greater than the zoo's property rights. This is the whole history of jurisprudence over the past 75 years—that property rights must give way to individual rights. In this case you have an ape that has ascended. (1977, p. 22)

Desmond (1979) writes of the ape language studies, "Apes 'growing up human' have created an unprecedented moral crisis for mankind, and a lobby is forming for radical changes in the law" (p. 59). As evidence, he cites a *Boston Law Review* commentary in which Stephen Burr insisted that "recognition is needed that animals have a right to live regardless of their usefulness" (ibid.).

During the same period that the ape was anthropomorphized in the public imagination, a number of books appeared which relied heavily on the baboon troop as a model for early hominid social structure (Ardrey 1966; Morris 1967; Tiger and Fox 1971). DeVore and Hall (1965) had described a highly organized troop structure in which the dominance relationships of the adult males provided group cohesion. This model has since been widely criticized as both sexist and anthropomorphic by individuals in a variety of disciplines (Haraway 1978; Reed 1978; Rowell 1972; Strum 1975). But these criticisms have been limited to a scholarly audience.

The Imperial Animal (1971) by Tiger and Fox is a particularly interesting case because it was written by social anthropologists and relies heavily on the DeVore-Hall baboon material and, to a lesser degree, the macaque studies of the Japan Monkey Center. Fox (1972, 1975*b*) had used these data to elaborate the tie between human and nonhuman primate behavior in a scholarly format. In both the popular and scholarly material, primate social structure is described as based on "hierarchy and competition for status, which determines access to resources and the privilege of breeding" (Tiger and Fox 1971, p. 31). Males dominate the political system, and older males dominate younger ones. Females may be influential in sending males "up the status ladder," but it is the dominant males who keep order, nurture, and protect the young.

> Among the terrestrial primates a division of labor among adult males, females, and young males already exists. Mature males control and defend the group; the females take care of the next generation; and the young males at the periphery act as guards and watchdogs. (Ibid., p. 86)

The cohesive element in these societies is the cooperative bonds between males, and it is the charisma of the dominant males that is the central focus for the whole structure. According to Tiger and Fox, "It will be quickly apparent that these rules apply to human beings as well as to many of the other primates" (p. 32). Culture is thus a thin covering over this presumed basic primate biogram:

> We can see that aristocracies, oligarchies, plutocracies, tyrannies, despotisms, democracies, and all other forms of political dominance, despite their obvious overt differences, all work according to the same basic processes. They differ in the way they institutionalize the basic features and how they emphasize different parts of the primate political biogram.
>
> Egalitarianism is often the stated goal of democratic idealists, indeed it is often adopted as a symbolic structure (Mr. President, Comrade Stalin, Citizen Robespierre) but here the possible hiatus between symbol and action is the most glaring—a continuing capacity in self-deception that is at once necessary and disastrous.

Necessary because without it there would be no democratic ideas; disastrous when it comes between us and a proper understanding of the limits within which those ideas can operate. (Ibid., p. 43)

The baboon model was compatible with, and tended to bolster, a Hobbesian and androcentric view of human society, while the use of chimpanzee behavior originally tended to reflect a more benign view (although this would change in the 1980s, when chimpanzee behavior too was brought under the umbrella of sociobiology). But the assumptions underlying the early use of ape and baboon behavioral data in models for hominid evolution were equivalent. Ape and monkey behavior were microcosms of human social behavior and political life.

The popularizations of the late 1960s and early 1970s derived from a trend in scholarly social science of the period toward the replacement of traditional human groups with nonhuman primates in evolutionary models. Ethnographic details of behavior among the !Kung San or Crow warriors were still invoked, but a frequent recourse was to use monkey and ape behavior as the analogue for early hominid evolution. Early social evolutionists such as Spencer (1896) and Westermarck (1894) mentioned nonhuman primates in their evolutionary schemata, but habitual recourse to nonhuman primate behavior by social scientists in evolutionary reconstructions did not occur until the 1960s, when modern primatology made detailed field observations available. The rejection of cultural evolutionism by modern anthropology made it untenable to trace the linear evolution of a behavior through living human groups, as, for example, the early evolutionist Morgan had done.

In *Ancient Society* (1877), Morgan wrote of

a part of the accumulating evidence tending to show that the principal institutions of mankind have been developed from a few germs of thought; and that the course and manner of their development was predestined as well as restricted within the narrow limits of divergence, by the natural logic of the human mind and the necessary limitations of its power. (Pp. v–vi)

The attempts to trace the origins of human social institutions through the nonhuman primates avoid the embarrassment of a

Morganesque cultural evolutionism by replacing traditional or ancient societies with a ubiquitous "primate" from whom the principal institutions of humans were supposed to be derived. The mode of analysis is structurally the same, and the fundamental errors of this approach are only magnified when monkeys and apes are slipped into the slot formerly occupied by traditional human groups.

Herskovits's 1955 introductory text *Cultural Anthropology* identifies for the student three postulates on which early cultural evolutionism was based:

> The postulate that the history of mankind represents a unilineal sequence of institutions and beliefs, the similarities between which, as discerned at the present time, reflect the principle of the Psychic Unity of Man.

> The comparative method, whereby the evolutionary sequence of human institutions and beliefs is to be established by comparing their manifestations among existing people who are assumed to be the living exponents of earlier stages of culture through which the more advanced societies are assumed to have passed.

> The concept of the survival of customs among peoples regarded as more advanced in their development; these survivals to be taken as evidence that such societies have passed through earlier stages whose customs, in vestigial form, appear in their present way of life. (P. 433)

The postulates of cultural evolutionism may be rephrased to fit the modern use of nonhuman primates in many evolutionary schemata as follows:

> That the phylogenetic history of the primates represents a unilineal sequence.

> The comparative method, whereby the evolutionary sequence of human institutions and behavior is established by comparing similar behaviors and institutions among nonhuman and human primates.

> The concept of the survival of biologically programmed primate behaviors in humans; the idea that these vestiges show the earlier stages through which the species has passed.

Thus, primates are the new missing link in modern evolutionary models. But nonhuman primates are as unwieldy a link as were the traditional groups of the early evolutionists. All living species of organisms have undergone separate histories combining both evolutionary and chance events. Yet modern theorists seem undismayed by the death of naive evolutionism in the social sciences and continue to use living species as missing links. It may be that certain styles of thought have such a pervasive appeal that exposure of their theoretical weaknesses has little impact.

In *Biosocial Anthropology* (1975a), Robin Fox is quite explicit about his use of nonhuman primates as a replacement for humans in traditional societies (italics added).

> Older theorists speculated on the "earliest conditions of man," and as we know debates raged between proponents of "primitive promiscuity" and "primitive monogamy." The former were usually seen as a prelude to "matriarchy" (now popular again) and the latter to "patriarchy." This has all been dismissed as ridiculous for well-known reasons. But I think we can now go back to the question in a different way. We know a great deal about primates which can tell us what is behaviorally available to our order in general and, therefore, what must have been available by way of a behavioral repertoire to our ancestors . . . "early man" then, in this sense, was less like modern man gone wild than like a primate tamed. *And even if we cannot deduce accurately the kinship systems of early man from those of the most primitive humans, we can do something better—we can distill the essence of kinship systems on the basis of comparative knowledge and find the elements of such systems that are logically, and hence in all probability chronologically, the "elementary forms of kinship."* (P. 11)

The differences between Fox's assumptions and Morgan's are negligible. Fox traced the evolution of human kinship through the primates, borrowing, as he admits, "somewhat recklessly from the jargon of social anthropology, descent and alliance" (ibid.). According to his analysis, these two elements are present in nonhuman primate social systems but are only combined in human groups. He divides primate social systems into two types, one-male and multimale groups, which all have in common

> a threefold division of the larger group into: a) adult males; b) females and young; c) peripheral males. We can look at any primate

social system, including our own, in terms of the "accommodations" made between these three blocks. (P. 13)

According to Fox, in one-male groups (gorillas and hamadryas baboons), the basic unit is the "polygenous family," while in the multimale group (common baboons, chimpanzees), "if the sexual relationship is brief and unenduring, the consanguineal relationship is long lasting and of central importance" (p. 15). The phylogenetic histories of different primates are thus collapsed into several categories with a certain internal consistency. But once the question of the relationship of complex human behaviors to nonhuman primate behavioral variation is raised, the evidence becomes a confusing array of bits and pieces of randomly chosen aspects of behavior among species with varying phylogenetic relationships to each other and to humans. Although nodding briefly at the issue of variation ("there will be a variety of different styles and content to rules, varying with the cultural experience, ecology, and history of different peoples [much the same is true of other primates as it happens"] [p. 10]), Fox goes on to the heart of his argument about nonhuman primates and human culture:

> The real question is do the rules represent more than a "labeling" procedure for behavior that would occur anyway?. . .
> If group A and B were called "Eaglehawk" and "Crow," and the various lineages "snake," "beaver," "bear," "antelope," etc., then a picture emerges of a proto-society on a clan moiety basis which would have delighted Morgan and McClellan (and Bachofen), but depressed Westermarck and Maine for sure. (P. 10)

Similarly, Morris (1967), another important popularizer of primate social behavior, wrote:

> The old-style anthropologist would have argued that his technologically simple tribal groups are nearer the heart of the matter than the members of advanced civilizations. I submit that this is not so. The simple tribal groups that are living today are not primitive, they are stultified. Truly primitive tribes have not existed for thousands of years. The Naked Ape is essentially an exploratory species and any society that has failed to advance has in some sense failed, "gone wrong" . . . the characteristics that the earlier anthropologists studied in these tribes may well be the very fea-

tures that have interfered with the progress of the groups concerned. (Pp. 10–11)

Morris's rationale for replacing traditional groups with nonhuman primates is thus that monkeys and apes are closer to the human ancestral state than the living, but "degenerate," human tribal groups.

Examples of this missing link approach to the use of nonhuman primate behavior abound in the literature from the 1960s to the present time. Many popularizations of this approach have had a wide audience (Comfort 1966; Morris 1967; Reynolds 1981). In one such account, Comfort, a sexologist and gerontologist, explains the presumed continual receptivity of human females as follows:

> At some point in primate evolution, the female became receptive all year round and even throughout pregnancy. This apparently trifling change in behavior was probably the trigger, or one of the triggers, which set off the evolution of man. Between baboons and higher apes we find the effects of this change. Baboons behave very like other pack-living animals. Higher apes, with sexual activity continuing all the year round, and unrelated to heat, develop a heterosexual social life which is not confined to the coital encounter. (1966, p. 13)

The order of ascent is baboon, ape, and human, and the character "continual sexual receptivity" is traced along this ladder in much the same way that Morgan traced kinship from savages to barbarians to civilized humans. ("Gorilla life is family life, where baboon life is a little more like that of a vast institution" [p. 13]). Comfort's apes are completely anthropomorphized into early ancestors. He attempts a Freudian primatology.

> We need not bother now with racial memory—evolutionary "memory" in the genes is a fully adequate explanation. If human sexuality had been brought forward into reproductive life, as it apparently has been, the oedipal reactions with their peculiar anxieties and their genital content could be part of the shift. (P. 24)

Similarly, E. O. Wilson (1978) slips chimpanzee tool-using into the slot traditionally occupied by human tribal technology:

> Each tool-using behavior recorded in Africa is limited to certain populations of chimpanzees but has a mostly continuous distribu-

tion within its range. This is just the pattern expected if the behavior had been spread culturally. Maps of chimpanzee tool-using recently prepared by the Spanish zoologist Jorge Sabater-Pi might be placed without notice into a chapter on primitive culture in an anthropology textbook. (P. 31)

And de Waal (1982) writes in his recent book on chimpanzee "politics":

> When I am observing the Arnheim chimpanzees I sometimes feel I am studying Freud's primal horde; as if a time machine has taken me back to prehistoric times, so that I can observe *droti de seigneur,* one of the forgotten products of Western culture. (P. 167)

As popularizers, Fox, Morris, and Comfort may seem at first glance to be straw figures in a serious critique of the use of scholarly primatological data. Whatever their naïveté about nonhuman primate behavior, they represented the beginning of a trend that blossomed vigorously in the work of serious primatologists like Hrdy (1977*b*), Symons (1979), and de Waal (1982). The use of primates as analogues for tribal humans continues to have an extremely powerful role in current evolutionary models.

When viewed in historical perspective, the use of primates by social scientists as analogues for traditional humans has a surprisingly long past and may be considered to have originated in the late nineteenth century. Herbert Spencer wrote in *The Principles of Sociology* (1896):

> Among sundry of the primates, gregariousness is joined with some subordination, some combination, some display of the social sentiments. There is obedience to leaders, there is union of efforts, there are sentinels and signals, there is some idea of property, there is adoption of orphans, and anxiety prompts the community at large to make efforts on behalf of endangered members. (Quoted in Zuckerman 1932, p. 13)

Similarly, Westermarck, in the first volume of his *History of Human Marriage* (1894), sought in the gorilla the "primeval habit" from which marriage developed. Briffault (1927), the early exponent of a matriarchal stage in human development, wrote:

> The animal family, out of which the human social group must be supposed to have arisen, is matriarchal . . . male anthropoids are not in general permanently attached to a given group, but join a

> female, or group of females, as does the orang, according as their instincts prompt them. (Ibid., p. 14)

Briffault believed that among nonhuman primates, females and young formed the only true permanent group and that this represented the traditional human condition, a theory that has recently been revived by some feminist primatologists. In 1932, Sir Solly Zuckerman criticized this use of nonhuman primates as analogues for early hominids.

> The similarity between anecdotal accounts of the habits of animals and ethnological accounts of the ways of primitive peoples makes it easy to understand why the two are so readily discussed together. Both are records of external forms of behavior, records amplified in the case of man by introspective analysis and embroidered in the case of the animal with anthropomorphic interpretation. (Zuckerman 1932, p. 17)

> To devise classificatory schemas of social behavior to include both animals and man, on the assumption that all behavior is fundamentally the same in kind, may be far more misleading than to conduct human sociological researches with implicit faith in the doctrine of man's separation from the rest of the animal world. (Ibid., p. 20)

Fifty years later, this trend has resurfaced with increasing popular persuasiveness.

The popularizations of the late 1960s and early 1970s shared a marked prescriptive attitude—that to understand and cure human social ills we must look at primate biological roots and attempt to align our own behavior more closely with our primate nature. In this spirit, popularizers Tiger and Fox (1971), Comfort (1966), Morris (1967), and Ardrey (1966) all discussed the concerns of the early ecology movement, such as the population explosion, the stresses of urban life, and the threat of nuclear war. Comfort entitles the final chapter of his book "Man as His Own Enemy—The Future of Human Nature." He writes:

> If we intend to survive our present achievements we must find vehicles through which we can both express and control our emotions, instead of letting them break out into violence or fragmentation, or hamper the proper use of the world's resources as they do today. (Comfort 1966, p. 184)

Morris (1967) derided modern architects for their lack of biological awareness: "One of the important features of the family territory is that it must be easily distinguished in some way from all the others" (p. 183). Thus, the anxiety about modern technology, concern for the natural environment, and the focus on animals (particularly primates) expressed in the modern animal rights movement are present in nascent form in many early popularizations of animal behavior. More recently, with the upsurge of activism, a cohesive theory ties together antitechnology, environmental issues, and animal rights, and animals have become the central focus for anxieties about humans' relationship to nature. That they should take on this iconographic meaning is not surprising considering the remodeling of natural categories of human and animal over the past twenty-five years of public interest in primatology.

The concept of continuity between humans and the world of nature has a long tradition in Western intellectual thought (Lovejoy 1936; Thomas 1983). The preevolutionary world view of a linear ordering of nature, in which forms may be placed on a ladder from simple to complex, was an important mode of thought long before the scientific theory of organic evolution. This concept persists in nineteenth-century and modern evolutionary discussions in covert form. It underlies the tradition of tracing a character (e.g., a bone or specific behavior) through the primates and then creating categories or groupings on the basis of one particular trait. All the attempts to trace the human division of labor or human kinship along a ladder of living primates exemplifies this persistent "Great Chain" approach. The enormous variability of primate species and the amount of phylogenetic distance between species undergoing evolutionary histories make a ladder of living forms meaningless; modern evolutionary theory recognizes the untenable nature of this approach. Nevertheless, the use of nonhuman primates as analogues for human ancestors continues unabated.

The paleontologist Osborn wrote in *The Origin and Evolution of Life* (1918) that

in the large vertebrates we are enabled to observe and often to follow in minute details this continuous adaptation not merely in one but in hundreds and sometimes in thousands of characters. . . . In the well-ordered evolution of these single characters we have a picture like that of a vast army of soldiers; the organism is like the army; the "characters" are like the individual soldiers; and the evolution of each character is coordinated with that of every other character. (P. 275)

Considerable light is shed on his optimism about orderly ladders of evolution when we realize that he also believed that the total geological time scale was sixty million years and the age of the mammals three million years. With seventy million years of separation for the primate order alone, and the consequent variability within the order, the "ladder" approach creates arbitrary, often absurd, categories.

Hodos (1970), a neuroanatomist, has criticized the persistence of this *scala naturae* or Great Chain concept in the neurosciences. For example, he cites the confusion between a phylogenetic scale or ladder and a phylogenetic tree. In neuroanatomical texts, the brains of the codfish, frog, alligator, goose, cat, and human are frequently compared as if they are in evolutionary order. But one living form is not ancestral to another. Such comparisons often imply that a particular species represents the essence of its type (e.g., the concept of the brain of "the reptile" or "the mammal"). Hodos's critique may be applied equally well to evolutionary models that have attempted to trace the evolution of a behavioral characteristic down the ladder from human to baboon, as Fox (1975a) does with human kinship. As we move up and down the phylogenetic scale, monkeys and apes are anthropomorphized, and behaviors of diverse species are used as simple analogues of human characteristics. This problem typifies much of the scholarly and popular evolutionary writing using nonhuman primate models of the early period of modern primatology. Group structure, kinship, and dominance behavior in nonhuman primates were viewed as precursors of human social structure and behavior. The influence of these models on popular attitudes toward the relationship of humans to animals has been profound.

In the mid-1970s, a shift occurred in which our own species is increasingly viewed as the end product of evolutionary trends that are not specific to humans (Hamburg 1971b; Hrdy 1977b; Symons 1979), just as earlier, nonhuman primates had been portrayed as protohominids. In this perspective, the human is animalized as the result of frequently unpleasant biological and evolutionary vicissitudes common to the primates and to animals in general. These approaches have received wide public attention, and their echo can be heard in much of the current animal rights literature.

The constructs underlying historical trends in primatology have been criticized recently, but, unfortunately, much of the analysis is couched in terms of language and theory inaccessible or objectionable to animal behavior specialists and not widely read by the lay public (Haraway 1978; Reed 1978). Both Haraway and Reed, for example, review the primatological literature from a feminist perspective. The anthropologists Sherwood Washburn (1978*b*) and Marshall Sahlins (1977), among others, have drawn attention to the pitfalls in the long exchange between biology and social science. Some social anthropologists have recognized the danger of reductionism in the use of nonhuman primate behavioral data for human evolutionary schemata. Burton Benedict has commented on the dangers of facile analogies (1979) and has noted of the nonhuman primate material, "How rudimentary is division of labor as compared with even the simplest human society" (1972, p. 13). But the view of nonhuman primates as primitive analogues of humans and the human as the "end result" of primate evolutionary trends continues unabated despite the increasing recognition among many scientists of its untenability.

To the early anthropomorphisms of Goodall, the ape language popularizations, and the portrayal of the baboon troop as a human political microcosm, the mid-1970s added the primatological animalizing of humans, and from this period to the present, a number of serious primatologists have increasingly portrayed humans as animal in nature. When as a result of insufficiently critical acceptance of this notion such mitigating considerations as phylogenetic distance, primate variability, and the role of human culture are thoroughly obscured, the portrayal becomes a self-fulfilling prophecy. Ultimately, the motif of nonhuman primates as missing links becomes implicit through repetition. The anthropomorphizing of nonhuman primates, the biologizing of humans, and the missing link role of monkeys and apes have restructured the modern idea of the primate.

Recent writings by the primatologists Hrdy (1977*b*), Symons (1979), Altmann (1980), and de Waal (1982), among others, exemplify this trend. Hrdy opens her sociobiological interpretation of langur behavior, *The Langurs of Abu* (1977*b*), with a comment on Shakespeare's play *Titus Andronicus*:

> Small wonder that a play replete with infanticide, dismember-ments, rape, and cannibalism has not weathered well the test of time. To modern audiences, these events seem implausible and unnatural. Nevertheless, if more primatologists had seen this play before going to the field, they might better have understood the behavior unfolding before them in the savannas and forests where monkeys are studied. The conflict of interest between Aaron and his mistress is basic to all sexually reproducing creatures where the genotype—and hence self-interests—of two consorts are nec-essarily not identical. (Pp. 1–2)

According to Hrdy, Shakespeare's human condition is but an elaboration of the basic animal "plan" seen in all sexually repro-ducing species (kin selection).

> The universality of conflict between the sexes is one reason that langurs might be of interest to human readers. A second reason is that the history of langur studies provides an obvious but all too relevant paradigm of our efforts to understand ourselves and creatures like us. (P. 2)

The paradigm is the modern recourse to genetic mechanisms as explanation for all behavior, and thus, by studying langur repro-ductive strategies, we can understand human social behaviors. Hrdy has been criticized by some nonsociobiological researchers of langur behavior on the basis of her interpretation of data (Boggess 1979; Dolhinow and Curtin 1978). But the zeitgeist is such that the appeal of this genetic reductionism is widespread, judging from the popularity of these sociobiological accounts in popular journals and newspaper stories. Infanticide as a socio-biological reproductive strategy may be the most widely dis-cussed concept in current popular animal behavior studies.

Symons wrote a popular sociobiology of human sexuality and discussed his ideas about the animal roots of human sexuality in such forums as the "Playboy Interview." Writing about the ro-mantic emotions of human adolescence in *The Evolution of Hu-man Sexuality* (1979), Symons hypothesizes that adolescent crushes are genetically controlled and have been selected in hu-man evolution as "guides" for parental decisions. Here he talks about anthropological data on parental mate choice among the Muria:

> These emotions may prove to be poor guides when adolescents are free to choose their own mates. Elwin's data, . . . for example, indicate that arranged Muria marriages are less likely to end in divorce than elopements are. (P. 170)

So implicit is the assumption that human behaviors (in this case, romantic attachments) represent simple adaptive characters that no elaboration of cultural factors seems necessary. The high divorce rate among Muria adolescents who have eloped thus "proves" that adolescent romantic attachments are not adaptive when they are allowed to guide mate choice. Thus, Symons hypothesizes that such emotions may have evolved as adaptations in the context of parental mate decisions, as useful guides to adults. Yet, in an earlier chapter, he has told us that the great majority of Muria marriages are arranged by parents

> primarily on the basis of family and economic considerations. Parents take into account whether potential spouses and their families are hard workers, free of scandal and the taint of witchcraft, and obedient to Muria traditions. An engagement is not simply a contract between individuals, but an alliance of families and clans. (P. 115)

Nowhere is it considered that in such a society extreme sanctions might be incurred by elopement. In this view, we are controlled by genetic mechanisms that have been adaptive over the course of human evolution, so the failure of elopements shows that romantic choice is biologically adaptive only in its presumed context of parental decision.

> Similarly, in an environment in which young people have relatively little say in spouse choice, selection might favor strong adolescent emotions about members of the opposite sex, emotions that have been designed by selection specifically to function in a milieu in which an adolescent's actual behavior will be constrained by the necessity to compromise with elders. (P. 169)

Jeanne Altmann, an exceptionally rigorous scientist who has made important contributions to both substance and methodology in modern primate studies, falls prey to similar "adaptationist" sociobiological assumptions in some of her recent work.

This mode of analysis pervades Altmann's *Baboon Mothers and Infants* (1980). Baboon maternal and infant behaviors are analyzed using cost-benefit analysis. Cost-benefit models have had great popularity in modern animal behavior studies and are derived through a process of naive translation from economics. Altmann writes:

> Models of the evolution of behavior are economic models; their major parameters include costs and benefits of behavior, usually measured in the "currency" of fitness of survival and reproduction, and of relative representation of genes in the next generation. (P. 5)

Using the cost-benefit model, Altmann analyzes restrictive and nonrestrictive modes of mothering among baboons and humans:

> Infants of high-ranking females are not as subject to the socially induced dangers of laissez-faire mothering as are infants of low-ranking mothers. Thus, by this argument, high-ranking mothers can in fact "afford" to be more laissez-faire, that is, laissez-faire mothering might be good mothering for a high-ranking infant, bad for a low-ranking one, and vice versa for restrictive mothering. (P. 188)

Thus, the restrictively raised baboon infant, although it may have a higher rate of survival during the earlier months, is less likely to survive the mother's death. Altmann goes on to point out possible implications for human groups.

> Many of the attempts to evaluate parental care in different Western social classes ignore the fact that not only the options that parents have but also the outcome situations to which infants must adapt may differ among these groups . . . if infant survival and adult adjustment, survival or reproduction, are reasonable criteria for good parenting, then the particular parental behavior that constitutes good parenting may vary considerably even within a given human or monkey society and must be considered within its normative context. (P. 188)

The implicit assumption is that these behaviors (restrictive versus nonrestrictive mothering) are genetically controlled adaptive reproductive strategies and that human class differences in child-rearing practices are in some sense equivalent to what is observed in baboons. But there is no discussion of the assumptions underlying the analogy between baboon dominance and human social class. Nor are data on ethnic, economic, or educational factors and human child-rearing practices introduced. Indeed, anything within the traditionally defined realms of human culture and history is ignored.

Again, the distinction between nonhuman and human primate is completely obliterated:

> In all aspects of the present study, one fact recurs: baboon mothers, like most primate mothers, including humans, are dual-career mothers in a complex ecological and social setting. They do not take care of their infants while isolated in small houses or cages as the rest of baboon life goes on. They are an integral part of that life and must continue to function within it. (P. 6)

This equation of baboon mothers to "dual-career" human mothers in modern technological society illustrates the modern trend that collapses the enormous complexity of human situations into a set of simple analogies to nonhuman primates.

De Waal's approach in *Chimpanzee Politics* (1982), a popular account of his observations of a chimpanzee colony at Arnheim, Holland, exemplifies all of the trends that have blurred the distinction between humans and other primates over the last twenty-five years. De Waal, a former student of the influential Dutch ethologist Van Hoof, opens his book, appropriately, with a foreword by Desmond Morris, who writes:

> We are closer to our hairy relatives than was previously held to be possible. The apes, when carefully studied, reveal themselves to be adept at the subtle political manoeuvre. The social life is full of take-overs, dominance networks, power struggles, alliances . . . arbitration . . .privileges and bargaining. There is hardly anything that occurs in the corridors of power of the human world that cannot be found in embryo in the social life of a chimpanzee colony. (P. 14)

The chimpanzees themselves are anthropomorphized; they are used as the missing link in the evolution of human politics, and finally, human political life is biologized. The following material from the book is illustrative of the total loss of boundary between animal and human:

> Mama enjoys enormous respect in the community. Her central position is comparable to that of a grandmother in a Spanish or Chinese family. (P. 56)

> We know from anthropological studies of primitive tribes that the chief exercises an economic role comparable to the control role: he gives and receives. He is richer but does not exploit his people, because he gives huge feasts and helps the needy. . . . This universal human system, the collection and redistribution of possessions by the chief, or his modern equivalent, the government, is exactly the same as that used by chimpanzees: all we have to do is replace "possessions" by "support and other social favors." It is perfectly reasonable to suppose that our forefathers had a centralized social organization long before material exchange began to play a role. The first system may well have served as a blueprint for the current one. (P. 204)

Thus, Trobriand Islanders are equivalent to the "chimpanzee stage" of hominid evolution.

> The Trobrianders do not seem to realize that it is the mother's husband who has fathered the children. Despite their lack of knowledge, it is above all the unconscious father who develops affectionate ties with the children, worries about them and takes risks to protect them. This example, described by Bronislaw Malinowski, proves that, in human beings as for chimpanzees, paternal care need not be based on rational thought. There undoubtedly existed strong ties between the human father and child long before man discovered the function of sex. (P. 173)

Human political behavior and social structure are derived from chimpanzee behavior, according to de Waal, and he decries the inability of some social scientists to accept this.

> Some social scientists seem unable to accept such things as human nature and the biological influence of parents, grandparents, and all the preceding generations right back to their animal forefathers. (P. 174)

The assumption that human and chimpanzee political behavior have the same roots is summed up as follows:

> This book . . . demonstrates something we had already suspected on the grounds of the close connection between apes and man: that the social organization of chimpanzees is almost too human to be true. Whole passages of Machiavelli seem to be directly applicable to chimpanzee behavior. The struggle for power and the resultant opportunism is so marked among these creatures that a radio reporter once thought to try and surprise me with the question: who do you consider to be the biggest chimpanzee in our present government? (P. 19)

The biologizing of human behavior is widespread and currently popular in fields other than primatology. Wilson (1978) views the mentally retarded as living analogues of a more simple state who

> represent a sudden and dramatic step downward in ability. . . . Their exchanges with others entail little that can be labeled as truly human communication. Cultural behavior thus seems to be a psychological whole invested in the brain or denied it in a single giant step, yet the non-cultural retardates retain a large repertory of more "instinctive" behavior the individual actions of which are complex and recognizably mammalian. (P. 41)

The use of retardates and criminals as representatives of earlier stages in human evolution originated with the eugenicists of the nineteenth century (Gould 1981) and has been reviewed by the modern biologizing of human behavior.

The relationship between modern primatology and popular ideas about animals, particularly about those most closely related to humans, is complex. Primate studies have reflected social concerns of the last two decades (e.g., the search for the causes of human aggression) and have had a powerful role in constructing popular images of monkeys and apes and their relationship to these concerns. Anthropological primatologists are uniquely situated in relation to questions about the human relationship to animals, first, because the study of primate social behavior within anthropology presupposes a continuum between humans and the nonhuman primates, and second, because the relationship of humans to the world of nature is a traditional and fundamental concern of social anthropology. This metaprimatological perspective connects primatological data to the traditional anthropological focus on world views, both by considering the role of modern primatology in the construction of modern categories of human and nonhuman and by recognizing the importance of the symbolic meaning of animals and of animal behavior studies to the construction of the modern natural cosmology.

An image has been created of animals on the border of humanity. This perception of blurred boundary between humans and the animal world in the modern period is reflected in the ideology of the animal rights movement. The cosmology of adherents of the movement is one available construction of a theory about animals, science, and nature which has a strong appeal at the present time and which has incorporated the anthropomorphized animal and animalized human categories of modern science. The anthropomorphic animals of the modern period have become rich symbolic projections of all that is most natural in humanity. To many advocates of animal rights, the scientific manipulation of primates represents a completely corrupt transgression, equivalent to experimenting on captive human populations. Ironically, the symbolic associations that fuel animal rights sentiment are an example of the distance between human beings, who spin such webs of significance, and the rest of animal life on earth.

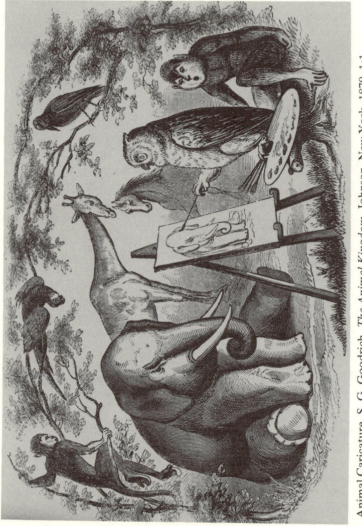

Animal Caricature, S. G. Goodrich, *The Animal Kingdom*, Johnson, New York, 1870. 1:1.

8

Conclusion

> Man is an animal suspended in webs of
> significance he himself has spun. I take cul-
> ture to be those webs, and the analysis of it
> to be therefore not an experimental science
> in search of law but an interpretive one in
> search of meaning.
>
> —Clifford Geertz

Trained in an approach to the evolution of human biology and behavior that stressed a strict adherence to hypothesis
testing and quantification, I have come gradually to appreciate the
strengths of the more interpretive approaches that explore human
meanings. Biological anthropology shares the search for laws
through hypothesis testing found in the other evolutionary and biological sciences rather than the interpretive traditions of cultural
anthropology. As a young graduate student in biological anthropology, I shared with my cohort a sense of our general supe-
riority—as "real scientists"—to our cousins in cultural anthropology. I have come to see this attitude as very much related to the
currently contested values of "hard" science, intellectual rationalism, and the "conquest of nature" that are often seen as functioning in opposition to the "soft" modes of interpretation. But the
associations that illuminate the meaning of much in human culture do not emerge through the pursuit of a strict empiricism that
models itself on the hard sciences; they must be sought in the webs
of significance that we spin. My research on the animal rights
movement compelled me to examine myself as subject as much as

it compelled me to examine the attitudes of my informants in the movement. The struggle to make sense of the passionate convictions of activists carried with it a mandate to examine my own approaches to studying complex behaviors and ideas. So, as I studied my subjects' attitudes, I studied my own, in an internal dialogue about the received wisdom of an education in biology and anthropology.

A comparative approach to the Victorian and modern protests against research with animals illuminated complex answers to my initial questions about the social determinants of such protest. The powerful movements for the abolition of animal research that have arisen twice within the last century did so in response to changes in attitudes toward animals, nature, and technology in both periods. The ideology of both movements has been rooted not merely in a renewed humane response to animal suffering but in an implicit critique of fundamental precepts of technological society, mediated through the culturally determined set of symbols available to movement adherents. Both movements reflect an acute anxiety about the human relationship to the world of nature, for which scientific research with animals is an important symbolic focus.

The Victorian antivivisection and modern animal rights movements share some aspects of millennarian and charismatic cults that have been described cross-culturally and historically. In both movements, research with animals is viewed as emblematic of the most pervasive social evils, and researchers are viewed as a kind of intransigent and immoral fraternity. The redemption of society is believed literally to hinge on the abolition of the use of animals by science. Charismatic cults place their adherents in a very special relationship to the powers-that-be in a given culture. Such movements, often viewed as typical of "simple" societies, seem to be flourishing in modern cultures as a renewal of religious cults with fundamentalist and evangelical bents take hold in many parts of the world. At the same time, a number of secular causes in technological society, such as the antiabortion and animal rights movements, also have a passionately charismatic tone. Attention to charismatic processes in technological society clarifies aspects of both animal rights and Victorian antivivisection and may help illuminate a number of other modern movements. Classically,

charismatic cults have appealed to the disenfranchised and alienated during periods of social upheaval. Anthropologists have
studied such cults but usually in tribal societies or non-
industrialized cultures under the impact of Westernization. It appears that today many middle-class people in American society
feel as alienated and removed from power over their lives as have
tribal peoples facing the incursions of technological cultures that
destroyed their traditional ways of life.

Shils (1982) has described charisma as a phenomenon of involvement, or oppositional involvement with the active centers of
social order, and of nearness to the center of the order of values,
beliefs, and symbols that govern a society. Thus, the charismatic
leader is able to empower followers by symbolically connecting
them to the centers of power, often by opposing these centers as
evil incarnate. The modern charismatic politician claims to empower his followers in a special way by putting them in touch with
great truths and fundamental values that are often in conflict with
the prevailing worldly power hierarchy, which is viewed as corrupt and greedy. By challenging the centers of power and their
values, we can feel related to these centers in a negative, but potent, way. Thus, individuals involved in charismatic cults feel
themselves to be in touch with the core of meaning in their society
and the central zone in which power resides. They perceive themselves as an elect who see through lies and manipulations to a re-
demptive truth. The new evangelical charismatics whose voices
crowd the American airwaves and the antiabortion and animal
rights movements represent, respectively, religious and secular
manifestations of acute alienation in modern life, channeled into
age-old symbols of good versus evil. Although these movements
differ profoundly in their political orientations from right to left,
they share some deep, structural similarities as responses to modern industrial culture and its anxieties.

Science and its practitioners are an important institution of authority in technological culture—a center and repository of symbols, beliefs, and values. According to Shils, "The central zone
partakes of the nature of the sacred. In this sense every society has
an 'official' religion, even when that society or its exponents and
interpretors conceive of it as a secular, pluralistic, and tolerant society" (1982, p. 73). The animal rights movement situates the ad-

herent in a profoundly oppositional position to what might be called the "sacred" central zone of science. The values of this central zone are perceived by many in our society as a hyperrational empiricism that seeks to conquer nature. By opposing the world view of modern science, animal rights becomes a vehicle for charismatic emotional expressions of alienation from these values. It is partly this fact that makes productive dialogue between researcher and adherent so frustrating and outrageous for both sides. The university, under siege by animal rights protest, attempts reform through the establishment of committees for the protection of animal subjects, better procedures for assuring compliance with laboratory animal care guidelines, and other practical reforms. Like their Victorian predecessors, activists see the struggle in very different terms. The perceived corruption, greed, and cruelty of the researcher predict an ecological apocalypse, and the use of animals by science must be ended so that human harmony with nature can once again be restored.

Charismatic beliefs are seen as antithetical to the mundane world of "rational-legal and traditional authority and organization" (Handelman 1985), which is the realm of the university administrator and researcher. But animal rights activists feel they are in touch with a very different level of meaning. They claim "the charismatic capacity to dissolve the integument of an integrated order" (ibid.). They challenge the fundamental assumption of border between human and animal as false and as emblematic of a hubris that is destroying the world. Activists feel they are in contact with "the very roots of existence, of cosmic, social and cultural order" (ibid.), while the university administrator talks about cleaner and larger cages.

These themes in the protest of animal research share some aspects of a potent and ancient myth of our culture, that of revolutionary millennarianism. In *Pursuit of the Millennium* (1961), the historian Norman Cohn limned the world view of millennarian European sects of the Middle Ages, in which charismatic prophets preached an apocalyptic vision to the disenfranchesed poor. About these movements, Cohn said, "One can recognize the paridigm of what was to become and to remain the central fantasy of revolutionary eschatology. The world is dominated by an evil, tyrannous power of boundless destructiveness" (p. 21). The elites of the clerical and political spheres, against whom judgment was applied with absolute vehemence, were viewed as avatars of the moral decay of society in much the same way that universities and researchers are viewed by some adherents of the animal rights movement. These themes have been played out in Western society for at least one thousand years, when certain kinds of social strains are channeled into a familiar frame of discourse about the boundless evil of the enemy, the torture of the innocents, and the revelatory perception of an elect who attack the specialist elite and posit a mystical holism of humans and nature.

But there are several elements of classic charismatic movements that are clearly absent in many modern secular philosophies with charismatic themes. Most dramatically missing in the animal rights or antiabortion movements, for instance, is a singular charismatic prophet preaching a religious vision to the disenfranchised poor. One does not have to be poor to feel alienated in modern society, however, and modern charismatic cults are not necessarily religious in theme, nor do they always have charismatic prophets. Changes in communication technology may open other vehicles for charismatic processes besides that of the singular prophet. Adherents of modern charismatic groups feel alienated from the centers of power and are drawn by the pull of a millennarian vision, despite the relative economic comfort of middle-class educations and incomes. In his famous depiction of the white-collar worker at midtwentieth century, C. W. Mills wrote, "He is pushed by forces beyond his control, pulled into movements he does not understand; he gets into situations in which his is the most helpless position. The white-collar man is the hero as victim, the small creature who is acted upon but who does not act" (1953, p. xii). Many members of our society feel at the present time like small helpless creatures, acted on by institutions over which they have little or no influence. In implicating some of these important institutions as evil manipulators and destroyers of animals, the animal rights movement fuels a powerful identification with science's "victims" waiting just beneath the surface of the modern sensibility. Thus, the disenfranchisement experienced by many in technological culture may find new outlets, but charismatic themes continue to exert a potent attraction.

Anthony F. C. Wallace (1956) has described millennarian and other revitalization movements as conscious efforts by members of a society to construct a more satisfying culture in the face of severe stress and the decreased efficiency of the culture to fulfill basic human needs. Revitalization is thus a unique kind of social phenomenon in which attempts are made to alter fundamental aspects of the cultural system rapidly. In the revitalization movements studied by Wallace cross-culturally, prophets have experienced dramatic moments of insight that permitted a new synthesis of values and meanings. Most of my informants underwent a personal and revelatory moment in their sudden apprehension of the concept of speciesism. In animal rights and other secular American movements, each individual is his or her own prophet. This is consistent with the high value placed on individualism and autonomy in our culture. Such moments of revelation have a positive value in allowing individuals to think beyond the normal boundaries of their society's rules and institutions. Many of the most important and, in their time, radical movements in Western history have had such millennarian underpinnings.

How have animals become linked to modern alienation and themes of redemption? In the natural cosmology of tribal societies, the first contrast is often between human and animal. In the cosmological scheme of the Lele of Central Africa, described by Douglas (1975), humans are thus distinguished by certain characteristics that animals do not have, for example, humans observe conventions of behavior such as appropriate forms of polite address and posture toward in-laws. Animals are regarded as lacking both manners and understanding in their social relationships, and thus it is on the basis of these distinctions that humans may hunt and kill them without shame. By introducing classification into the potential chaos of human experience, order is obtained. It is the classificatory "otherness" of animals for the Lele, and for many other groups, which allows them to understand the appropriate attitudes and behaviors toward animals and to hunt them for food, keep them for their various products, and use them for their labor.

The last century has seen a vast scientific remodeling of the relationship between animals and humans, particularly those animals most closely related to our species, the nonhuman primates. During the late Victorian period, evolutionary theory threatened the integrity of the Victorian cosmology in which human and animal were sharply demarcated. The new physiology began to use animal subjects as analogues for the human body, and the developing field of immunology created the technique of vaccination in which dead viruses derived from animal cells were injected into the human body. From the modern vantage point, it is hard to realize what a cognitive assault these changes were for many individuals. The educated urban middle and upper classes, already removed from daily contact from farm animals (and thus from the distinctions between human and animal implicit in agrarian life), were the first group subject to this shattering of cosmological boundaries. There is evidence from this period that women and individuals attracted to the revelatory vision of Victorian Evangelicalism were, for many reasons, most acutely sensitive to the impact of these changes.

Pets had become the animals with which the urban Victorian had habitual contact. Pets occupy an intermediate status between animal and human; they live within the home, they are called by human names, and they are never eaten. It is the pet, with its inherently anomalous status, that signified the category "animal" for the urban Victorian. In the face of enormous anxiety about the new medical technologies, the antivivisectionists developed a cult of animals as victims of the worst human impulses. According to this cult, the symbolic remedy for pervasive social ills and moral pollution was the abolition of vivisection on animals. Alienated and made anxious by the new technologies and their invasions of the body, the antivivisectionists developed a charismatic cult of the animal. The passion informing Victorian antivivisection and much of its emotional hyperbole are explained by the symbolic meaning of the act of vivisection. The abolition of animal research became the magical remedy that would restore natural order.

Currently, our society is witnessing a resurgence of protest against the use of animals in research unparalleled since the Victorian era, and there are important similarities in the ideological and social parameters of protest in both periods. The same sector of society that proved most responsive to Victorian antivivisection, that is, the educated urban middle class, is again in the forefront of activism. Women and people interested in philosophies of personal revelation are particularly drawn to the movement. As in the Victorian period, it is individuals far removed from daily contact with working animals who constitute the membership in the new groups.

The impact of technology is all around us in the urban environment, as it was increasingly in the Victorian period. Anxiety about the incursion of human industry into the natural environment is a feature of both periods, and the British Victorians have been viewed as the first to experience the large-scale impact of industrialization (Thomas 1983). Similarly, our society has undergone, in recent decades, an important scientific and popular discourse about the relationship of animals to humans. Modern animal behavior studies, particularly those of the nonhuman primates, have had an enormous popular audience. The cognitive abilities of primates and other animals, their complex social behaviors, and the ability of apes to perform as subjects in experiments involving acquisition of human language skills are now part of the popular image of animals. As was true for the Victorians, pet-keeping is widespread. In fact, the degree of attention to pets in the developed Western nations is of a magnitude unparalleled in other parts of the world, historically or in the present.

A high degree of concern about pollution and technological manipulation of the environment and living organisms is expressed by most adherents of the modern animal rights movement. Many increasingly view our species as subject to materialistic technological forces antithetical to nature and as facing a potential ecological apocalypse with other species. Animal rights has emerged in recent years as a response to these anxieties about the human relationship to nature much as occurred in the Victorian era.

The talking apes and matrilineal monkeys standing at the border of our cosmological village have inspired a radical redefinition of the line separating human and animal. For animal rights activists, the work of the present and foreseeable future is the abolition of science's use of species that deserve to be granted rights reserved in the past for humanity alone. The degree to which the movement succeeds in attaining its goals will ultimately reflect how deeply many of us feel about the present alignments of humans, animals, and technology.

Postscript

Talking Across the Abyss

Time has confirmed my impression that the animal rights movement was in a nascent stage in 1983 and 1984. Several years after my research, the movement has grown in size, visibility, and credibility and has succeeded in achieving some major victories in its efforts to stop animal research. Structural changes have occurred as some groups gain ascendance over others. For example, Mobilization for Animals, despite its early successes in organizing the yearly primate center rallies, has been eclipsed in influence and visibility by People for the Ethical Treatment of Animals (PETA), which is now the most active group at the national level.

In 1984, many researchers were uncertain about whether adherents really sought reform in the treatment of laboratory animals or the total abolition of research. It was clear to me from my discussions with animal rights activists that for most the ultimate goal was total abolition and the issue of reform merely a stepping-stone to this end. It is now widely recognized that the new groups are committed to antivivisection, although there is evidence that for political reasons, activists still hesitate to refer to themselves as antivivisectionists. The term is still too evocative of fringe fanatics in the minds of many people.

In late 1986, I watched a video on animal research produced by one of the new animal rights groups. It was an exegesis of the millennarian vision that has informed the protests of animal experimentation for a century. Juxtaposed images of crippled children and vivisected animals appeared, while the commentator spoke of the indoctrination of physicians by modern biomedicine. Dead puppies, a small monkey with its eyelids sewn shut, thalidomide victims, human victims of vaccination reactions crowded the screen to the accompaniment of a frightening and awesome musical refrain. A famous neurophysiologist appeared in one frame, and the commentator suggested that he may well have performed bizarre surgeries on hospitalized psychiatric patients. The video was long, and it seemed there might be no end to the horrible images spilling off the screen. The shedding of innocent animal blood, said the commentator, was socialization for the shedding of innocent human blood. The religion of modern medicine required animal sacrifices, and this was the reason for animal experimentation. All human suffering and disease would be prevented in the future through vegetarian diet and healthful environments, because all disease was caused by the pollution of the natural body with unnatural foods, vaccines, and chemicals. In the millennium of mercy that was to come, all animal experiments would be abolished, and our species would return to a perfect harmony with nature. In the meantime, the greed and corruption of the researchers, their secrecy and deception, would be exposed by the movement at every opportunity. These themes, which emerged as buds in the statements and beliefs of my informants, had blossomed vigorously in this video production and in much recent literature of the movement.

The concept of animal rights and many of its claims have become familiar through numerous articles and television programs. For instance, in the northern California *Jewish Family Bulletin* of June 1985, in an article about several of the San Francisco Bay area activists entitled "Jewish Activists Pushing Animal Rights," one activist is quoted as saying, "The same blind spot these researchers have toward animals is, I'm sure, the same blind spot Mengele had toward Jews in the concentration camps" (Krantz 1985). Other activists point out that Jews have traditionally emphasized social justice and have had a history of involvement in other progressive causes. Similarly, the January 1985 issue of the *New York Review of Books* contained a long review of the literature and history of the animal rights movement by Peter Singer. Singer compares animal rights to the abolition of slavery and writes of animals, "We treat them as if they were things to be used rather than as beings with lives of their own to live" (Singer 1985). The animal rights movement's analogies between laboratory animals and slaves or concentration camp victims can now be found in publications with broad and varied readerships.

Another important development in the mid-1980s has been the movement of animal rights activists into some local and national humane societies. In 1985, what the press described as a "surprise coup" at the wealthy Peninsula Humane Society in San Mateo, California, brought about the resignation of conservative members of its board of directors and their replacement by animal rights advocates. One board member is quoted as saying, "I am resigning because I do not agree with the philosophy of extreme activists" (McCabe 1986). According to an article on the movement published in 1986, some other prestigious humane groups, including the American Society for the Prevention of Cruelty to Animals and the half-century-old Animal Protection League, have recently assumed a moderately antivivisectionist stance. This is a significant accomplishment by the movement, although PETA's vocal activist, Ingrid Newkirk, may be overstating the case when she says, "Humane societies all over the country are adopting the animal rights philosophy, becoming vegetarian, and working harder to get inside labs" (ibid.). But Mariela Gordon, an informant whom I revisited in 1986, was not impressed with changes in the humane movement and thought that they were exaggerated by the press. Some societies had adopted animal rights stances cautiously, but, from Mariela's point of view, there was far to go. She still viewed the humane movement as fundamentally conservative but felt that change was in the wind and that the humane movement along with everyone else was adopting a more responsive attitude to animal rights.

As of 1986, there were eighty bills pending in state legislatures to restrict animal research, but the most pervasive influence of the movement thus far has been in the nonlegal realm. The chill on animal research is palpable to anyone in contact with the research community. The long-range effects of animal rights on the practice of science in America are far from manifest and may occur in the gradual discouragement and fear surrounding the use of animal subjects rather than in the realm of laws and restrictions. This is similar in many ways to the effect that antivivisection had on late

Victorian British physiology, which consisted, above all, in discouragement of animal research and a dampening of its appeal to younger researchers (French 1975).

The movement's radical wing, the Animal Liberation Front (ALF), has been increasingly active, claiming credit for numerous laboratory break-ins. Such tactics have received qualified public approval from some movement luminaries (see Singer's review of animal rights in the January 17, 1985, *New York Review of Books*). Raids on laboratories at the University of California at Riverside, the City of Hope National Medical Center in Duarte, California, and, most notably, at the University of Pennsylvania have achieved wide media coverage. In May 1984, the ALF raided the Head Injury Clinic at the University of Pennsylvania and seized sixty hours of videotapes taken by researchers during NIH-funded studies on the effects of brain injuries on baboons. This research involved simulating effects of automobile accidents on baboons in order to examine neurological aspects of injury and to develop more effective treatment strategies.

Unfortunately for both the researchers and their baboon subjects, the tapes displayed a number of abuses in animal treatment and laboratory protocol. In the videotapes, researchers smoke cigarettes in the laboratory and perform nonsterile surgeries on poorly anesthetized monkeys. In the short video that PETA edited from the original tapes and circulated widely through the media, the scientists are shown grotesquely joking about their baboon subjects. This is the picture of researchers as callous abusers that the animal rights movement had painted and that the research community denied. Here were scientists at a highly regarded institution making fun of their injured subjects. It could not have been more damning if staged by the movement. It seemed to me that the jokes in the laboratory were very familiar territory and, ironically, had to do with the particular anxiety that is aroused by procedures that are upsetting to perform. It is a kind of humor familiar to anyone who has worked in the realm of medical manipulations of the human body. I thought as I viewed the tapes that the researcher's black humor represented a very superficial callousness that was an attempt to control the universal discomfort of these alarming experiences by the distancing effect of joking.

The National Institutes of Health and the U.S. Department of Agriculture tried to secure copies of the full taped record for examination, but PETA refused to turn them over. Between April and May 1985, selected tapes were given to the USDA, which passed them on to NIH, which began an investigation into whether or not the Head Injury Clinic had failed to comply with guidelines for animal care. At the same time, the University of Pennsylvania commenced its own investigation into the alleged abuses. In June, NIH made a report to Congress citing the value of the research done at the Head Injury Center and stating that the center would continue to receive support under its existing grant. A new grant would be considered after completion of the investigation. In their report to Congress of June 24, 1985, NIH confirmed the value of the studies.

> The care of human victims of head and neck injury has improved because of methods developed by the University of Pennsylvania research group to monitor and control intercranial pressure, [and to develop] diagnostic criteria and treatments that have been beneficial to human patients. (NIH Fact Sheet, 1985)

A report on August 2, 1985, specifically justified the importance of using animal models in head injury research.

> The [animal] model allows scientists to study what happens in the brain at different times after specific types of trauma, and to test, in a controlled way, different therapies and interventions. A major contribution of the model has been in the study of diffuse axonal injury . . . which involves a damaged brain stem as well as torn brain axons [nerve cells]. (Ibid.)

PETA's reaction was swift, with the group staging a dramatic sit-in outside the National Institutes of Health. On July 18, 1985, Secretary of Health and Human Services Margaret Heckler intervened to suspend all NIH funding for the University of Pennsylvania laboratory. Later, the NIH Office for Protection from Research Risks cited the laboratory for noncompliance with NIH policy for the care and use of laboratory animals and the USDA imposed a civil penalty on the university of $4,000.

There are two aspects of the University of Pennsylvania case which mark significant gains in the movement's fight to end animal research. For the first time, Congress used evidence obtained through an illegal break-in during discussions of possible revisions of animal welfare legislation. It also marked the first time that an administration official has ever intervened in the allocation of NIH funding to a grantee. Public officials and their constituents were beginning to speculate about whether the conditions in the Head Injury Clinic were unique.

Not surprisingly, there is reported evidence that the animal rights community has greater consensus in its endorsement of illegal entries as a means of gaining evidence against researchers. The success of the ALF at the University of Pennsylvania provided a clear justification to many movement adherents for such extraordinary tactics. In September 1985, the movement held a conference in Minnesota at which the Pennsylvania incident was cited as a major victory. Summing up the effect of ALF tactics, one activist stated:

> The climate of fear in the research community is causing them to spend more money on security, reducing the amount of funds for research. It may also discourage young scientists from going into animal research since they fear their chances of advancement may be jeopardized if they become the target of a liberation. In this way, the actions of the ALF save many more animal lives than the ones that are actually liberated. (McCabe 1986, p. 154)

The research community has begun to publicly express its anxieties about the impact of the movement on science. University administrators and researchers are now worried about the future of important areas of medical research and the health of the biomedical research professions. Referring to the effects of the 1985 break-ins, a recent article critical of the movement quotes several researchers:

> "Worse than the dollar value," notes Stanford's Dr. Hamm, "are the personal costs. I see a number of colleagues leaving the field because they can't adjust to the harassment of the activist group."

> For obvious reasons, security has become a major concern—and expense—at research facilities. According to Dr. Arthur Butterfield, director of the Research Resources Facility at Georgetown University's new multimillion dollar animal-research center, "security was the overriding factor" in the facility's design.

At the University of California at San Francisco—where recent animal-rights activism has cut off the supply of dogs for cardiovascular research—Dr. Joseph Spinelli says, "We are losing some faculty because of the problems with large-animal availability. Younger researchers are not going to go someplace where their work and their chances of advancement are impeded."

Says Dr. Frederick Goodwin, director of intramural research programs for the National Institute of Mental Health: "My people speak more and more of extreme fear and demoralization." (Ibid.)

A study carried out in 1984 by the Society for Animal Protective Legislation, an animal welfare group, reviewed USDA inspection reports on laboratory animal care under the Freedom of Information Act. Sampling 188 of the 1,400 research facilities, they found that approximately 23 percent had problems of compliance with standards of caging, sanitation, veterinary care, and other aspects of treatment. In response to such findings, Congress has asked the National Academy of Sciences to conduct a two-year study of animal laboratory conditions in an effort to tighten controls on research.

One evening in fall 1986, I visited with Mariela Gordon in the apartment where we had talked two years earlier over a pot of coffee. With Jack Hill, Mariela had been one of the chief architects of the Berkeley animal rights movement, which has focused so much passionate energy on laboratory animals at the University of California. The apartment was now full of boxes, and we found a small clear space in the kitchen to sit down. Mariela had finished business school since we had last met, and she and her husband were in the process of moving to a suburban area nearby. One important reason for the move, she told me, was their impending adoption of a sixteen-year-old Filippino boy who had lived on the streets of Manila for most of his life. Mariela and her husband had no children, and the teenager had never been outside the Philippines, so she knew they would all be making considerable adjustments. Her hair was shorter and somehow she looked more serious and mature than she had the last time we spoke. She told me that she had recently had her thirty-first birthday and was feeling old. The shirt she wore was really the only thing about her now that seemed related to her student days—a T-shirt with an antifactory farming message and a picture of a steer.

I asked Mariela if she thought there had been important changes in the perception of the movement or the treatment of animals since we had last talked. Her response was a complicated one, because while she believed enormous changes had occurred in public perceptions of animal rights, she felt that the treatment of laboratory animals had changed very little. She thought that the visibility and credibility of the movement over a several-year period had increased, and she attributed this to the growing strategic sophistication of the new groups. The early and emotional spokespersons were being replaced now by experts who could represent the animal rights position with real authority. The movement's whole political strategy had evolved, and activists were learning about American politics and how power was negotiated in American life. The important thing was to convince legislators that animal rights should be on their agendas; it did not matter at first how they felt about the issue, but they needed to see that many people—many of their constituents—really cared about animals:

> "The legislative response has changed dramatically. There are more and more people in the federal government and state legislatures for whom this is part of their agenda. Actually, there are now some legislators for whom this is the largest issue on their agenda right now. I used to write letters to these people and not get many responses. Now I always get a letter back."

Mariela has also seen signs of changing attitudes in her work life. Most of the people she knows at work have never been to a rally in their lives. Five years ago, they had probably viewed animal rights as a weird fringe phenomenon, a group of radicals with whom they had nothing in common. Now everyone knew about the movement, and people were quite conversant with the issue of animal rights. She pointed out with great excitement that the much-admired writer Alice Walker had recently said in an interview that the two causes for which she would do a benefit were Winnie Mandela, the South African antiapartheid leader, and the animal rights movement. Mariela thought that the next phase would come when people like those with whom she works started to get interested enough to look at the movement more deeply, and she was very heartened by the speed with which animal rights had come to be accepted by many people in contrast to how long past social reforms had taken. Children, she believed, had been viewed very differently "for thousands of years and finally, about one hundred years ago, people changed their attitudes toward them. Animal rights has caught on much faster." She attributed these changes to the growing ability of the movement to mobilize its energies:

> "I think the animal rights community has gotten better at what it does. We've seen a lot of specialization recently, for instance. There was a problem with the fact that we thought we could all do everything. Now, you have a group like Attorneys for Animal Rights which has made a tactical decision to specialize in certain areas. We've gotten more sophisticated in our ways of approaching people—nonconfrontationally and confrontationally—we're more organized."

We talked about the events at the University of Pennsylvania Head Injury Clinic, and Mariela asked me if I had seen the PETA tapes. I said I had seen them and agreed that they were upsetting. Mariela commented:

> "There's no way we could have made that up. When the tapes came out I thought, 'This is it, people are going to get wise.' These are well-educated people doing this, with supposedly lofty goals, and they're doing worse things than your average street punk would do. I'm very suspicious of an ideology that thinks it's acceptable to do such things when they're balanced by loftier goals."

Despite her optimism about the current impact of the movement on public opinion, when I asked Mariela if she thought that the treatment of laboratory animals had improved, she was not optimistic, and a shadow seemed to fall across our conversation. Not much had changed for the animals, she said, but she had to hope that the future would be different:

> "If I didn't really think that things were going to change for animals, I wouldn't want to live. It's that simple. Just like if you thought that the nuclear bomb was going to hit in five years, you probably wouldn't really want to live now."

I did not feel inclined to dispute her statement, although I was sure that I disagreed with her that the idea of an impending apocalypse made life in the present meaningless. It had seemed to me for years that a fundamental part of the human enterprise was to be engaged in life in the face of inevitable extinction. I knew I did not believe in the coming of the millennium, although in many ways I envied my informants their utopian visions.

I asked Mariela if any of her own ideas had changed. She replied:

> "I'm still a zealot. I'm in a totally different environment now because nearly all the women I work with have fur coats, which has involved terrible, monstrous pain for animals. But some of these people are friends of mine, and I'm able to talk to them and respect them in other realms. I'm a vegetarian, which for me took quite a while. I knew in my heart that I had to go that way, and I kicked and screamed a lot . . . now I'm fighting a personal battle over cheese. I don't know where the cheese has come from, and, in a way, it's actually better to eat the chicken than the egg, because you know that the chicken is dead and no longer suffering."

While many aspects of Mariela's life had changed—she was no longer a student, for instance—her principles and advocacy of animal rights were clearly as steadfast as ever.

As I got ready to leave, I wished her luck with the forthcoming adoption and her new home. She looked at me quizzically and said, "You know, I've wondered why you did a dissertation on the animal rights movement. I mean, what does that *make* you, an expert on animal subjects, or a bioethics specialist, or what?" Like all of the other activists with whom I spoke, she had not asked me about my attitude toward the rights of animals. It seemed that the role of interviewer and anthropologist put me outside the realm of moral judgments. Now, in parting, I felt Mariela playing with me by turning the anthropologist-informant relationship upside down. As she questioned my enterprise, I felt that she reduced it to an esoteric and possibly silly pursuit. I defended my work by saying that I thought the movement was interesting and important because it questioned fundamental assumptions about the human place in nature. Since anthropologists study natural cosmology in other societies, why not our own? She said that she liked this idea and agreed that the animal rights movement was connected to a redefinition of categories, that this "felt right" to her.

Clearly, the animal rights movement has developed over the last several years in its ability to make an impact on public attitudes, but a siege mentality and lack of communication still plague the whole arena of reform in animal research practices, and the lines are being more clearly drawn between those defending animal research and those opposed to it.

As in the Victorian period, science has begun to mobilize a united effort to defend the achievements of animal research. In 1983, national and local groups emerged to represent the interests of the biomedical research community. One day late in summer 1986, I went to talk with Sandra Bressler, executive director of the California Biomedical Research Association (CBRA), a non-profit educational and lobbying group representing the interests of animal research. The association has as members the University of California as well as about thirty other large biomedical research institutions in the state. Two related national organizations now exist which are devoted to lobbying and educational efforts on behalf of animal research.

Sandra struck me as a woman comfortable in the public and private places where power is negotiated. She is an attorney, and with her composure, verbal mastery, and neat American good looks, she could easily be a young congresswoman or rising corporate attorney. In the discipline of law, Sandra said she had found an approach that was elegantly rational, and rationality is something that she values very highly. In fact, she told me she considered herself to be a very emotional person and she believes that the ability to apply rational judgments is of paramount importance in human interactions. The themes of rationality and irrationality threaded through our conversation that afternoon. When I thought about our meeting later, I realized that another discourse was woven through our talk, just below the issues of human lives saved through medical advances based on animal research. The whole notion of the human right of ascendance over the animal world reflects Western concepts of what the nature of a human being is. The millennarian visions of many of my informants are based on a concept of human perfectibility. Before the Fall, according to the Christian millennarian sects, humanity lived in perfect harmony with animal creation. The Golden Age would revive this peaceable kingdom. In the early modern period, Europeans were sometimes treated to living diaramas of this vision in which predator and prey were displayed together in harmony.

> It had always been a feature of the Christian millenarian ideal that wild animals would one day lose their ferocity and live once more, as in Eden, on peaceable terms with man. At fairs it was common to display booths foreshadowing this golden age to come. Thus in 1654 a lamb and a lion living on friendly terms with each other were put on public show in London; and in 1831 on one of the London bridges a showman exhibited animals in a state of reconciliation: cats, rats and mice in one cage, hawks and small birds in another. In their Utopian novel *Millennium Hall* (1762) Elizabeth Montague and Sarah Scott depicted a sanctuary where man was no longer 'a merciless destroyer' and where animals moved unmolested. (Thomas 1983, p. 288)

Many of my informants expressed views that are part of this tradition of hope for the redemption of human nature, for a future in which humanity lives at peace with other species. I was struck by Sandra's contrasting views of human nature, which she expressed in her vision of people as fundamentally predatory. We began to talk about the vegan activists we had each met who tried to eliminate all animal products from their lives. Sandra felt that veganism flew in the face of human evolutionary history, that as a species we were adapted to a carnivorous existence, which is what had gotten us where we are today. In Sandra's words, I heard part of an old dialectic in European thought—the other side of the dream of human perfectibility—and part of a crucial contest for the definition of human nature:

> All that remained was the Hobbesian view, justifying the human species in anything it felt necessary for its survival. The rights which brutes had over us, declared Spinoza, we had over them. The objection to killing animals was 'based upon an empty superstition and womanish tenderness, rather than upon sound reason.' Civilization would be impossible if humanity acted justly towards nature; man could not survive without being a predator. . . . The whole of nature . . . was "one great slaughterhouse." (Ibid., pp. 298–299)

Sandra was a proponent of sound reason as my informants were proponents of love above reason; her reason showed her that humans and animals inhabited a world of nature that was red in tooth and claw, in which people had best look out for their own species' interests. One species gain would inevitably be another's loss, but this was the way of the world. Sandra's vision of human nature threaded through our conversation about the pragmatics of head injury research and animal models in the war on AIDS.

It was hard not to notice that CBRA's office was discreetly situated. Although we did not discuss it, my sense was that it was thought best not to attract too much attention, specifically, the kind of attention that the radical groups had begun to pay to their perceived enemies. The office was small and pleasant, with neatly stacked Fact Sheets, which the association prepares to educate the public about the necessity for animal research. The Fact Sheets made strong, rational arguments for animal models as critical to important health issues. For example, the AIDS pamphlet states the following:

> What has animal research revealed about AIDS? Through animal research it has been discovered that AIDS is caused by a newly evolved human virus called HTLV III, LAV or ARV. This discovery has already resulted in the rapid and reliable tests used in the nation's blood banks to reduce the risk of transmitting AIDS by blood transfusions. . . . Researchers at U.C. Davis and at the New England Primate Center in Boston have recently found that a disease closely resembling AIDS occurs naturally in monkeys. These primates have been carefully observed and studied and represent an important step toward establishing an animal model for more intensive study of AIDS.

Over our lunch of Szechwan eggplant and rice, I asked Sandra what had attracted her to a job in which she represented biomedicine. She told me that, although she is an attorney, most of her work has been in the public interest rather than in a law firm. During the energy crisis, for example, she worked with a geothermal energy project and, more recently, represented University Hall, the statewide administrative branch of the University of California, in collective bargaining issues. The topic of biomedical research had immediately attracted her, and she had no question about her attitude with regard to the issue of animal research. She had long been fascinated by health-related research and medicine and believed that she might well have gone into one of these areas professionally. But the life of a researcher, with its isolation in the laboratory, did not appeal to her. In a sense, her work representing biomedicine was the next best thing, and it engaged her particular strengths in the public realm.

One thing that had struck her immediately about animal rights was the irrationality of the activists: "I recognized the real danger and fanatical quality of the people who were out there raising cain." When I asked her if she felt there had been recent changes in the way the issue of research was being debated, she said:

> "One thing that's very clear is, if there ever was a voice of reason and genuine concern for the welfare of animals, it is simply not being heard. The entire scene is dominated by the antivivisectionists, whether they call themselves that or not."

I spoke of an "abyss of misunderstanding," that is, the protestor and researcher or administrator are talking about completely different issues. Sandra agreed:

> "In some sense, I recognize that abyss rather clearly, and I do not think it is very useful to address those that are totally and fundamentally opposed to animal research. What I think is important is that they do not have sole access to communication about this issue, because you have a group of radical fanatics dominating public debate and getting all the attention."

Sandra envisions her role as that of providing "rational and accurate" information about biomedical research, and she describes her fight against the movement's "irrationality" as a contest for the hearts and minds of the public. She has, however, sometimes engaged in debate with activists for the purpose of public education, with "mixed results." For instance, Sandra described taking part in an audience participation television show put on by one of the local affiliates. The audience was packed with animal rights activists, and when she and the few other probiomedicine participants identified themselves, there was chaos. People in the audience pushed into the aisles and grabbed the moderator's sleeves. "It was the wildest experience I had ever had," Sandra said, and, according to her, it was also the wildest experience the moderator, a local news anchorman, had ever had. Afterward, the newsman chastised the activists for their unruly behavior.

Before we began our conversation, Sandra rapidly read through some material that I had written about the movement and told me that she agreed that the whole phenomenon of animal rights seemed to be related to an underlying critique of modern life. She felt that animal rights appealed to people's basic sense of alienation and that this could be a dangerous advantage:

> "They will get their way by small increments of emotional response. A lot of people may not be fanatic in their disaffection with the modern world, but everybody feels it. It's stressful to know that we have this capability of nuclear power, and what, in God's name, can we do about it? And so everyone is vulnerable to the kinds of sentiments that get expressed and if not given some notion of what the choices are, and what's at stake, may make dreadful mistakes."

Thus, according to Sandra, it is crucial to apply reason to these emotionally charged issues, and she believes in framing the question of animal research differently. Once the question is reframed, most people will not want to abolish animal research:

> "Understand that you fundamentally have chemotherapy and coronary bypass and all kinds of prenatal care from the use of animals in research. Start there, and then throw into the whole equation that you care about animals and don't want to make them suffer unnecessarily. That's a legitimate concern. But make sure that you understand what's at stake as we proceed with this particular enterprise."

In Sandra's view, what is at stake is progress in key areas of research affecting human health and life. She points out that since the NIH withdrawal of funding at the University of Pennsylvania, no one is conducting research on head injury, a major cause of death and disability in young adults in the United States. There are serious problems, she says, in the attitudes of many researchers toward the movement, and several times she expressed her frustration at the unwillingness of some researchers to make known their positions through the media. Then again, she noted that many researchers are not effective communicators, and no one wants to listen to a "talking head" mumble about an obscure hypothesis. Another problem she identifies has to do with the traditional liberalism of academics:

> "The academic community is traditionally a liberal community itself, and the liberal failing and the liberal strength is the notion that there can be a compromise, that you can work things out. Compromise does not work here, at least insofar as you're dealing with extremists, and there's an enormous failure on the part of a lot of people to understand that in the academic community. They keep trying and it isn't working."

Sandra and I spoke of the new Animal Welfare Act and the revised NIH guidelines for laboratory animal care. According to her, there are problems with these reforms, even though she agrees that they are partly beneficial:

> "To be in compliance with the new NIH funding requirements is enormously burdensome, and the cost of doing it is substantial. The question is, is the benefit worth the cost? If you're taking money to do this, then it's not being given to do that. We don't live in a perfect world, and you have to make some choices. People want the results, but they have no idea what it takes to get them."

The passionate convictions that characterize both sides in the animal rights debate are expressions of an old dialectic in Western thought. My conversation with Sandra Bressler and my conversations with animal rights activists reflected vast differences in views about the human place in nature held by people in our society. It has become clear that both sides in the argument over animal rights do not represent a mere difference of opinion. These contested world views, supported in each case by some dubious and some compelling arguments, are interwoven with older meanings. The vision of humanity living in harmony with the world of nature has deep roots in Western history. In the past, it has been tied to religious ideas about redemption and the coming of the millennium, and now it appears in the new cloth of a secular struggle for nature's creatures. The animal rights activists believe in the perfectibility of a human species currently immersed in death, greed, and cruelty. The technological manipulations of nature in the modern world represent a polluting of all that is pure and good. The researchers are accused of indifference to suffering; they are avatars of the moral decay of society. The ecological apocalypse and death of all species must be averted by a struggle for human redemption through the recognition of animal rights.

I heard reflected in Sandra's words the theme of humanity's fundamental separation from nature. For many, it is the human mandate to acknowledge that separation and to study it through the exercise of human rationality. The conquest of knowledge through rationality and the human separation from animals on the grounds of our distinctive rationality were the tradition Sandra represented:

> Descartes had only pushed the European emphasis on the gulf between man and beast to its logical conclusion. A transcendent God, outside his creation, symbolized the separation between spirit and nature. Man stood to animal as did heaven to earth, soul to body, culture to nature. (Thomas 1983, p. 35)

The university administrator, biomedical or behavioral researcher working with animal subjects, and animal rights activist confront each other across an abyss, with these contested visions of the human place in nature echoing through the empty space below. Their words are lost in a cacophony of new and old utterances. As reform in the treatment of laboratory animals is inevitably achieved, the dissonance between the world views of activist and researcher only becomes more manifest. If there is any hope of communication across the abyss, both sides will eventually have to address these old themes of the place of human and animal in the Western cosmology.

Bibliography

General

Adams, R.
   1978   *The plague dogs.* London: Knopf.
Ainsworth, M.
   1976   Discussion of papers by Suomi and Bowlby. In *Animal models in human psychobiology,* eds. G. Serban and A. King. New York: Plenum Press.
Altmann, J.
   1980   *Baboon mothers and infants.* Cambridge: Harvard University Press.
Animal Welfare Institute
   1970   *Basic care of experimental animals.* Washington: Animal Welfare Institute.
Ardrey, R.
   1961   *African genesis.* New York: Dell.
   1966   *The territorial imperative.* New York: Dell.
Asad, T.
   1973   *Anthropology and the colonial encounter.* London: Ithaca Press.
Aspinall, J.
   1976   *The best of friends.* New York: Harper and Row.
Bachofen, J. J.
   1967   *Myth, religion and mother right: Selected writings of J. J. Bachofen.* Trans. Ralph Manheim. Bollingen Series. Princeton: Princeton University Press. London: Routledge and Kegan Paul.
Barker-Benfield, B.
   1972   The spermatic economy: Nineteenth-century views of sexuality. *Feminist Studies* 1 (Summer 1972):45–74.
   1976   The horrors of the half-known life: Male attitudes toward women and sexuality. In *Nineteenth-Century America.* New York: Harper and Row.

Bauer, C.
  1973   *The sexual politics of sickness.* Old Westbury, N.Y.: Feminist Press.
Bauer, C., and L. Ritt
  1979   *Free and ennobled: Source readings in development of Victorian feminism.* Oxford: Pergamon Press.
Benedict, B.
  1969   Role analysis in animals and men. *Man* 4 (2):203–214.
  1972   Scale and roles among the primates. Burg Wartenstein Symposium 55, Scale and Social Organization. Unpublished paper.
  1979   The dangers of analogy. *Behavioral and Brain Sciences* 2(1).
Bentham, J.
  1789   *Principles of morals and legislation.* New York: Hafner. Reprinted 1961.
Berger, J.
  1980   *About looking.* New York: Pantheon.
Berry. W.
  1977   *The unsettling of America.* San Francisco: Sierra Club Books.
Boggess, J.
  1979   Troop male membership changes and infant killing in langurs (P. entellus). *Folia Primatologica* 32:65–107.
Bowker, G. K., ed.
  1949   *Shaw on vivisection.* London: George Allen.
Briffault, R.
  1927   *The mothers: A study of the origins of sentiments and institutions.* New York: Johnson Reprint Corp. Reprinted 1969.
Burghardt, G., and H. A. Herzog, Jr.
  1980   "Beyond conspecifics: Is "Brer Rabbit our brother?" *Bioscience* 30(11):763–767.
Carroll, L.
  1875   Some popular fallacies about vivisection. *Fortnightly Review* xxiii:854.
Carson, G.
  1972   *Men, beasts and gods.* New York: Charles Scribner's Sons.
Chance, M., and C. Jolly
  1970   *Social groups of monkeys and apes.* New York: E. P. Dutton.
Clifford, J., and G. Marcus, eds.
  1986   *Writing culture: The poetics and politics of ethnography.*

Berkeley, Los Angeles, London: University of California Press.

Cobbe, F. P.
1872a   The consciousness of dogs. *Quarterly Review,* vol. cxxxiii.
1872b   *Darwinism in morals and other essays.* London and Edinburgh: Williams and Norgate.
1872c   Dogs whom I have met. *Cornhill Magazine,* vol. xxvi.
1891   *The significance of vivisection.* London: Victoria Street Society.
1894   *Life of Frances Power Cobbe.* Vol. II. Boston: Houghton, Mifflin & Co.
1888   *The duties of women.* London and Edinburgh: Williams and Norgate.

Cobbe, F. P., ed.
1884a   *The antivivisection question.* London: Victoria Street Society.
1884b   *The moral aspects of vivisection.* 6th ed. London: Victoria Street Society.

Cohn, N.
1961   *The pursuit of the millennium.* New York: Oxford University Press.

Coleman, S.
1924   *Humane society leaders in America.* Albany: The American Humane Association.

Coleridge, S.
1916   *Vivisection: A heartless science.* London: John Lane.
1918   *Great testimony.* London: John Lane.

Comfort, A.
1966   *The nature of human nature.* New York: Harper and Row.

Cook, J. M.
1975   *In defense of Homo sapiens.* New York: Farrar, Straus and Giroux.

Corbett, P.
1972   Postscript. In *Animals, men and morals,* eds. S. Godlovitch and J. Harris. New York: Taplinger.

Curtin, R., and P. J. Dolhinow
1978   Primate social behavior in a changing world. *American Science* 66:468–475.

Curtis, P.
1980   *Animal rights: Stories of people who defend rights of animals.* New York: Four Winds Press.

Daly, M.
   1978   *Gyn-ecology: The meta-ethics of radical feminism.* Boston: Beacon Press.
Dembeck, H.
   1965   *Animals and men.* New York: The Natural History Press.
Desmond, A.
   1979   *The ape's reflexion.* New York: The Dial Press.
DeVore, I., and K. R. L. Hall
   1965   Baboon social behavior. In *Primate behavior: Field studies of monkeys and apes,* ed. I. Devore. New York: Holt, Rinehart and Winston.
De Waal, F.
   1982   *Chimpanzee politics: Power and sex among apes.* New York: Harper and Row.
Diner, J.
   1979   *Physical and mental suffering of experimental animals.* Washington, D.C.: Animal Welfare Institute.
Dolhinow, P.
   1969   *Primates: Studies in adaptation and variability.* New York: Holt, Rinehart and Winston.
Dolhinow, P., ed.
   1972   *Primate patterns.* New York: Holt, Rinehart and Winston.
Dolhinow, P., and R. Curtin
   1978   Primate social behavior in a changing world. *American Scientist* 66:468–475.
Douglas, M.
   1966   *Purity and danger.* London: Routledge and Kegan Paul.
   1973   *Natural symbols.* New York: Vintage.
   1975   *Implicit meanings.* London: Routledge and Kegan Paul.
Doyle, D. E., M.D.
   1983   The making of an animal activist. *Mainstream* 4(1):20–21. Publication of Animal Protection Institute, Sacramento.
Durkheim, E.
   1951   *Suicide: A study in sociology* (first published 1897). New York: Free Press.
Ehrenreich, B., and D. English
   1973   *Witches, midwives, and healers: A history of women healers.* Old Westbury, N.Y.: The Feminist Press.
Eibl-Eibesfeldt, I.
   1979   *The biology of peace and war.* New York: Viking.
Fairholme, E. G., and W. Pain
   1924   *A century of work for animals: The history of the RSPCA 1824–1924.* London: John Murray.

Fee, E.
    1974   The sexual politics of Victorian social anthropology. In
            Clio's consciousness raised, eds. M. Hartman and I. Ban-
            ner. New York: Harper and Row.

Firth, A.
    1886   *Voices for the speechless: Selections for schools and private
            reading.* Cambridge: Riverside Press.

Fossey, D.
    1983   *Gorillas in the mist.* Boston: Houghton Mifflin Co.

Foucault, M.
    1975   *The birth of the clinic.* New York: Vintage.

Fox, J. L.
    1984   Lab animal welfare issue gathers momentum. *Science* 233
            (February 3):468–469.

Fox, M.
    1980   *Returning to Eden.* New York: Viking Press.

Fox, Michael Allen
    1985   *The case for animal experimentation.* Berkeley, Los
            Angeles, London: University of California Press.

Fox, R.
    1968   The evolution of human sexual behavior. *New York Times
            Magazine,* March 24. Pp. 32ff.

    1972   Sexual selection and the evolution of human kinship sys-
            tems. In *Sexual selection and the descent of man,* ed. B.
            Campbell. Chicago: Aldine.

    1975a   *Biosocial anthropology,* ed. New York: John Wiley and
            Sons.

    1975b   Primate kin and human kinship. In *Biosocial anthropology.*
            New York: John Wiley and Sons.

French, R. D.
    1975   *Antivivisection and medical science in Victorian society.*
            Princeton: Princeton University Press.

Gallup, Jr., G., et al.
    1977   A mirror for the mind of man, or will the chimpanzee create
            an identity crisis for Homo sapiens? *Journal of Human
            Evolution* 6:3111.

Gardner, A. R., and B. Gardner
    1969   Teaching sign language to a chimpanzee. *Science* 165:666.

Geertz, C.
    1973   *The Interpretation of Cultures.* New York: Basic Books.

Godlovitch, S., and J. Harris, eds.
    1972   *Animals, men and morals: An inquiry into the maltreatment
            of non-humans.* New York: Taplinger.

224 BIBLIOGRAPHY

Goldman, D.
1978   Special abilities of the sexes: Do they begin in the brain? *Psychology Today* 12(6):48ff.

Goodall, J.
1965   Chimpanzees of the Gombe Stream Reserve. In *Primate behavior*. ed. I. DeVore. New York: Holt, Rinehart and Winston.
1968*a*   A preliminary report on expressions, movements and communications in the Gombe Stream chimpanzees. In *Primates,* ed. P. C. Jay. New York: Holt, Rinehart and Winston.
1968*b*   The behavior of free living chimpanzees in the Gombe Stream Reserve. *Animal Behavior Monographs* 1:3.
1971   *In the shadow of man.* Boston: Houghton Mifflin Co.
1979   Life and death at Gombe. *National Geographic* 155(5):597–620.

Gould, S. J.
1980   Vision with a vengence. *Natural History* 89(9):16–20.
1981   *The mismeasure of man.* New York: W. W. Norton and Co.

Griffin, A., and J. Sechzer
1983   Mandatory versus voluntary regulation of biomedical research. *Annals of the New York Academy of Sciences, The Role of Animals in Biomedical Research* 406:187–200.

Griffin, S.
1982   *Pornography and silence.* New York: Harper and Row.

Grodsky, P. E.
1983   Public opinion on animal-based research: The unknown factor in ethical and policy decisions. *Annals of the New York Academy of Science, The Role of Animals in Biomedical Research* 406:157–158.

Hall, K. R. L., and I. DeVore
1965   Baboon social behavior. In *Primate behavior,* ed. I. DeVore. New York: Holt, Rinehart and Winston.

Hamburg, D.
1963   Emotions in the perspective of human evolution. In *Expression of emotion in man,* ed. P. H. Knapp. New York: International University Press. Pp. 300–317.
1970*a*   Recent evidence on the evolution of aggressive behavior. *Engineering and Science* 23:15–24.
1970*b*   Sexual differentiation and the evolution of aggressive behavior in primates. In *Environmental influences on genetic expression: Biological and behavioral aspects of sexual dif-*

ferentiation, eds. N. Kretchmer and D. Wakner. Washington, D.C.: National Institutes of Health. Pp. 141–151.

1971*a*   Aggressive behavior of chimpanzees and baboons in their natural habitat. *J. Psychiatric Res.* 8:385–398.

1971*b*   Psychobiological studies of aggressive behavior. *Nature* 230(March 5):12–22.

Hamburg, D., and J. Goodall

n.d.   Factors facilitating development of aggressive behavior in chimpanzees and humans. Unpublished manuscript.

Handelman, D.

1985   Charisma, liminality, and symbolic types. In *Comparative social dynamics: Essays in honor of S. N. Eisenstadt,* eds. M. Lisak and U. Almagor. Boulder: Westview Press.

Haraway, D.

1978   Animal sociology and a natural economy of the body politic. *Signs* 4(1):21–60.

1979   The biological enterprise: Sex, mind, and profit from human engineering to sociobiology. *Radical History Review* 20(SpringSummer):206–234.

1985   A manifesto for cyborgs: Science, technology, and Socialist Feminism in the 1980s. *Socialist Review,* no. 80, pp. 65–108.

1987   Primate visions. Unpublished manuscript.

Hartman, M., and I. Banner

1974   *Clio's consciousness raised.* New York: Harper and Row.

Harwood, D.

1928   *Love for animals and how it developed in Great Britain.* New York: Columbia University Press.

Hayes, H.

1977   The pursuit of reason. *The New York Times Magazine,* June 12.

Hediger, H.

1969   *Man and animal in the zoo.* New York: Delacorte Press.

Held, J. R.

1983   Appropriate animal models. *Annals of the New York Academy of Science, The Role of Animals in Biomedical Research* 406:13–19.

Herskovits, M.

1955   *Cultural anthropology.* New York: Knopf.

Himmelfarb, G.
  1962   *Darwin and the Darwinian revolution*. New York: Anchor
            Books.
Hodos, W.
  1970   Evolutionary interpretation of neural and behavioral stud-
            ies of living vertebrates. *The Neurosciences* 2.
Hodos, W., and C. B. G. Campbell
  1969   *Scala naturae*: Why there is no theory in comparative psy-
            chology. *Psychological Review* 76(4):337–350.
Hrdy, S.
  1976   Hierarchical and relations among female hanuman langurs.
            Science 193:4256.
  1977a   Infanticide as a primate reproductive strategy. *American
            Scientist* 65:40–49.
  1977b   *The langurs of Abu: Female and male strategies of reproduc-
            tion*. Cambridge: Harvard University Press.
Hubbard, R., et al., eds.
  1979   *Women look at biology looking at women*. Cambridge:
            Schenkman.
Hume, C. W.
  1962   *Man and beast*. London: United Federation of Animal
            Welfare.
Illich, I.
  1977a   *Medical nemesis*. New York: Bantam Books.
  1977b   *Toward a history of needs*. New York: Bantam Books.
Jordanova, L. J.
  1980   Natural facts: A historical perspective on science and sexu-
            ality. In *Nature, culture, and gender,* eds. C. MacCormack
            and M. Strathern. Cambridge: Cambridge University
            Press.
Keen, W.
  1914   *Animal experimentation and medical progress*. Boston:
            Houghton Mifflin Co.
Kevles, Bettyann
  1980   *Thinking gorillas: Testing and teaching the greatest ape*.
            New York: E. P. Dutton.
Kitcher, P.
  1985   *Vaulting ambition*. Cambridge: MIT Press.
Klingender, F.
  1971   *Animals in art and thought*. Cambridge: MIT Press.
Krantz, Marshall
  1985   Jewish activists pushing animal rights. *Northern California
            Jewish Bulletin* 134(2):1, 25.

Kroeber, A.
  1917   The superorganic. *American Anthropologist* 19:163–213.
  1943   Structure, function, and pattern in biology and anthropology. *Scientific Monthly* 56(February):105–113.

Lansbury, C.
  1985   *The old brown dog: Women, workers and vivisection in Edwardian England.* Madison: University of Wisconsin Press.

Leach, E.
  1966   Anthropological aspects of language: Animal categories and verbal abuse. In *Directions in the study of language,* ed. E. H. Lenneberg. Cambridge: MIT Press.

Leach, M.
  1961   *God had a dog: The folklore of the dog.* New Brunswick: Rutgers University Press.

Lovejoy, A.
  1936   *The great chain of being.* Cambridge: Harvard University Press.

McCabe, Katie
  1986   Who will live, who will die. *The Washingtonian.* August, pp. 112–117.

MacCormack, C., and M. Strathern
  1980   *Nature, culture and gender.* Cambridge: Cambridge University Press.

McGreal, S.
  1983   The gibbon that got away. *Mainstream* 14(1):17–19. Publication of Animal Protection Institute of America, Sacramento.

Magel, C.
  1981   *A bibliography on animal rights and related matters.* Washington, D.C.: University Presses of America.

Maine, Sir H. H. S.
  1897   *Ancient law: Its connection with the early history of society and its relation to modern ideas.* 6th ed. London: Murray.

Maple, T.
  1980   *Orang-utan behavior.* New York: Van Nostrand Reinhold.
Marmor, J., and V. W. Bernard et al.
  1960   Psychodynamics of group opposition to health programs. *American Journal of Ortho-psychiatry* 300:330–345.

Martin, P.
  1982   *The animal rights movement in the United States: Its composition, funding sources, goals, strategies, and potential impact on research.* Unpublished, prepared by Harvard University Office of Government and Community Affairs.

Merchant, C.
  1980   *The death of nature: Women, ecology, and the scientific rev-olution.* San Francisco: Harper and Row.
Midgley, Mary
  1983   *Animals and why they matter.* Middlesex: Penguin.
Mills, C. W.
  1953   *White collar: The American middle classes.* New York: Ox-ford University Press.
Moretti, L. A.
  1983   Review, *The cancer syndrome* by R. W. Moss. In *Agenda* 3(2):26. Publication of Animal Rights Network.
Morgan, L. H.
  [1877]   *Ancient society.* New York: Holt, Rinehart and Winston.
Morgan, R.
  1980   *Love and anger: An organizing handbook.* Westport: Ani-mal Rights Network.
Morris, D.
  1967   *The naked ape.* New York: McGraw Hill.
Morris, F. O.
  1875   All the articles of the Darwin faith. London. Unpublished.
  1890   The demands of Darwinism on credulity: A homethrust at the wretched and shallow infidelity of the day, and its twin sister the cowardly cruelty of experimentors on living ani-mals. London. Unpublished.
Mosedale, S.
  1978   Science corrupted: Victorian biologists consider "the woman question." *Journal of the History of Biology* 11(1).
Murray, J. H.
  1982   *Strong-minded woman.* New York: Pantheon Press.
Nadler, R.
  1981   Laboratory research on sexual behavior of the great apes. In *Reproductive biology of the great apes,* ed. C. E. Gra-ham. New York: Academic Press.
National Institutes of Health
  1985   Head injury research at the University of Pennsylvania. NIH Fact Sheet. Bethesda, Md.: National Institutes of Health.
Nelson, I.
  1972   Duties to animals. In *Animals, men, and morals,* eds. S. Godlovitch and J. Harris. New York: Taplinger.
O'Flaherty, T.
  1984   How man treats his best friends. *San Francisco Chronicle,* June 22, p. 38.

Ortner, S. B.
 1974   Is female to male as nature is to culture? In *Women, culture, and society,* eds. M. Rosaldo and L. Lamphere. Stanford: Stanford University Press. Pp. 67–88.

Osborn, H. F.
 1918   *The origin and evolution of life.* New York: Charles Scribner's Sons.

Oyama, S.
 1985   *The Ontogeny of information.* Cambridge: Cambridge University Press.

Patterson, F.
 1978   Conversations with a gorilla. *National Geographic* 154(4):437–465.

Paton, W. D. M.
 1983   Animal experiments: British and European legislation and practice. *Annals of the New York Academy of Sciences, The Role of Animals in Biomedical Research* 406:201–214.

Pond, G.
 1873   Darwinism in literature. *Galaxy Magazine* 16(May 1873):68–75.

Poole's Index to Periodical Literature
 1802–   Revised edition. Boston: Houghton Mifflin.
 1906

Poovey, Mary
 1986   Scenes of an indelicate character: The medical "treatment" of Victorian women. In *Representations* 14(Spring):137–168. Berkeley, Los Angeles, London: University of California Press.

Pratt, D.
 1976   *Painful experiments on animals.* New York: Argus Archives.
 1980   *Alternatives to pain.* New York: Argus Archives.

Premack, D., and A. Premack
 1972   Teaching language to an ape. *Scientific American* 227:95.
 1984   Proposed change in American Physiological Society guiding principles in the care and use of animals. *The Physiologist* 27(3).

Rabinow, P.
 1986   Representations are social facts: Modernity and Post Modernity in Anthropology. In *Writing culture,* eds. J. Clifford and G. Marcus. Berkeley, Los Angeles, London: University of California Press. Pp. 234–261.

Reed, E.
 1978 *Sexism and science*. New York: Pathfinder.
Regan, T.
 1982 *All that dwell therein: Essays on animal rights and environ-mental ethics*. Berkeley, Los Angeles, London: University of California Press.
 1983 *The case for animal rights*. Berkeley, Los Angeles, London: University of California Press.
Regan, T., and P. Singer
1976 *Animal rights and human obligations*. Englewood Cliffs, N.J.: Prentice-Hall.

Rendall, J.
 1984 *The origins of modern feminism: Women in Britain, France, and the United States: 1780–1860*. New York: Schocken Books.
Reynolds, P.
 1981 *On the evolution of human behavior: The argument from animals to man*. Berkeley, Los Angeles, London: University of California Press.
Roberts, C.
 1980 *Science, animals, and evolution: Reflections on some unre-alized potentials of biology and medicine*. Westport: Green-wood Press.
Rollins, B. E.
 1981 *Animal rights and human morality*. New York: Prometheus Books.
Rosaldo, M., and L. Lamphere, eds.
 1974 *Women, culture, and society*. Stanford: Stanford University Press.
Rowan, A.
 1982 Twenty years of effort—and failure—at America's regional primate centers. *The Humane Society News* 27(4):22–25.
 1984 *Of mice, models, and men*. Albany: State University of New York Press.
Rowell, T.
 1972 *The social behavior of monkeys*. Baltimore: Penguin.
Rowland, B.
 1973 *Animals with human faces: A guide to animal symbolism*. Knoxville: University of Tennessee Press.
Ruesch, H.
 1978 *Slaughter of the innocents*. Bantam: New York.

Rumbaugh, D., ed.
  1977   *Language learning by a chimpanzee: The Lana project.*
          New York: Academic Press.

Russell, W., and R. Burch
  1959   *The principles of humane experimental technique.* London:
          Methuen.

Ryder, R.
  1972   Experiments on animals. In *Animals, men, and morals,*
          eds. S. Godlovitch and J. Harris. New York: Taplinger.

  1975   *Victims of science.* London: Davis-Poynter.

Sahlins, M.
  1977   *The use and abuse of biology: An anthropological critique
          of sociobiology.* Ann Arbor: University of Michigan Press.

Salt, H. S.
  1892   Animal rights. London. Unpublished. Reprinted, new edi-
          tion, Clark's Summit, Pa.: Society for Animal Rights, 1980.

Schleifer, A.
  1983   A look at the grass roots: An interview with Quebec's Ka-
          ren Urtnowski. *Agenda* 3(2):4–6. Publication of Animal
          Rights Network.

Schultz, W.
  1959   Animal protection. *Encyclopedia of the social sciences.*
          Vol. II. New York: Macmillan.

Sechzer, J.
  1983   The ethical dilemma of some classical animal experiments.
          *Annals of the New York Academy of Sciences, The Role of
          Animals in Biomedical Research* 406:5–12.

Sechzer, J. A., ed.
  1983   *The role of animals in biomedical research.* Annals of the
          New York Academy of Sciences, vol. 406. New York: New
          York Academy of Sciences.

Shell, M.
  1986   The family pet. *Representations* 15(Summer 1986):121–
          153.

Shelley, M. W. G.
  1818   *Frankenstein.* London: Lackington, Hughes, Harding,
          Mavor, and Jones.

Shils, E.
  1982   *The constitution of society.* Chicago: University of Chicago
          Press.

Sigsworth, E. M., and T. J. Wyke
  1972   A study of Victorian prostitution and venereal disease. In

Suffer and be still, ed. M. Vicinus. Bloomington: Indiana University Press.

Singer, P.
1975   *Animal liberation.* New York: Avon.
1985   Ten years of animal liberation: A review of ten recent books. *New York Review of Books,* vol. 31, nos. 21 and 22 (January 17, 1985):46–52.

Smelser, N.
1962   *Theory of collective behavior.* New York: Free Press.

Smith, G.
1983   The problems of reduction and replication in the practice of the scientific method. *Annals of the New York Academy of Sciences, The Role of Animals in Biomedical Research* 406:1–4.

Smith-Rosenberg, C.
1972   The hysterical women: Sex roles and role conflict in nineteenth-century America. *Social Research* 39(Winter 1972):652–678.

Snyder, G.
1969   *Turtle Island.* New York: New Directions.

Spencer, H.
1896   *Principles of sociology.* New York: D. Appleton.

Star, S. L.
1979   The politics of right and left: Sex differences in hemispheric brain asymmetry. In *Women look at biology looking at women,* eds. R. Hubbard et al. Cambridge: Schenkman.

Stevenson, L. G.
1956   Religious elements in the background of the British anti-vivisection movement. *Yale Journal of Biological Medicine* 29:125–57.

Stevenson, R. L.
1886   The strange case of Dr. Jekyll and Mr. Hyde. Reprinted in *The Merry Men and Other Tales and Fables.* New York: Charles Schribner's Sons, 1906.

Strum, S.
1975   Life with the pumphouse gang. *National Geographic,* May.

Symons, D.
1979   *The evolution of human sexuality.* Oxford: Oxford University Press.

Taylor-Bell, C.
1884a   For pity's sake. In *The antivivisection question,* ed. F. P. Cobbe. London: Victoria Street Society. Pp. 1–17.

1884*b*   Vivisection: Is it justifiable? In *The antivivisection question,*
            ed. F. P. Cobbe. London: Victoria Street Society. Pp. 1–
            24.
Temerlin, M.
1976   *Lucy: Growing up human.* London: Souvenir Press.
Thomas, K.
1983   *Man and the natural world: A History of the modern sensi-*
         bility. New York: Pantheon.
Tiger, L., and R. Fox
1971   *The imperial animal.* New York: Holt, Rinehart, and Win-
         ston.
Tondorf, F., ed.
1923   *A vindication of vivisection.* Washington: Georgetown
         Medical School.
Turner, E. S.
1964   *All heaven in a rage.* London: Michael Joseph Ltd.
Turner, J.
1980   *Reckoning with the beast: Animals, pain, and humanity in*
         the Victorian mind. Baltimore: Johns Hopkins Press.
Ulrich, R.
1979   Some thoughts on human nature and its control: I am my
         neighbor and my neighbor is me. *Journal of Humanistic*
         Psychology 19:29.
U.S. Department of Agriculture and Animal and Plant Health
            Inspection Service
1972   *Animal welfare act: Regulations and standards.* Hyattsville:
         U.S. Department of Agriculture and Animal and Plant
         Health Inspection Service.
U.S. Department of Health, Education and Welfare
1973   *Grants Administration Manual.* Washington, D.C.: De-
         partment of Health, Education and Welfare.
U.S. Department of Health, Education and Welfare and National
            Institutes of Health
1972   *Guide for the care and use of laboratory animals.* Bethesda:
         National Institutes of Health.
Vicinus, M.
1972   *Suffer and be still.* Bloomington: Indiana University Press.
Vicinus, M., ed.
1977   *A widening sphere: Changing roles of Victorian women.*
         Bloomington: Indiana University Press.
Walkowitz, J.
1977   The making of an outcast group: Prostitutes and working
         women in nineteenth-century Plymouth and Southhamp-

ton. In *A widening sphere,* ed. M. Vicinus. Bloomington: Indiana University Press. Pp. 72–93.

Walkowitz, J. R., and D. J. Walkowitz
  1974   We are not beasts of the field: Prostitution and the poor in Plymouth and Southampton under the Contagious Diseases Acts. In *Clio's consciousness raised,* eds. M. Hartman and I. Banner. New York: Harper and Row.

Wallace, A. F. C.
  1956   Revitalization movements, *American Anthropologist* 58:264–281.
  1972   *Handsome Lake: The death and rebirth of the Seneca.* New York: Random House.

Washburn, S. L.
  1978*a*   Animal behavior and social anthropology. In *Sociobiology and human nature,* eds. M. S. Gregory et al. San Francisco: Jossey-Bass.
  1978*b*   Human behavior and the behavior of other animals. *American Psychologist* 33:405–418.
  1978*c*   What we can't learn about people from apes. *Human Nature,* November, pp. 70–75.

Wells, H. G.
  1896   *The island of Dr. Moreau.* [London:] Stone and Kimball. Reprint ed. Garden City, N.Y.: Garden City Publishing Co., Inc.

Westermarck, E.
  1894   *The History of human marriage.* New York: Macmillan. Reprint, 5th ed. 3 vols. London: Macmillan, 1921.

Williams, R.
  1975   *The country and the city.* St. Albans: Paladin.

Willis, R.
  1974   *Man and beast.* New York: Basic Books.

Wilson, E. O.
  1978   *On human nature.* Cambridge: Harvard University Press.

Windeatt, P.
  1983   The Move rallies: Be there. *Agenda* 3(2):22. Publication of Animal Rights Network.

Winick, M.
  1983   Nutrition and early development. *Annals of the New York Academy of Sciences: The Role of Animals in Biomedical Research* 406:140–143.

Wood, Ann D.
  1973   The fashionable diseases: Women's complaints and their

treatment in nineteenth-century America. *Journal of Interdisciplinary History* 4(Summer 1973):25–52.

Young, R. M.
  1970   *Mind, brain, and adaptation in the nineteenth century.* Oxford: Oxford University Press.

Zuckerman, Sir S.
  1932   *The social life of monkeys and apes.* London: Routledge and Kegan Paul. London: Butler & Tanner.

Ephemera

American Antivivisection Society
  n.d.   *Vivisection: Subject matter of nightmares.* Pamphlet.
  1983*a*   *Pilate washes his hands.* Pamphlet.
  1983*b*   *Vivisection is cruel, brutal, futile.* Pamphlet.

Animal Protection Institute of America
  n.d.   *Agony in the labs.* Sacramento: Animal Protection Institute of America. Pamphlet.
  1983   *Animal experimentation.* Sacramento: Animal Protection Institute of America. Pamphlet.

Animal Rights Connection
  n.d.   *Animal rights: No laughing matter.* Berkeley: Animal Rights Connection. Pamphlet.

Attorneys for Animal Rights
  1984   *Newsletter,* winter.

Buddhists Concerned for Animals
  1983*a*   *Newsletter,* no. 1.
  1983*b*   "Dear Friends." *Newsletter,* no. 2.
  1983*c*   "World day for laboratory animals." *Newsletter,* no. 2.

Cantor, A.
  1983   *The club, the yoke, and the leash. Ms.,* pp. 27–30. Reprinted as pamphlet by Feminists for Animal Rights.

Corea, G.
  1984   *Dominance and Control. Agenda,* May-June, pp. 20ff. Reprinted as pamphlet by Feminists for Animal Rights.

Feminists for Animal Rights
  n.d.   *Animal rights is a feminist issue.* Pamphlet.

Hamilton, P.
  n.d.   Letter, in *A respect for all life.* Vancouver, B.C.: Lifeforce. Pamphlet.

Health Action
  [1982]   *Dog ailments may be tied to fluoride in pet food.* Reprinted
            from Grand Rapids Press, August 14, 1981. Pamphlet.
Help Laboratory Animals
  1983   Pamphlet, no title. Menlo Park, Calif.: Help Laboratory
            Animals.
Horrobin, D., M.D.
  [1982]   *Science and deception.* Pamphlet. [Transcript of] Canadian
            Broadcasting Company broadcast, October 17, 1982.
Humane Society of the United States
  1983   *Looking for alternatives.* Washington, D.C.: Humane Soci-
            ety of the United States. Pamphlet.
McGreal, S.
  1981   *Monkeys go to war.* Reprint from *Mainstream,* winter, pp.
            20–22. Sacramento: Animal Protection Institute of Amer-
            ica. Pamphlet.
[Miller, B.]
  n.d.   Pamphlet, no title. San Francisco: Buddhists Concerned
            for Animals.
[Mills, E.]
  1976   *Thinking the unthinkable.* Action for Animals. Pamphlet.
  1981   Racism, sexism, speciesism . . . three of a kind. Transcript
            of speeches by Sally Gearhart and John George, April 25,
            1981, San Francisco, Calif. Unpublished.
  1983   *Enriching and expanding the animal movement.* Interview
            with Sally Gearhart. *Agenda,* September-October. Re-
            printed as pamphlet by Action for Animals.
  1984   *Calendar—June 1984.* Action for Animals.
Mobilization for Animals
  1983   *Mobilization for Animals.* Columbus, Ohio: Mobilization
            for Animals. Pamphlet.
Progressive Animal Welfare Society (PAWS)
  1983   *Animal experimentation.* [Lynnwood, Washington: Pro-
            gressive Animal Welfare Society.] Pamphlet.
Stiller, H., M.D.
  n.d.   *Animal experiments and the welfare of man,* trans. from
            German. Jenkintown, Pa.: American Anti-vivisection So-
            ciety. Pamphlet.

Index

Designer: U. C. Press Staff
Compositor: A-R Editions
Text: 10/12 Times Roman
Display: Goudy